Bloom's Modern Critical Views

SALMAN RUSHDIE

Edited and with an introduction by
Harold Bloom
Sterling Professor of the Humanities
Yale University

D0209857

CHELSEA HOUSE
PUBLISHERS
A Haights Cross Communications Company

Philadelphia

©2003 by Chelsea House Publishers, a subsidiary of
Haights Cross Communications.

A Haights Cross Communications ✦ Company

Introduction © 2003 by Harold Bloom.

Printed and bound in the United States of America.

10 9 8 7 6 5 4 3 2 1

Library of Congress Cataloging-in-Publication Data

Salman Rushdie / edited and with an introduction by Harold Bloom.
    p. cm. -- (Bloom's modern critical views)
Includes bibliographical references and index.
  ISBN: 0-7910-7400-5
 1. Rushdie, Salman--Criticism and interpretation. I. Bloom, Harold.
II. Series.
  PR6068.U757 Z844 2002
  823'.914--dc21
                                    2002152674

Chelsea House Publishers
1974 Sproul Road, Suite 400
Broomall, PA 19008-0914

http://www.chelseahouse.com

Contributing Editor: Anne Marie Albertazzi

Cover designed by Terry Mallon

Cover photo by © Matthew Mendelsohn/CORBIS

Layout by EJB Publishing Services

Bloom's Modern Critical Views

Bloom's Modern Critical Views

Contents

Editor's Note

My Introduction follows Salman Rushdie himself by arguing the case for the purely aesthetic achievement of *The Satanic Verses*.

M.D. Fletcher finds Rushdie's *Shame* an *apologia pro vita sua*, after which Henry Louis Gates, Jr. defends both Wole Soyinka and Rushdie against the forces of censorship.

To Catherine Cundy, *Grimus* marks an entrance into Rushdie's work, while K.M. Newton spins a fine web of literary theory that seems to me sublimely irrelevant to Rushdie's sufferings.

The palpably cinematic elements in *The Satanic Verses* are set forth by Nicholas D. Rombes, Jr., after which Vijay Mishra sees Rushdie's mode as diasporic narrative.

I find little in common between the work of Toni Morrison and Salman Rushdie, despite the argument of Eleni Coundouriotis.

Paul A. Cantor shrewdly focuses on Rushdie's excursions into Spanish history in *The Moor's Last Sigh*.

The influence of *Midnight's Children* on national narratives of the eighties is outlined by Josna E. Rege.

Brian Finney, approaching the heart of the matter, deals with the demonic in *The Satanic Verses*, while John Clement Ball examines traditions of satire in *Midnight's Children*.

Stephen Baker illuminates aspects of *The Moor's Last Sigh*, after which Ayelet Ben-Yishai considers complexities of representation in *Shame*.

Introduction

The Satanic Verses clearly is fated to be Salman Rushdie's most notorious book. After rereading it against *Midnight's Children* and *The Moor's Last Sigh*, it seems to me also Rushdie's largest aesthetic achievement.

Though I allow myself some remarks in the Editor's Note upon the essays collected in this volume, they possess in common a great disinterest in the question of the aesthetic. Since their interests are theoretical, historical, Marxist, Post-Colonial, they scarcely are interested in asking and answering the question: how good a book is *The Satanic Verses*? Rushdie fortunately is not of their number. He passionately defends his book as an aesthetic value, as a figurative work that transcends political and religious considerations.

Audacity is the keynote of *The Satanic Verses*. Though an Enlightened sensibility, Rushdie writes of Mahound with insight, humane reverence, and awakened imagination. As a historical portrait of the prophet of Islam, Rushdie's Mahound is persuasive and properly enigmatic.

Unfortunately, 1988 was not a good year to publish *The Satanic Verses*. Indeed, 2002 would be even worse. The Ayatollah Khomenei is dead and his fatwah (I believe) is void, but now that militant Islam and the West are, more or less, at war, Rushdie remains in a somewhat precarious condition, even in the United States. And of course he must be haunted, by the eleven deaths and sixty injuries that accompanied *The Satanic Verses* into our world.

To his everlasting credit, Rushdie has broken with the motley crew of postcolonialism, the rabblement of lemmings who might have seen him as a martyr according to the Gospel of Foucault. He has proclaimed *The Satanic Verses* as a figurative achievement, a cunning and beautiful structure of rhetorical tropes. His book's purpose is neither to exalt nor to debase Islam, or its prophet, but to tell an enchanting story, and to add strangeness to beauty.

Rather than quote Rushdie upon Rushdie, I turn instead to the text of *The Satanic Verses*, to the fearful moment in which Mahound executes the poet Baal:

1

The General, Khalid, had wanted to have Baal executed at once, but Mahound asked that the poet be brought to trial immediately following the whores. So when Baal's twelve wives, who had divorced stone to marry him, had been sentenced to death by stoning to punish them for the immorality of their lives, Baal stood face to face with the Prophet, mirror facing image, dark facing light. Khalid, sitting at Mahound's right hand, offered Baal a last chance to explain his vile deeds. The poet told the story of his stay at The Curtain, using the simplest language, concealing nothing, not even his final cowardice, for which everything he had done since had been an attempt at reparation. But now an unusual thing happened. The crowd packed into that tent of judgment, knowing that this was after all the famous satirist Baal, in his day the owner of the sharpest tongue and keenest wit in Jahilia, began (no matter how hard it tried not to) to laugh. The more honestly and simply Baal described his marriages to the twelve 'wives of the Prophet', the more uncontrollable became the horrified mirth of the audience. By the end of his speech the good folk of Jahilia were literally weeping with laughter, unable to restrain themselves even when soldiers with bullwhips and scimitars threatened them with instant death.

"I'm not kidding!" Baal screeched at the crowd, which hooted yelled slapped its thighs in response. "It's no joke!" Ha ha ha. Until, at last, silence returned; the Prophet had risen to his feet.

"In the old days you mocked the Recitation," Mahound said in the hush. "Then, too, these people enjoyed your mockery. Now you return to dishonour my house, and it seems that once again you succeed in bringing the worst out of the people."

Baal said, "I've finished. Do what you want."

So he was sentenced to be beheaded, within the hour, and as soldiers manhandled him out of the tent towards the killing ground, he shouted over his shoulder: "Whores and writers, Mahound. We are the people you can't forgive."

Mahound replied, "Writers and whores. I see no difference here."

I think that is the heart of *The Satanic Verses* and of Rushdie's aesthetic stance against Islam. For Baal is Rushdie's surrogate, who like his author recognizes no jurisdiction except that of his muse. As Baal is led out to be beheaded, he shouts: "Whores and writers, Mahound. We are the people you can't forgive." And Rushdie then burns his book's eloquence into a single sentence: "Mahound replied, 'Writers and whores. I see no difference here.'"

At that moment, Rushdie is permanently subversive of Islam, at least of an Islam that ends poetry by beheading.

M.D. FLETCHER

Rushdie's Shame *as Apologue*

*S*hame is described in its jacket blurb as "captivating fairy-tale, devastating political satire and exquisite, uproarious entertainment". While jacket blurbs may not be the most precise contributors to genre studies, this does indicate the need to explore the basis of coherence in this work. The argument in this article is that *Shame* is essentially an apologue which strategically employs parody, ridicule, and the fantastic to achieve its purpose.

The term apologue is from Shelson Sack's *Fiction and the Shape of Belief*, and his distinction between satires and apologues as coherent works of fiction is apposite. In Sacks' terms, a satire is a work in which each part is employed to the single purpose of ridicule, while an apologue is a work "organized as a fictional example of the truth of a formulable statement or closely related set of such statements".[1] Both are distinguished from what Sacks calls "represented actions" (or "novels"), in which "characters about whose fate we are made to care are introduced in unstable relationships which are then further complicated until the complications are finally resolved by the complete removal of the represented instability",[2] or works in which the reader's attention and interest are focused on characters and on their interaction and development.

Authors of effective satires and apologues will, of course, arouse reader interest in characters as much as possible without obscuring the purpose of

From *The Journal of Commonwealth Literature* 21, no. 1 (1986): 120-132. © 1986 by *The Journal of Commonwealth Literature*.

the work,[3] and Rushdie is a master story-teller. Nevertheless, it is clear from the treatment of characters in this work and from the abundance of other clues (including especially authorial interventions) that *Shame* is not a "represented action", or simply an "entertainment". At least on the surface, however, it does evidence characteristics of both satires and apologues. The continuation of this analysis will be facilitated by outlining the "plot" or at least locating the characters of the work.

Shame relates the interaction between the Harappa family and the Hyder family. Iskander ("Isky") Harappa at forty abandons his dissolute life and becomes the civilian Prime Minister of a country that is "not quite Pakistan" (p. 29). Raza ("Old Razor Guts") Hyder, restored to military prominence by Isky on the premise that Raza will not cause trouble, replaces him in a military coup. Raza has Isky killed to avenge personal humiliations, as Isky has vengefully had his own cousin, Little Mir, killed.

Isky is married to Rani, Raza's cousin, and they have a single daughter, Arjumand ("the virgin Ironpants"), who worships her father and becomes politically involved on his behalf. Raza is married to Bilquis, and their two daughters are Sufiya Zinobia and Naveed ("Good News"). Naveed marries the police captain, Talvar Ulhaq, rejecting an arranged marriage with Isky's nephew, Haroun Harappa, on the eve of the wedding. Haroun, in turn, rejects Arjumand, who sees in him the duplication of her father—the potentially great man given over to dissipation. Sufiya, rejected as the "wrong miracle"—a girl instead of the anticipated boy—is called "Shame" by her mother. Mentally retarded and therefore "pure", she becomes the repository of all the shame not felt by others, which becomes "a beast" within her. Eventually the beast takes over her body entirely, stalking the country-side as incarnate, avenging violence and bringing down Raza's regime.

Omar Khayyam Shakil, ostensibly the central protagonist of the work, is the "hero" as bystander or peripheral person. He is conceived and raised under bizarre circumstances by three sisters in the Shakil mansion, boarded up to be inaccessible and supplied through a booby-trapped dumb-waiter. He eventually escapes the prison of his "motherland" to become both a brilliant doctor and a dissolute, "shameless" person. He attaches himself to Isky as companion in debauchery and, after Isky's reform, to Raza as Sufiya's doctor and then husband. The narrative begins with his birth and childhood and ends with his death at the hands of the beast, "Sufiya".

While the "public" plot focuses primarily on political rivalries, the "private" lives of the women are equally important and, as the author intervenes to inform us, "refract" or perhaps even "subsume" the male plot (p. 173).

It is obvious that Pakistani politics is being ridiculed via the portrayal of Isky and Raza, and that many of the standard techniques of satire are employed. At the same time, the tragic effects on others of the actions of those ridiculed are seriously depicted. If *Shame* were a satire, then the purpose of this serious side might be to avoid the danger of trivializing the consequences of the actions of the ridiculed, as Heller's use of the macabre and macro-grotesquery function in *Catch-22*. Similarly, the introduction of the "Eastern" concept of "shame" might be seen as a way of introducing a basis for evaluation into a context in which "the death of God and of tragedy" (p. 115) are accepted.

As a coherent work, however, *Shame* holds together much better when viewed as an apologue in which ridicule and the techniques of satire constitute one of the strategies. If that is the case, then the "statement" or closely related set of statements of the work must be discernable. In fact, Rushdie provides such a set of statements in authorial interventions: "Repression is a seamless garment; a society which is authoritarian in its social and sexual codes, which crushes its women beneath the intolerable burdens of honour and propriety, breeds repressions of other kinds as well". "Shamelessness, shame: the roots of violence.... Humiliate people for long enough and a wilderness bursts out of them." "In the end ... it all blows up in your face." (pp. 173, 116–17, 173).

If one strategy of the work is the use of ridicule, another is to structure the work as a parody of revenge tragedies. Rushdie has said that the work combines a plot comprised of "the stuff of tragedy" but with a cast of "gangsters, clowns, hoodlums", necessitating that it be written "like a farce, a kind of macabre black farce".[4] Isky orders the murder of his cousin, Little Mir, and Mir's son, Haroun, carries it out. Raza has Isky and Talvar killed and shoots Omar's "brother", Baber (also conceived and raised by the Shakil sisters, twenty years after Omar), in the line of duty. Omar's mothers kill Raza, either directly or through Omar, after Bilquis has died of malaria (or poison) in their house. Sufiya kills Omar and then explodes in the final sentences of the book. In the meanwhile Naveed commits suicide and numerous minor characters die or are killed. It is a parody because although virtually everyone dies or is killed, in most cases the depiction of the characters denies them tragic stature. At the same time, this is not true of all the characters, and there is an additional dimension of seriousness in that the consequences of the antics of the major male characters are depicted as indeed tragic for others. The parodying of revenge tragedies, then, appears to be part of the structural strategy of the work rather than a characterization of its nature.

The third major strategy is the use of the fantastic in the role played by Sufiya Hyder. *Shame* is referred to as a fairy tale by the author as well as by the jacket blurb and by some of the early reviews (pp. 70, 257), and the narrative includes references to beauty and the beast, sleeping beauty, and the forty thieves. But Sufiya metamorphosed into an animal of superhuman strength does not make this a fairy tale. Fairy tales provide a consistent expectation of supernatural happenings, while the fantastic is characterized by the depiction of events that contradict expectations established by the text, and to which the reader responds with ambiguity or hesitation concerning their natural or supernatural nature.[5] Similarly, while metamorphosis is often used in satire, either to ridicule by levelling or to provide a "worm's eye view" (or both, as in *The Golden Ass*), Sufiya's is not of that nature.[6] She is inhabited by the beast of violence resulting from shame.

The major clue to the overall organization of *Shame* is provided by the authorial comment that the work includes both a "male" and a "female" plot but that both are the same story after all (p. 173). These two plots are approached differently. The story of the males is treated primarily from the "satiric" perspective of ridicule employing standard satiric techniques. Those emphasized in this article are parody, irony, clownish language, grotesquery and a mock-satiric protagonist, and there are also humourous names, puns, jokes and folk sayings (and misapplied folk sayings). The plot of the wives and daughters is more realistic and tragic in its presentation, while the theme of women's role generally lies in between and is dealt with in styles ranging from the tragic to the mildly amusing.

There are, in addition, the stories of Omar and Sufiya, which begin separately but converge during the narrative. Sufiya, as "shame", epitomizes the "female" plot.[7] Omar is tied to Sufiya as her doctor and later as her husband, and through the theme of hypnotism/mesmerism and general marginality. He also begins as the embodiment of shamelessness, counterpoised to her identity as shame. Omar is linked to the male story through his personal attachment to Isky and then to Raza and in his role as "satiric" hero. The various plots are therefore integrated in circular fashion into one story: from Omar through Isky and Raza to the wives and daughters to Sufiya and back to Omar, with Sufiya also cutting across the diameter of the circle to complete the violent destruction of the male sphere in the end.

Omar Khayyam Shakil appears in the world at the beginning of *Shame* in true "satiric" fashion, with three mothers and no father. The three Shakil sisters—Chhunni, Munnee, and Bunny—had long ago determined to have a child in common, and they fulfil this plan with the anonymous assistance of an "Angrez" officer at a ball held when their father dies. They do not emerge from the house again, nor does Omar until the age of twelve. He is ugly and fat, often referred to by other characters as "pigmeat tub" (e.g., p. 94) and at one stage crushes a horse he is attempting to ride (p. 80). He loses weight to the extent that he is no longer "a cartoon" only in response to the sexual activity provided by Sufiya's ayah as surrogate for his adolescent, mentally retarded wife (p. 212). He is a voyeur, his first sexual experience is achieved by hypnotizing Farah Zoroaster while they are still students, and he re-enters the story in adult life as Isky's companion in debauchery. He is also characterized as misogynist, possibly from the need to take revenge on his mothers (p. 40).

He is subject to vertigo and feels "a person apart" (p. 24), "living at the edge of the world, so close that he might fall off at any moment" (p. 21) and convinced of his own worthlessness (pp. 22, 24). As the author intervenes to ask, "What manner of hero is this?" (pp. 25, 42), and how can his sincerity ever be trusted (pp. 142, 144–45)? The approach here is clearly in the satiric tradition, and its self-consciousness is revealed by the author's having provided a genealogy to set off the hero's "obscure" origins (opposite p. 11). And yet Omar does not play the role of satiric target or of naïve exposer.[8]

Without losing his marginality or bystander role, Omar ceases his life of dissipation when Isky "reforms" and abandons him, becoming Sufiya's doctor and exhausting himself in his work. He becomes attached to Raza not only through Sufiya but also as ringside physician when Raza attempts to restore army morale by losing a long series of wrestling matches to individual soldiers. It is at this stage that Omar's general nature seems to change. When he refuses to kill Sufiya with a painless injection despite the danger posed to him by her increasingly violent symptoms, and attempts to confront her instead, even the author ascribes courage to him ("and courage is a rarer thing than evil") (p. 235).

If Omar is ostensibly a "satiric hero" who does not, in fact, play that role, Isky and Raza are ridiculed via standard satiric techniques. They represent civilian and military Pakistani politics for satiric purposes, and also patriarchal oppression and neglect in the broader terms of the apologue. The author describes the locale of this narrative as "not quite Pakistan" (p. 29), and lists the abuses that he would have to discuss if this were a realistic novel about that country (pp. 68–70). Thus, he continues the mock satiric by claiming the work to be a fairy tale, in the tradition of satires inhibited by censorship, while deliberately undermining his own subterfuge. Karachi and Islamabad are cities in the fiction, while Zia and Bhutto, the Islamic revival, events after partition, and recent jokes and stories from Pakistan are all included in authorial interventions. In terms of the central statement of the apologue, the extreme misogyny of Indian culture is perceived as being re-fortified by Pakistan's Islamic revival.

Isky rises to power as civilian Prime Minister through oratory and personal charm, as the voice of the people. But his idolatrous epitaph turns out to exist only in Arjumand's imagination (p. 177). His only depicted acts as Prime Minister involve the effective harassment of a long line of US ambassadors, a kind of game or joke with little positive effect, however much such treatment may be justified. The activities of his debauchery with Omar are ironically detailed as his great sacrifice for the people (p. 125), and his sartorial splendour gives way to green Pierre Chardin Red Guard suits (p. 150).

Even his oratorical virtuosity is ridiculed. On one occasion he bares his chest during a public speech, as did, we are told, the young Richard Burton in the title role of the film *Alexander the Great* (p. 180). Isky is, of course, Alexander's namesake, and the film reference reinforces the belittling comparison with *the* Iskander.[9] As Bilquis states later, in reference to Raza, "Once giants walked the earth.... Now the pygmies have taken over, however" (p. 271).

Isky's eloquence is also paralleled, and undermined, by his fluency with oaths and obscenities. Although he alters his public language to match his political ambitions—except in the countryside, where his prodigious repertoire is worth votes—it is his tirade against Raza while he is under house arrest that precludes his release, and another against Raza's ADC, Colonel Shuja, that costs him his life. As Shuja has remarked laconically after the first occasion, "Just look where bad language will get you" (p. 226). The relationship between sex and death, in terms of a balancing between reproduction and destruction, is mythologically universal, and obscenities relate anthropologically to the breaking and/or ritualizing of taboos.[10] In *Shame*, particularly with Isky but also with Little Mir, Farah Zoroaster and anonymous soldiers, the power of the sex act and of obscenity is portrayed as having been largely defused into banality by its uncalculated and persistent usage. While the author is able to enlist Isky's language for the purpose of humour, Isky's efforts to employ it as a weapon are also depicted as ultimately ineffectual.

In addition to the undermining ridicule, direct indictment is levelled at Isky by Rani. Abandoned to the loneliness of the rural Harappa estate, she embroiders a total of eighteen shawls depicting in miraculously fine detail his many crimes (pp. 191–95).[11] Although at that stage her accusations are an isolated counter to the events revealed in the narrative and to Isky's heroic stature in the eyes of his daughter, they are subsequently substantiated (e.g., pp. 209, 216). Isky's sense of infallibility as the voice of the people has produced even greater repression and bloodshed than that experienced under his predecessors.

The military is also exposed to ridicule, both directly and through Raza. When the results of the first election divide entirely on geographical lines, with an advantage to the East Wing, the caretaker president, General "Shaggy Dog", must "restore a sense of proportion" to the Easterners by military means (p. 179). Although a northern war during the hot season is initially welcomed, the series of reported victories culminates in defeat (pp. 179–80), and in the total demoralization of the military (and the division of the country).

Raza has become a hero in earlier military actions against tribals by capturing a high mountain valley—"and you must not believe the propaganda which says that the enemy did not bother to defend the place" (p. 79). Presumably, however, we may believe the revelation by his mother that he invented his own nickname, "Old Razor Guts" (p. 82). Subsequently losing favour and being effectively demoted in his appointment to head the military academy, he is consequently the only General not discredited in the Bangladesh war. He is therefore able to restore army morale. Although the staged wrestling matches help, the coup is the real key to the army regaining its morale, and it is urged on Raza in precisely those terms.

Raza is undermined by the author primarily through irony and demonstrations of inconsistency. While Isky begins his political reign in the catastrophe of the East-West war, Raza begins his by nearly bungling his coup against Isky. During a telephone conversation with the Joint Chief, Tunglak, Raza realizes to his great embarrassment that he has forgotten to warn his superior (p. 222). In spite of his conspicuously religious nature, he makes post-coup promises with his hand on the Holy Book that he will later break (p. 223). He justifies Islamic punishments by emphasizing the sanitary manner in which hands will be cut off (p. 245), sees his wife "regularly" when he takes her to his weekly television interview (p. 248), and keeps the religious bruise on his forehead renewed by praying on camera at the beginning of those interviews (p. 248).

He cynically rejoices in the Soviet invasion of "the country of A." (obviously Afganistan), knowing that that will ensure American military support for his own regime (pp. 255–56), and when provided with evidence that Tunglak, Shuja and Ulhaq are plotting a coup because he wants to get rid of each of them for personal reasons (p. 250). Raza is a religious man, and does not use Isky's language,[12] but his deeds are undermined by Isky's colourful description of them: "Fuck me in the mouth, yaar, everybody knows those tribals are running wild out there because Hyder kept hanging innocent people by the balls" (p. 119).

Raza's indecisiveness is signalled by the popular meaning attributed to the intials CMLA (Chief Martial Law Administrator), namely, Cancel My Last Announcement (p. 227). More telling still is the description of Raza as having two monkeys on his shoulders, Isky and the religious fanatic Dawood after they both have died (e.g., pp. 238, 276). Isky provides "useful tips" in the form of quotes from Machiavelli while Dawood pushes a "Khomeni" line of abstinence, prayer and punishments. While these voices begin by paralyzing Raza with confusion, they end in a vicous combination of political opportunism and religious fanaticism.

Isky and Raza also are almost, but not quite, accorded "satiric" deaths. Bakhtin has argued that "clownish death", in which the horror of death *per se* is combined with the humour of the manner in which it occurs, is a major sub-category of satirical grotesquery as exemplified in Rabelais' writings; later satire has often simply added humorous detail to otherwise gruesome descriptions of death to achieve grotesquery with a different emphasis.[13] Comic deaths do abound in this tale, mainly in the cases of minor characters: Old Mr Shakil commits his soul to Hell as he exits, and Omar is born in the death-bed (pp. 11–14, 21); Yakoob Balloch, who builds the lethal dumb-waiter for the Shakil sisters, is presumed to have died, not from being poisoned by them to keep him quiet, but from "the genuinely fatal banality of peritonitis. Or some such thing" (pp. 17–18); Hashma Bibi, the ayah of Omar's childhood, allows himself to be hypnotized by him, and likes it so much that she wills herself "deeper and deeper" into death at the alleged age of 120 (p. 34); Bilquis' father, Marmoud, is blown up in his own cinema for attempting to screen a Moslem/Hindu double bill, and thereby alienating everyone—tolerance was his "fatal personality flaw" (p. 62). Even Baber's death is comically exalted, recorded only in the imagination of his mothers; he is transformed into an angel, a process almost completed by the time the bullets actually kill him (p. 132).

Naveed, overwhelmed by the arithmetical progression of children she is producing, hangs herself after filling the room with the scent of "Joy by Jean Patou, the most expensive perfume in the world"—which is, of course, Joy's advertising slogan (p. 228). But Naveed is close to a main character, and victim, and the humour is dwarfed by the tragedy in her case. At the other extreme from clownish death, Little Mir's is totally macabre.

In the cases of Isky and Raza, only minor humorous details detract from the grim reality. The scene in which Raza is forced into the Shakil contraption includes a humorous description of his towel slipping, leaving him naked, but the detailed description of the specific parts of his body pierced by the dumb-waiter's eighteen-inch stiletto blades adds little to the humourous aspect of an almost entirely gruesome death (p. 282). In Isky's case only the companionship of flies in his death cell, "fornicating on his toenails" (p. 229), reminds us of the earlier "satiric" tone.

The police play a relatively subordinate role, represented by Talvar Ulhaq. Talvar is physically the classic hero (p. 163), which allows him to win Naveed from under Haroun's nose, and he is elevated from police chief to head of the Federal Security Force in Isky's government. In an advance on the standard satiric exposure of police as equating arrest with guilt, Talvar is clairvoyant, which allows him to foresee and prevent crimes and acts of treason.

Rushdie's comment that his "male" and "female" plots are after all the same story has been noted above, and the fiasco of Naveed's wedding recreates the "male" plot in miniature. Because the wedding is held on the day when rioting in the streets has precipitated the first coup, by "Shaggy Dog" fronting for Isky, the guests have arrived in their oldest clothes to avoid attracting attention on the way. They fail to eat because added to that shock is the erratum slip announcing a change in the players, Talvar substituting for Haroun in the role of groom, just as the series of coups replaces one leader for another. During the ceremony itself Sufiya attacks Talvar and, although restrained from ripping his head off, sends blood spurting everywhere with a near-fatal bite to the neck, "so that all of her family and many of the camouflaged guests began to resemble workers in a halal slaughterhouse" (p. 171).

The role of women is culturally defined in terms of marriage and childbearing: the male must be older (p. 84); the women's definition of a "good" man is one who does not beat his wife (p. 76); marriage is a woman's fate, and brains are less than an asset (pp. 158, 161); the hypocrisy and ill-will of female in-laws is to be expected (e.g., p. 165); wives are not to enjoy sex or even be known to have it except by the birth of children (pp. 88, 74); and to have a female child rather than a male is to suffer defeat.

Both Isky and Raza effectively abandon their wives after the birth of daughters—Isky for a mistress, Pinky, whom he really does seem to love but "sacrifices" for his political career, and Raza for abstinence, although he is also interested in Pinky until her preference for Isky is rudely demonstrated. Rani sits on the verandah of the Harappa homestead producing her shawls, while Bilquis slowly goes crazy.

But the statement that *Shame* is making involves the consequences of sexual oppression, not the suggestion that women are inherently superior to men. Arjumand's battle to overcome her woman's body and to disguise its great beauty leaves her loveless, nicknamed "the virgin Ironpants" (e.g., p. 126). Desiring no man (or woman) except Haroun, and he only to reform him in her father's image, she idolizes and emulates her father and is exposed by the author in many of the same ways that Isky is. Her response to the election, for example, is treated with irony. She applaud's Isky's victory in the West, over-whelming if not entirely legally achieved, as *"rough justice ... but justice all the same"*, and she regards the subsequent assassination of Sheikh Bismillah in the East as the "sort of behaviour one expects from types like that" (cf. the series of killings in the West) (p. 179). She sexually teases the naïve and decent captain of the guard while she and Rani are under house arrest and has him tortured after a reversal in their fortunes. And, also like Isky, she attempts to use language as a weapon. To her, Omar is a monkey and Rani a burrowing owl (p. 126), while the people in the East Wing are inhuman "jungle bunnies" (p. 179).[14]

Naveed, who is "Good News" (but only to her mother—she is tacitly known not to be Raza's child), is the opposite of Arjumand, having willed herself to be attractive from an unpromising start and having fallen for Talvar because of his looks. Talvar picks her, however, because he perceives her ability to have babies. She is soon inundated and suffocated in the offspring of Talvar's male pride, as the arithmetical population explosion of first one child, then twins, etc., unhinges everyone in the household (p. 227). Her lack of compassion for her older sister is expressed in her statement after the wedding fiasco that Sufiya should have been drowned at birth (p. 171), and in aggressive vegetable epithets: "Turnip. Beetroot. Angrez radish" (p. 136).

To have no male children is to bring collective shame on the family (p. 84), but Sufiya, as the "wrong miracle", becomes shame itself, attracting her mother's hate and the epithet (rather than nickname) "Shame" (p. 119). The term Rushdie invokes, in yet another authorial intervention, is *sharam*: "not only shame ... but also embarrassment, discomfiture, decency, modesty, shyness, the sense of having an ordained place in the world, and other dialects of emotion for which English has no counterparts" (p. 115). It is also that which results from injured pride or honour (p. 115). These comments seem designed to suggest the cultural bases of meanings rather than to denigrate English as a language (as one reviewer has alleged[15]), and they underlie the uses to which the term is commandeered in this work.

If "satiric" techniques are used to expose Isky and Raza, and applied to Arjumand to a lesser extent and to Naveed still less until they disappear altogether in the depiction of Rani and Bilquis, with Sufiya the author employs the fantastic. As indicated above, Rushdie claims to have made

Sufiya an idiot to preserve her purity (p. 120), and she is therefore suitable as the repository of all the shame not felt by others (p. 122). She blushes from birth, and blushes red hot even before the violence begins (pp. 90, 121–22). Initially, she fights against the beast. Her first violent attack is against Pinky's domestic turkeys, and she falls into a coma after the episode (pp. 138–39). She then diverts the violence against herself, as the oppressed and shamed often do, and her life is barely saved by Omar through hypnotism after a total immunological collapse (pp. 140–41). She again lapses into coma after the attack on Talvar, and she attempts to control the beast in its first attack on Omar (p. 236). Between those latter two episodes she has killed four youths after having sexual intercourse with them, having been forbidden that latter experience with her husband because she is retarded and a minor (pp. 216–18).[16]

Eventually, however, the beast takes over totally. Escaping into the countryside on the night that Isky is killed, the beast appears everywhere at once in a form described by witnesses as that of a white panther, killing animals and people indiscriminately (pp. 252–53). This menace to the countryside is described as "the time-honoured man-eater scare" with a terrifying difference in the manner of the killings (p. 253), and with the same caveat we also recognize similarities to the universal concept of the phantom-woman. The beast mesmerizes it victims, rips of their heads, and pulls their "guts" up through their necks to eat (pp. 138, 253).

The details of the victims being beheaded and having their entrails eaten link the beast's *modus operandi* to that of the goddess Kali, and despite the beast's whiteness in contrast to Kali's blackness the nudeness, matted hair, terrifying eyes, "blood-curdling howls", nauseating stench of death, and ability to be everywhere at once also fit.[17] Similarly, Sufiya's trances and mesmerizing powers, paralleled by Omar's vertigo and hypnotic abilities, suggest the alleged power of yoga in both its inner, self-overcoming, and its outer, magical, properties. But in both cases there is suggestiveness without equation. *Shame* is clearly not a religious allegory in which, for example, Sufiya "stands for" Kali.

There is another sense in which allegorical implications must be considered, however, namely that Sufiya "stands for" the destructive power of the violence resulting from an overdose of shame. There is no question that the exploits of the beast are depicted as actually happening in the narrative, with numerous witnesses for each occasion to preclude the "natural" interpretation that the beast is meant to be an illusion or the imaginings of one character. But the question of whether the superhuman strength and other characteristics of the beast are to be explained naturally or supernaturally is left open. The author states that what is involved is "one of those supernatural beings, those exterminating or avenging angels, or werewolves, or vampires" (p. 197); but he also has Omar, the brilliant doctor, offer a "scientific" explanation in terms of mind over matter, similar to the psychosomatic nature of blushing (p. 234). Ultimately, there is allegorical intent, with the personification in Sufiya of the violence resulting from shame, and there is also the rule-shattering use of the fantastic as fictional strategy to break through the illusions about human nature and "given" reality that support sexual and political discrimination and oppression (cf. pp. 197, 199–200).

Sufiya, then, plays a number of roles in the narrative. She blushes to expose acts of shame, beginning with her own birth and the reaction thereto. She judges. And she avenges. She brings down the regime of Raza, her father, who, disguised as a woman, flees to the house of the Shakil sisters and is killed there. She kills Omar, the last survivor among the major male characters, and then explodes.

The strategies of this work include parody, "satiric" ridicule and the fantastic. All three, however, are subordinated to the major task of exemplifying in fictional form a closely related set of statements. Sexual, cultural and political repression and humiliation are all part of a seamless web that lead to shame; shame becomes violence, and in the end it all blows up in your face.

NOTES

(Page numbers in brackets in the text refer to Salman Rushdie, *Shame*, London: Jonathan Cape, 1983.)

1. Sheldon Sacks, *Fiction and the Shape of Belief*, Berkeley: University of California Press, 1964, pp. 7–8 and more generally pp. 1–60.

2. Sacks, *Fiction*, p. 15.

3. Sacks, *Fiction*, p. 57.

4. Salman Rushdie, 'PW Interviews', *Publishers Weekly*, November 11, 1983.

5. Tzvetan Todorov, *The Fantastic*, trans. Richard Howard, Cleveland: The Press of Case Western Reserve University, 1973, 1970. See also, e.g., Rosemary Jackson, *Fantasy: The Literature of Subversion*, London: Methuen, 1981.

6. Obviously, also, Sufiya's is not a self-willed metamorphosis of the type discussed by Irving Massey in *The Gaping Pig: Literature and*

Metamorphosis, Berkeley: University of California Press, 1976. Nor is it the type of metamorphosis either magically induced as punishment or simply included as a miraculous addition to the entertainment as in various parts of *The Arabian Nights Entertainments*, the *Ramayana*, the *Mahabharata*, etc.

7. Shame, not frailty, thy name is woman. Burton indicates that the Arabic word "aurat", meaning shame, reappeared in Hindustani jargon with the meaning "a woman" or "a wife"; note 10, 'Sinbad's Third Voyage', *The Arabian Nights Entertainments*, trans. Sir Richard Burton, New York: The Heritage Press, 1955, Vol. I.

8. Compare, for example, the role of the main protagonist and the author's spuriously pejorative comments on his "hero" in Vladimir Voinovich, *The Life and Extraordinary Adventures of Private Ivan Chonkin*, trans. Richard Lourie, New York: Farrar Straus Giroux, 1977, 1969. See also, e.g., William Riggan, *Picaros, Madmen, Naifs and Clowns: The Unreliable First Person Narrator*, Norman: University of Oklahoma Press, 1981.

9. "Harappa" was one of the two major Indus Valley cities of the Bronze Age, *c.* 2500 B.C. Among recent demogogues, Perón also performed the ritual of removing his shirt during a speech to the masses.

10. The relationship between taboos and verbal abuse is discussed in, e.g., Edmund R. Leach, 'Anthropological Aspects of Language: Animal Categories and Verbal Abuse', *New Directions in the Study of Language*, ed. Eric H. Lenneberg, Cambridge: MIT Press, 1964, pp. 23–63.

11. Rabelais' *Gargantua and Pantagruel* includes reference to the tapestry made by Philomela to convey the story of her rape by Tereus, who had also cut out her tongue to prevent disclosure; François Rabelais, *The Histories of Gargantua and Pantagruel*, trans. J. M. Cohen, Harmondsworth: Penguin Books Ltd., 1955, p. 454.

12. Only at the end does Raza lapse, when Bilquìs has been left, uncleaned, to die of malaria (or perhaps poison): "I'll make them pick up turds with their eyelashes and stuff them up their nostrils" (p. 280). A variation of this form appears in *Pantagruel*—the punishment of removing with one's teeth a fig leaf from a mule's "private parts", reappearing in *Private Chonkin*, for example, in a description of voting as removing a slip of paper from someone's bare backside with one's teeth. This point is not to suggest borrowing, but rather the cross-cultural nature of images and the close relationship between "satire" and bodily functions.

13. Mikhail Bakhtin, *Rabelais and His World*, trans. Helene Iswolsky, Cambridge: MIT Press, 1968; Wolfgang Kayser, *The Grotesque in Art and Literature*, Bloomington: Indiana University Press, 1963; Geoffrey Galt

Harpham. *On the Grotesque*, Princeton: Princeton University Press, 1982. See also, e.g., Joseph Heller's *Catch-22* as a contemporary example.

14. In addition to his oaths, Isky refers to the Shias as "bedbugs" (p. 123). The animals Arjumand invokes—e.g., monkeys and burrowing owls— also have negative connotations in her cultural context. On the general topic, again see, e.g., Leach, 'Animal Categories and Verbal Abuse'.

15. D.J. Enright, 'Forked Tongue: *Shame*', *New York Review of Books*, 8 December, 1983.

16. Note the similarity to, e.g., Demetrio Aguilera-Malta, *Seven Serpents and Seven Moons*, trans. Gregory Rabassa, Austin: University of Texas Press, 1979, 1970.

17. The role of Kali in Indian religion and mythology is, of course, complex, with different emphasis in various contexts and time periods, but her association with death and destruction is consistent. See, e.g., David R. Kinsley, *The Sword and the Flute: Kali and Krsna, Dark Visions of the Terrible and the Sublime in Hindu Mythology*, Berkeley: University of California Press, 1975.

HENRY LOUIS GATES, JR.

Censorship and Justice:
On Rushdie and Soyinka

D oes it do any good for us as scholars and critics of literature to speak out when the lives of writers like Salmon Rushdie are threatened? At the outset, let us be perfectly clear about one thing. We are not in dialogue with Mr. Rushdie's persecutors. For dialogue is something they do not countenance. We speak to and among ourselves. Our charge is not diplomacy. What we can do—what people did in public forums throughout the world during the weeks following the Ayotollah Khomeini's pronouncement—is to reaffirm our commitment to freedom of expression. Censorship is to art what lynching is to justice. In this case, the two have come together. But that is why it is important to remind ourselves of all the ways that the Rushdie case is *not* unique. From Chile to Czechoslovakia, men and women languish in prison for a dissidence not of deeds but of words. We must remind ourselves that censorship is not just a form of savagery practiced in distant, alien lands. As the Spector-Green bill introduced in the United States Senate illustrates, it is an ever-present danger in countries that pride themselves on their respect for freedom of expression.

In England, where Rushdie is a citizen, Prime Minister Thatcher stoutly declared her devotion to a concept of freedom that the supposedly intolerant, heathen East had transgressed. Yet she herself threatened to abolish independent television groups that challenged her veracity. And her

From *Research in African Literatures* 21, no. 1 (Spring 1990): 137-139. © 1989 by the Indiana University Press.

government oversaw the closing of newspapers that offended the prejudices of her constituency.

Well, what goes around comes around. Rushdie and his publisher were privately prosecuted in the British courts for "blasphemous libel." The precedent for the legal case against him was a court case, decided about ten years ago, in which the common-law offense of blasphemy was invoked to shut down a gay newspaper and sentence its editor to prison. These cases are related in a very important way. One can't preach tolerance about religious matters and practice intolerance toward unpopular minorities. Freedom of speech doesn't exist just for the protection of masterpieces. Anyone who thinks it does may soon discover that there are no masterpieces left to protect.

The Satanic Verses was not a hard case for most of us to judge. It hardly challenged the limits of *our* tolerance. But our test will come. And when it does, we won't see a great novelist, no, *we* will see a purveyor of smut or hatred. It won't be about religious blasphemy; and it won't be an affront to the prophet. The thin end of the wedge will look very different. It will speak to the rights of victims, as the Spector-Green bill did. It will speak to our compassion and ethical commitments—to our conception of human dignity. We will see not an offense to a prophet but perhaps to our children.

When *our* ideals, *our* principles, are being challenged, when it really hits home, will we—those of us who say we believe in freedom of expression—will we speak out then? Will? Where is the meaning of free expression taught in the United States? In the schools? According to a group that monitors book banning in schools, the incidence of this sort of censorship has been steadily increasing at an annual rate of 35%. Among the books most frequently banned: *The Diary of Anne Frank*, *The Adventures of Huckleberry Finn*, Richard Wright's *Black Boy*. Americans are teaching their children an important lesson, but perhaps we should think about what that lesson is.

Courageous Moslem students in Iowa and elsewhere organized readings of Rushdie's *Satanic Verses* to demonstrate—if it needed demonstrating—that Khomeini did not speak for all Islam. Yet his sway was powerful, mortally so. It was not hard to take a stand in New York or London. Elsewhere in the world, the risks were real. In Lagos, Wole Soyinka did not keep silent: he spoke out in Rushdie's defense and against the Ayatollah for what he called the "implicit blasphemy in his arrogation of a Supreme Will." In the streets of Lagos, crowds of thousands called for his death: shouts against Rushdie segued into the chant, "Death to Soyinka." No big surprise: In Nigeria, when you say, "I am Salmon Rushdie," they take you at your word.

In the statement that Soyinka issued at this time, he declared:

> The world recognizes courage, and cowardice. It is easy for any leader of a nation, protected and cushioned by the entire machinery of state, to issue death warrants on a solitary writer.... It is also cowardly ... and impious.
>
> If Salmon Rushdie dies, then his work must be unleashed upon an expanding readership by every available means.
>
> If Salmon Rushdie is unnaturally and prematurely silenced, the creative world will launch its own Jihad. It has the will, it has the resources and above all, it has the imagination. The zombies and dacoits of unreason, no matter how well sheltered...will not stop it, nor will a million acts of terrorism organized against the innocent. It will outlast the Ayatollah Khomeini's great grandchildren; it will, in fact, become a permanent feature of a world that has mastered the art of communication.

These are fighting words, but the fight is really everyone's fight.

The Iranian government announced at one point that it had killed all its political prisoners. Well, not quite; not yet. Rushdie is in effect a political prisoner, of no fixed abode, a heresiarch hostage to an Imam's edict.

I do not know Salmon Rushdie personally, but Soyinka is my friend, and one of his poems articulately poses the question that we must all answer for ourselves. "What If Thus He Died?" was written in solitary confinement, on toilet paper, when the Nigerian government imprisoned Soyinka for his own writings.

> ....The wrongs of day
> And cries of night burnt red fissures
> In chambers of his mind
> And so he set upon the quest
> Seeking that whose plenitude
> Would answer calls of hate and terror
>
> ...
> He lit the torch to a summons
> Of the great procession—and, what of it?
> What of it if thus he died
> Burnt offering on the altar of fears.

In asking this question, Soyinka has called upon all of us to remember that freedom of expression lies at the heart of the enterprise in which we are all engaged.

NOTE

These comments were originally made in a somewhat different form at the Lincoln Center rally for Rushdie on March 13, 1989.

CATHERINE CUNDY

"Rehearsing Voices": Salman Rushdie's Grimus

Rushdie's first novel *Grimus* offers an important insight into stylistic and thematic preoccupations developed more fully in the author's later work. The models for *Grimus* within both Eastern and Western traditions are diverse—Dante's *Divine Comedy*, Farid ud-din Attar's *Conference of the Birds (Mantiq Ut-tair)*, even Johnson's *Rasselas*, with the hero Flapping Eagle and his sister choosing to escape the particular social restrictions and conformities of their own less-than-Happy Valley. At this stage in Rushdie's development, the diversity remains just that; the elements insufficiently blended to make the novel appear a skilfully amalgamated whole.

Viewed from the standpoint of *The Satanic Verses*, *Grimus* allows us to see areas of debate which are handled with greater depth and maturity in Rushdie's later work—ideas of personal and national identity, the legacy of colonialism, the problems of exile and even the first signs of a tendency to demonize female sexuality. A crucial aspect of these discussions in Rushdie's later novels is his use of a specific geographical setting, not only to evoke a particular atmosphere but, through its cultural and historical associations, to raise certain issues for the reader. For Timothy Brennan in *Salman Rushdie and the Third World*, *Grimus*'s lack of a specific and identifiable geographical location is its chief failure:

From *The Journal of Commonwealth Literature* 27, no. 1 (1992): 128-137. © 1992 by *The Journal of Commonwealth Literature*.

It would be hard to find a novel that demonstrated better the truth of Fanon's claim that a culture that is not national is meaningless.... they must be anchored in a coherent "structure of feeling", which only actual communities can create.[1]

Fanon's discussion of the need for a post-colonial national culture in *The Wretched of the Earth* highlights Rushdie's own problem, in *Grimus* and beyond it, of producing a new kind of literature; a new kind of cultural representation that is an amalgam of both the Eastern and Western influences that comprise his experience. The native intellectual experiences the desire "to shrink away from that Western culture in which they all risk being swamped",[2] says Fanon, but then encounters the obstacle whereby the "national culture" to which s/he turns

can hardly supply any figureheads which will bear comparison with those, so many in number, and so great in prestige, of the occupying power's civilisation.[3]

This is, in a sense, the "problem" of *Grimus*—its desire to incorporate a variety of literary styles and products into a framework which, as Brennan puts it, "'tries on' cultures like used clothing".[4]

In so far as *Grimus* is located anywhere, its depiction of the Amerindian culture of the Axona makes tentative first steps towards an examination of post-coloniality. As with the inhabitants of Johnson's Happy Valley, "no Axona had ever descended from this plateau to the plains beneath".[5] The voyage out is both an exploration of alternative societies and a confrontation with the forces of change, here linked to the image of an oppressive white power. Phoenix, Flapping Eagle's first port of call, combines the material trappings of progress with the soulless conformity of Western capitalism: "automobiles and launderettes and juke boxes and all kinds of machines and people dressed in dusty clothes with a kind of despair in their eyes".[6] The Axona, for all their own prejudices, possess customs and a social framework that offer a sense of community and identity which the people of Phoenix lack.

The link with *Rasselas* may also hint at the concern with post-coloniality that is the undeveloped side of *Grimus*. Johnson's full title, *The History of Rasselas, Prince of Abyssinia*, provides a link to a minor and somewhat feeble comic motif in *Grimus*. The mysterious Nicholas Deggle, expelled from the town of K for his attempted destruction of the source of Grimus's power, first encounters Flapping Eagle in Phoenix and, eventually and unwittingly, leads him towards his final confrontation with Grimus:

[Deggle] came and went his unknowable way, sauntering in and out of Mrs Cramm's villa on the southern coast of Morispain, and every time he left, he would wave unsmilingly and say:- Ethiopia!

It was a complex and awful joke, arising from the archaic name of that closed, hidden, historical country (Abyssinia ... I'll be seeing you) and it drove Flapping Eagle out of his mind every time it was said.[7]

This mention of Rasselas's kingdom may indicate just how submerged the question of post-coloniality is in the novel. As the only African country never to be colonized, Abyssinia/Ethiopia continues to hold a particular significance for all those whose identities are a product of colonialism.

The links to Johnson's tale of utopian disaffection are reinforced when Flapping Eagle drinks the elixir of life brought to him from Grimus by his sister Bird-Dog. His centuries-long sea journey illustrates the burden of perpetual existence for Flapping Eagle. The problems of longevity are equally oppressive to Rasselas:

He had been before terrified at the length of life which nature promised him, because he considered that in a long time much must be endured.[8]

Rushdie's familiar preoccupations with protagonists of confused or mysterious parentage is there in Flapping Eagle's characterization, alongside the customary whiteness of his skin that sets apart the hero, like Rushdie himself, from the majority of his compatriots. In his various guises of Born-from-Dead, Joe-Sue and Flapping Eagle, Rushdie's hero prefigures the divided identities of Gibreel and Saladin in *The Satanic Verses*. As the demonized Saladin is informed, it is the fate of the migrant post-colonial subject to be "invented" by his oppressors, and to succumb to the requirements of that character invention. The mutations of Flapping Eagle's identity demonstrate a growing awareness of the cultural and political implications of names. Just as Saladin Chamcha re-embraces India through the identity of Salahuddin Chamchawala, so Flapping Eagle is granted true Amerindian status by the eagle that names him, leaving behind the stigmata of androgyny and posthumous birth.

Flapping Eagle's voyage away from Phoenix elicits a passage of illuminating if rather self-indulgent prose. The deployment of a multiplicity of narrative voices has been one of Rushdie's most notable achievements. It is an idea he is clearly grappling with notionally in this passage. Flapping Eagle encounters an Eliot-like figure on his travels:

> A man rehearsing voices on a cliff top: high whining voices, low gravelly voices, subtle insinuating voices, voices honeyed with pain, voices glinting with laughter, the voices of the birds and of the fishes. He asked the man what he was doing (as he sailed by). The man called back—and each word was the word of a different being:- I am looking for a suitable voice to speak in.[9]

It is not so much that *The Satanic Verses* speaks in one voice, but that Rushdie's "ear" for dialogue, and the ease with which he moves between cultures and historical periods is more sophisticated in his later work. This passage shows an alternative narrative voice breaking out, but the skilful manipulation of polyphony and the endless readings this can produce is debated here rather then embarked on.

Alongside the reference to polyphony goes a description of Flying Eagle's chameleon nature, constantly adapting to the changes in his environment and others' attitudes towards him.

> Stripped of his past, forsaking the language of his ancestors for the language of the archipelagos of the world, forsaking the ways of his ancestors for those of the places he drifted to ... he lived, doing what he was given to do, thinking what he was instructed to think, being what it was most desirable to be ... and doing it so skilfully ... that the men he encountered thought he was thus of his own free will and liked him for it.[10]

This is surely an attempt at assessing the condition of the migrant post-colonial that stops short of the direct and personalized accounts that we find in *Shame* and *The Satanic Verses*. The prose touches on the acquiescence of the native subject in his own reinvention, but fails to push its argument home. Flapping Eagle is at one and the same time the hero of a nascent and tentative study of migrant identity, and a chaotic fantasy with no immediately discernible arguments of any import. The voyage of discovery buckles under the weight of the different elements it seeks to assimilate.

Where *Grimus's* links with *Rasselas* are largely thematic, Rushdie's borrowings from Dante consist of topographical and stylistic devices. His most obvious debt to Dante is the use of Virgil Jones as Flapping Eagle's guide. As the poet Virgil leads Dante through Hell and Purgatory to a vision of God in Paradise, so Virgil Jones leads Flapping Eagle in his ascent of Calf Mountain towards Grimus.

In the introduction to her translation of the *Divine Comedy*, Dorothy L. Sayers notes that, in popular tradition, Virgil was often regarded as a white magician. In this vein, Virgil Jones is able to master many of the supernatural obstacles on the path to Grimus and protect his charge. When the poet Virgil assumes his role as Dante's guide in Canto I of *Hell*, he indicates that a worthier soul than he will actually lead Dante to his culminating vision of Paradise. This figure is Beatrice. For Flapping Eagle, Virgil Jones's place is taken by the far-from-beatific Media, a whore from Madame Jocasta's brothel in K.

The topography of both Dante's Hell and Rushdie's Calf Mountain is such that their navigation entails journeys within journeys. The routes up Mount Purgatory and Calf Mountain require travellers to negotiate other dimensions existing simultaneously with the overriding geographical features in the narratives. Cantos V to VIII of *Hell* correspond almost exactly to the movements of Flapping Eagle and Virgil Jones in two chapters of *Grimus*. In the latter the travellers enter the Inner Dimension of Calf Mountain. They must negotiate a series of concentric circles in order to be brought back into a waking state. They journey on bicycles through a tunnel which takes them to a river bank. In the distance is a lake with a tall, stone circular building at the centre. Flapping Eagle passes across to the tower in a boat and, after his encounter with the goddess Axona, is brought back to consciousness.

In the *Divine Comedy*, Dante and Virgil begin their descent through the circles of Hell in Canto V. They find Hell-Gate in the wilderness of Mount Purgatory and cross the River Acheron on the edge of Upper Hell. In Canto VII they spy the watchtower by the marsh of Styx and in Canto VIII a boat is despatched to fetch the two men to the tower. Just as Calf Mountain both rests on and effectively *is* Calf Island, so Mount Purgatory, as Sayers informs us, is "a lofty mountain on an island in the Southern Hemisphere".[11] Both are banked by sandy shores and both Dante and Flapping Eagle have to negotiate forests and bad weather on their ascents. The final, less directly transferred correspondence between the two texts is the use of a symbolic rose in both narratives. The Stone Rose is the source of Grimus's power which must be broken to destroy his continuing control over the mountain and the people of K. The Celestial Rose in Dante's *Paradise* is a symbol of divine love—rather than the authority of a mystical deity—and depicts the saints in heaven on each of its white petals.

Grimus does not restrict its eclecticism to Western literary models. The most direct Eastern influence upon its construction is the *Conference of the*

Birds (Mantiq Ut-Tair), a twelfth-century religious poem by the Sufi mystic Farid ud-din Attar. Despite Rushdie's declaration in a 1984 interview that his interest in Sufism had diminished,[12] it is to some of the figures within Attar's narrative that he returns in *Haroun and the Sea of Stories*. It is possible to speculate on the comfort offered by such a model to a writer as beleaguered as Rushdie was when writing *Haroun*. Despite its more sophisticated handling, there was something of a return to the earlier "innocence" of Grimus in the move. The return to Sufi symbolism may mark an attempt to reconcile the fundamental conflict between the expression of unity that is the basis of Islam—"There is no god but God"—and Rushdie's own movement towards, and increasing embrace of, multiplicity: cultural, social, linguistic and spiritual. The professed project of a union between Islamic culture and the demands of post-colonial post-modernity (for those who do not believe or care that it was achieved in the *Verses*) will perhaps require the influence of Sufism to reassert itself in his writing.

The *Conference* depicts the search of the bird "kingdom" for a ruler. That ruler is the Simurgh (of which Grimus is an anagram) who dwells on Kaf (Calf) Mountain. The birds are led by the Hoopoe (who also figures in *Haroun*), who is singled out by his markings as particularly favoured. He examines the birds to see who is willing and able to undertake the journey to the Simurgh. The Hoopoe sets out the difficulties of the journey ahead in a way that similarly describes the mysterious power of Grimus:

> We have a true king, he lives behind the mountain called Kaf. His name is Simurgh and he is the king of the birds. He is close to us but we are far from him. The place where he dwells is inaccessible, and no tongue is able to utter his name … He is the sovran lord and is bathed in the perfection of his majesty. He does not manifest himself completely even in the place of his dwelling, and to this no knowledge or intelligence can attain.[13]

As with *Rasselas*, there is a link to ideas of longevity and immortality. The poem mentions the water of life drunk by Al Khizr in the time of Abraham which conferred the gift of immortality on him.

The notion of the quest is central to Sufism. It is the means by which the adherent moves towards the divine centre, where the multiplicity of existence is seen to be gathered into totality and unity. The birds in the *Conference* thus discover that their ultimate goal is realization of their unity with the Simurgh. Only thirty of them survive the quest—Simurgh itself means "thirty birds"—and are taken up into a unity of being with their creator:

... they did not know if they were still themselves or if they had become the Simurgh. At last, in a state of contemplation, they realized that they were the Simurgh and that the Simurgh was the thirty birds.[14]

The cosmic mountain of Kaf/Qaf in Sufism has a significance beyond the merely topographical detail it provides in *Grimus*. That mountain-climbing for Rushdie, Dante and Attar possesses some symbolic significance is evident, but it varies between the texts. For Rushdie, it would seem no more than a stylistic device that an arduous ascent is called for from Flapping Eagle in order to achieve his desired goal, though reunion with his sister Bird-Dog seems somewhat lame as a directing force for such a generally aimless character. Timothy Brennan sees it as a representation of the social climbing of the emigrant,[15] but such a meaning is too deeply buried in the text to validate this argument. Its spiritual rather than social symbolism is far greater. For the Sufi:

> mountain climbing corresponds to the inner aspects of life ... One needs a guide to climb: one can climb a mountain by many paths, but one needs to follow one made by experienced people ... one passes the tree-line and enters the world with-out forms. One passes from form to formlessness, from sensible to intelligible. The name of the person who reaches the top of the cosmic mountain is Simurgh.[16]

The topography is repeated in *Grimus*: there is a point at the edge of the Forest of Calf where the travellers enter alternative states. The Sufi quest entails a passage through four Gardens of Paradise: the gardens of the Soul, Heart, Spirit and Essence. The Fountain of Life or Immortality is encountered in the Garden of the Heart, while the Garden of Essence requires of the Sufi-to-be a surrender of individual identity. Brennan sees the goal of the quest in *Grimus* as "a transcendent vision of heterogeneity."[17] This in some ways is the central quest of Rushdie's writing—the assimilation of cultural diversity within artistic unity and not the homogeneity, so often ascribed to post-colonial writing, which he berates in his criticism. Rushdie arguably loses—or at least fails to establish—his own authorial identity in *Grimus*. The successful assertion of heterogeneity and hybridity comes much later.

Rushdie's failure to engage fully with questions of migrant identity in *Grimus* has led to a dissipation of critical interest, away from the seeds of the engagement and towards more abstruse theorization of the novel's complex structure. A rare assessment of the novel, Ib Johansen's essay "The Flight of the Enchanter"[18] acknowledges a Prospero/Caliban relationship between Flapping Eagle and *Grimus*, but fails to explore the novel's (admittedly flimsy) treatment of post-coloniality. Johansen likens *Grimus* to the forms of Menippean satire as defined by Bakhtin. *Problems of Dostoevsky's Poetics* reveals the close links between the genre and Rushdie's construction of *Grimus*. According to Bakhtin, Menippean satire:

> is characterized by an extraordinary freedom of plot and philosophical invention ... [while its] bold and unrestrained use of the fantastic and adventure is internally motivated, justified by and devoted to a purely ideational and philosophical end: the creation of extraordinary situations for the provoking and testing of a philosophical idea, a discourse, a truth, embodied in the image of a wise man, the seeker of this truth.[19]

Brothels and taverns we are told; such as Madame Jocasta's and the Elbaroom in *Grimus*, are the kind of place where the adventures of Menippean satire occur. The confusion of genres and philosophies in *Grimus* means that the truth sought by Flapping Eagle is never clear, never entirely spiritual in a Sufi sense, nor entirely secular, as the book's modernist tendencies might seem to demand. The undeclared quest for the explication and reintegration of the post-colonial identity is side-stepped, and the goal of the journey dissolves in the final moments of the novel's apocalyptic dénouement.

At this stage of Rushdie's writing, *Grimus* offers little more than a mirror of the techniques and conventions of Menippean satire as Bakhtin sees them. But there is within Bakhtin's study an interesting precursor to the treatment of multiple realities and divided identities in Rushdie's later work:

> Dreams, daydreams, insanity destroy the epic and tragic wholeness of a person and his fate: the possibilities of another person and another life are revealed in him, he loses his finalized quality and ceases to mean only one thing; he ceases to coincide with himself.[20]

Grimus can only register that disjunction and multiplicity through a jarring blend of fantastic episodes and philosophies. The *Verses*, with its integral use of dream sequences and its implicit and explicit concern with "cultural schizophrenia", is the exemplification of Bakhtin's idea within the context of post-colonial writing.

The notion of Flapping Eagle's "difference" is established without recourse to any examination of the "othering" of the post-colonial subject. Flapping Eagle is too white for the Axona and different from them by the manner of his birth. But there is nothing about him to suggest any fundamental difference from the figures of oppression that appear in the novel. He is no Saladin Chamcha; the ubiquitous "Paki" confronting the prejudices and bigotry of Proper London. The idea of exile within the novel subsequently retains a Joycean rather than migrant aspect—the misunderstood young man, forced to leave home on a literal and figurative voyage of discovery. There are, however, glimpses of the greater understanding of exile as intimately connected to the condition of post-coloniality. Flapping Eagle, newly arrived in K, sees through a window an old woman examining her past in the form of a photograph album. "It is the natural condition of the exile—putting down roots in memories."[21] In this context, the statement is almost a *non sequitur*. The link between the old woman's nostalgia and the concept of exile is a tenuous one. It is as if the important concerns and messages of Rushdie's writing as a whole are attempting to surface through the confusions of this bizarre narrative. Later, Virgil Jones's ex-wife reads to Flapping Eagle from Virgil's diary of how Calf Island was created and how Grimus plans to populate it with figures from different dimensions. It serves as an acknowledgement of the problems of cultural integration in society.

> Will there be a problem in assimilating immigrants from these different planets in the one society? Grimus is cheerfully optimistic. The differences are too minute to matter, he says. I trust he is right.[22]

Though peripheral in some ways to the admittedly obscure project of *Grimus*, the novel's treatment of women and of female sexuality is interesting in that the embrace of women's rights to social, political and sexual autonomy seems equally matched by the tendency to demonize female sexuality. If Rushdie's agenda for women is to depict their lives and loves without fear or favour, he seems curiously obliged always to demonstrate both rather than neither. In Liv Jones, we get the first of many "ice-women" in his novels—someone who embodies a kind of crystalline perfection (in this case limited to Liv's beauty and sexual prowess) while at the same time maintaining the air of being unapproachable and unassailable. Both Farah Zoroaster in *Shame* and Allie Cone in the *Verses* have the epithet of ice-woman ascribed to them. With mysterious women such as Liv and Farah, this may simply be a way of depicting the distance they seem to desire between themselves and those, particularly the men, around them. But in a character as live and "explicable" as Allie Cone, it smacks of a perverse desire to establish the otherness of woman, particularly as a sexual being.

Similarly the use of the brothel as "a place of refuge"[23] in both *Grimus* and the *Verses* suggests the ambivalence if not outright confusion that Rushdie seems to feel when confronting overt manifestations of female sexuality. The "tart with a heart" he so fondly depicts is as much a male construction as Islam's concepts of female purity and untouchability, so derided by him elsewhere. As with the image of the brothel, female sexuality contains both a promise and a threat. It is at once liberating as an expression of individual identity and oppressive in itself when it reminds man of his own weakness. In Flapping Eagle's journey through the Inner Dimension, the threat/promise dichotomy of female sexuality is embodied in Bird-Dog. Having been the woman who initiated him in to the pleasures of sex, her body under Grimus's thrall becomes a labyrinthine tunnel, in a passage that displays the more disturbing traits in Rushdie's presentation of women:

> The hole between her legs yawned: its hairs were like ropes. Ten yards away. She was a house, a cavern lying red and palpitating before him, the curtain of hair parting. He heard her booming voice.—Why resist, she was saying. Give up, little brother. Come in. Give up. Come in.[24]

The two women in the town of K who find their attention drawn to Flapping Eagle, Elfrida Gribb and Irina Cherkassova, in themselves represent this dichotomy. Irina, sexually rapacious and worldly, Elfrida, innocent and naive. It is arguable that Rushdie's treatment of women in later novels represents something more complex than a division between virgins and whores, but Grimus seems disturbingly simplistic on this count. Much of the novel's sexual content is gratuitous, adding nothing to the story-line or the development of character (witness Virgil's oft-repeated, rather tedious breast fetish) while sexual degradation as a means of controlling women occurs too regularly for comfort. Whatever problems still adhere to Rushdie's treatment of women in his later novels, he is at least able to allegorize, politicize and humorize the sex according to demand. Here it is purely mechanized.

Rushdie's desire to draw on the genre of science fiction may account in part for some of the ingenuousness of the narrative, even perhaps for its presentation of women; sadly two-dimensional in much male science fiction. In a *Scripsi* interview, Rushdie says he turned to the genre because it was "traditionally a good vehicle for the novel of ideas".[25] But as Eric S. Rabkin points out in *The Fantastic in Literature*:

> a good work of science fiction makes one and only one
> assumption about its narrative world that violates our knowledge
> about our own world and then extrapolates the whole narrative
> world from that difference.[26]

This is clearly not the case with *Grimus*. Here, the reader is expected not
only to suspend all normal narrative expectations and enter "an other world",
but also to be and remain as fully in tune with the real world, its literature,
philosophies and religions as is intellectually possible. Rushdie is nothing if
not a demanding read.

Rabkin posits the notion of a narrative continuum along which science
fiction moves, embracing more and more elements of fantasy to take it away
from the recognizable-but-not-quite-real situation of "true" science fiction.
Such "technology" as appears in *Grimus*, most notably the powers of the
Stone Rose, is clearly at the fantastic end of Rabkin's scale, while Rushdie's
own working definition of sci-fi as the novel of ideas would seem inadequate
as a reason for employing the genre.

Elsewhere Rabkin speaks of the feelings of alienation and
transformation that prompt much science-fiction writing[27] and it is perhaps
these moods that Rushdie is trying to recreate in *Grimus*. The alienation is
not as yet politicized, the transformation is still more of a fantastic than a
social nature. The desire to employ specific genres at this stage, however
inappropriate they might ultimately prove, is perhaps a defence against the
impending loss of narrative control that might come from the attempt to
create the truly hybrid novel.

Grimus represents the beginning of a conception of literature as an
orchestration of voices—one in which the art of the oriental story-teller is
blended with a diversity of literary techniques to form something entirely
individual. The "baggyness" of *Grimus's* narrative is of a different nature to
that of, say, *Midnight's Children*. One can accept Elfrida Gribb's views on
narrative without feeling that Rushdie successfully implemented them in the
novel:

> I do not care for stories that are so, so tight. Stories should be like
> life, slightly frayed at the edges, full of loose ends and lives
> juxtaposed by accident rather than some grand design.[28]

Grimus is clearly a novel of a period when Rushdie had not yet achieved
the synthesis of diverse cultural strands and narrative forms. He rightly

attributes the novel's failure to this lack of a defined voice at its heart, or even, to borrow from Sufism, a unified voice which expresses its own diversity:

> I feel very distant from [Grimus], mainly because I don't like the language it is written in. It's a question of hearing your own voice, and I don't hear it because I hadn't found it then.[29]

NOTES

1. Timothy Brennan, *Salman Rushdie and the Third World*, London: Macmillan, 1989, p. 70.

2. Frantz Fanon, *The Wretched of the Earth*, Harmondsworth: Penguin, 1967, p. 168.

3. *ibid.*, pp. 176-7.

4. Brennan, *op. cit.*, p. 71.

5. Rushdie, *Grimus*, London: Grafton Books, 1989, p. 17.

6. *ibid.*, p. 21.

7. *ibid.*, p. 28.

8. *The Oxford Authors: Samuel Johnson*, ed. Donald Greene, Oxford: OUP, 1984, p. 340.

9. *Grimus*, p. 32.

10. *ibid.*

11. D. L. Sayers, Introduction to Dante Alighieri's, *Purgatory*, Harmondsworth: Penguin, 1949, p. 69.

12. Rushdie interviewed in *Scripsi*, III, 2-3, 1985, p. 125.

13. Farid ud-din Attar, *Conference of the Birds*, trans. S. C. Nott, London: Janus Press, 1954, p. 12.

14. *ibid.*, p. 131.

15. Brennan, *op. cit.*, p. 72.

16. Laleh Bakhtiar, *Sufi: Expressions of the Mystic Quest*, London: Thames and Hudson, 1976, pp. 27-8.

17. Brennan, *op. cit.*, p. 77.

18. Ib Johansen, "The Flight of the Enchanter: Reflections on Salman Rushdie's *Grimus*", *Kunapipi*, VII, I, 1985, pp. 20-32.

19. Mikhail Bakhtin, *Problems of Dostoevsky's Poetics*, from *Theory and History of Literature, Volume 8*, ed. and trans. Caryl Emerson, Manchester: Manchester UP, p. 114.

20. *ibid.*, pp. 116-7.

21. *Grimus*, p. 107.

22. *ibid.*, p. 212.

23. *ibid.*, p. 133.

24. *ibid.*, p. 71.

25. Rushdie interviewed in *Scripsi, op. cit.*, p. 125.

26. Eric S. Rabkin, *The Fantastic in Literature*, Princeton: Princeton UP, 1976, p. 121.

27. *Science Fiction: A Historical Anthology*, ed. Eric S. Rabkin, New York: OUP, 1983, p. 4.

28. *Grimus*, p. 141.

29. *Scripsi, op. cit.*, p. 125.

K.M. NEWTON

Literary Theory and the Rushdie Affair

Does literary theory have anything to contribute to the Salman Rushdie affair? Up to now the conflict between him and his opponents has been discussed mainly in terms of such issues as free speech and free expression, but on its own the freedom question is not likely to have much impact on Muslim opinion. Muslims can easily point to anomalies and contradictions in the arguments of defenders of the right to free speech and free expression. For example, the fact that there is a law against blasphemy in this country which applies only to Christianity, even if it is almost never enforced, would appear to discriminate unfavourably against the Islamic religion. One also sees free expression curtailed in other areas without protest, a point made forcibly by a Rushdie supporter, Kathy Acker:

> Most of the western writers who have discussed the issues around *The Satanic Verses* have proclaimed, as writers and artists, their right to 'freedom of speech'. (A freedom not publicly applauded when the matter in hand isn't anti-Muslim, if that's what *The Satanic Verses* is, but is rather anti-Zionist, and, as in the case of Jean Genet's final book, pornographic, etc.)[1]

From *English: The Journal of the English Association* 41, no. 171 (Autumn 1992): 235-247. © 1992 by The English Association.

It may, therefore, be more productive to shift the ground from freedom of expression to the question of reading. Rushdie himself has moved the debate into this area: whereas Muslim readers interpret certain passages in *The Satanic Verses* as blasphemous Rushdie has asserted that this is an inappropriate way of reading the novel since it is a work of art and should not be read in such a literal manner. In his essay 'In Good Faith' he says that the novel 'aspires to the condition of literature' and that 'people on all sides of the argument have lost sight of this fact'.[2] He rejects the view that the novel is deliberately offensive to Muslims as this is to ignore its literary aspect: 'It has been bewildering to learn that people *do not care about art*' (p. 397). Is it possible to demonstrate convincingly that Muslim interpreters of the novel are guilty of misreading or are they justified in reading the novel as they do? Though literary theory may have little or no direct influence on fanatics who are determined to kill Rushdie, it surely has a responsibility to attempt to resolve or at least to clarify the issues that are at stake in this conflict since clearly they have wide and important ramifications.

It may be useful to compare the conflict between Rushdie and Muslim readers as to how *The Satanic Verses* should be read with a dispute about reading between M. H. Abrams and J. Hillis Miller in regard to Wordsworth's lyric 'A Slumber Did My Spirit Seal'. In an essay called 'Construing and Deconstructing' Abrams attacked Miller's deconstructive reading of the poem as an 'over-reading' and advocated a return to 'construing' the plain meaning of the poem.[3] Miller replied as follows to Abrams's critique of his reading:

> The major misunderstanding in Abrams' essay might be approached by way of his title, 'Construing and Deconstructing'. If these two terms are translated into their more traditional equivalents, Abrams' title would be 'Grammar and Rhetoric' … Abrams' error is the aboriginal one of assuming that the grammar of a language … is a first and fundamental level of easily identifiable meaning to which figurative language, the deviant realm of tropes, is added as a nonessential layer open to what Abrams, in a nice little play of double meaning of his own, calls 'over-reading'. First there is under-reading, or the construing of plain grammar, and then, if you happen to want it (though why should you?) there is over-reading, the interpretation of figures, what is sometimes called deconstruction.

Miller goes on to argue that 'All good reading is ... the reading of tropes at the same time as it is the construing of syntactical and grammatical patterns' and that 'there is no such thing as that plain under-reading which Abrams hypothesizes'.[4]

Using this model, Muslim readers of *The Satanic Verses* may be seen as 'under-readers' of the text who take the words on the page literally whereas Rushdie could claim that his text requires 'over-readers'. Another way of putting this is to say that Muslim readers read the text 'grammatically' whereas the text requires that one looks beyond the grammatical or literal to the rhetorical or the figurative. On the face of it, then, if one accepts Miller's argument, one can accuse Muslim interpreters of Rushdie's text of misreading it because they restrict its meaning to the grammatical level and refuse to recognise its more powerful rhetorical or figurative dimension. Rushdie himself, in defending the novel against Muslim attacks on it, has emphasised its figurative nature. The passages that have particularly offended Muslims do not aim 'to vilify or "disprove" Islam, but ... portray a soul in crisis' (p. 397); a reference to 'Salman the Persian' is not intended to 'insult and abuse' the Prophet's companion Salman al-Faris but is rather 'an ironic reference to the novel's author' (p. 399). Rushdie claims that 'such highlighting is a proper function of literature' (p. 400). Similarly, the 'shocking' representations of the Prophet's wives as whores are not to be taken literally but rather as images which juxtapose antithetically 'the sacred and profane worlds' (p. 401).

However, one difficulty of this parallel is that such an eminent critic as M. H. Abrams, if one accepts Miller's characterisation of him as an 'under-reader', becomes implicitly an ally of Muslim readers of *The Satanic Verses*, and one could find numerous critics who would much prefer to 'under-read' Wordsworth in the manner of Abrams than to 'over-read' him in the manner of Miller. Miller's dismissal of under-reading and his claim that 'There is only and always, from the beginning, one form or another of over-reading, the reading of grammar and tropes together, more or less adequately'[5] may therefore do the Rushdie case more harm than good unless we explore the issue further.

Now of course one cannot say that reading 'grammatically' without taking account of the rhetorical or figurative is wrong in itself. In most forms of discourse 'under-reading' is quite adequate to serve our normal purposes. Indeed to attempt to read all texts rhetorically would be absurd. But though it may be pragmatically necessary to restrict certain discourses to the level of the grammatical, this does not mean that Miller is wrong to assert that the rhetorical dimension can never be excluded from any text. A motorist who interprets a 'Keep Left' road-sign figuratively as a political slogan may find himself or herself in practical difficulties but this does not mean that the language of the text is not open to such a reading. Rather, pragmatic considerations demand that road-signs be restricted to a grammatical or literal interpretation with any possible rhetorical dimension of the text being ignored. Miller would not, I feel sure, deny this. His claim that good reading demands that the rhetorical have priority over the grammatical implicity applies only to certain forms of discourse, most obviously literature. Nor surely, would Abrams deny that rhetoric is crucial in any reading of a literary text; his difference with Miller is about how far one should go in interpreting literature rhetorically. Both Miller and Abrams would almost certainly agree that a rigidly grammatical reading of a literary text that ignored its rhetorical aspect was inadequate. Rushdie therefore, if *The Satanic Verses* is recognised as a work of literature, would be likely to have the backing of both in the conflict.

On the face of it, literary theory would appear to be on the side of Rushdie since it can provide support for the view that the language of literary texts cannot be read in a straightforward, 'grammatical' manner. Certainly the claim that *The Satanic Verses* is a work of art and therefore a literary text is central to Rushdie's strategy in his fight against his opponents, and he continually asserts in speeches and interviews that the text has to be read as such. What Rushdie can be interpreted as asserting is that his novel is not open to accusations of blasphemy since in art or literature the figurative necessarily dominates. One could illustrate how such a view may affect reading by considering a canonical literary text, *Richard III*, which could also be accused of bias and factual inaccuracy. The question as to whether the historical Richard was in fact the psychopathic monster and murderer Shakespeare depicts him as being could be seen as irrelevant in any consideration of the play as a work of art. Read as a literary text, it may be argued, the play does not operate on such a factual or literal plane and anyone who condemned it on these grounds would be responding wrongly to it. Even if convincing documentary evidence emerged which indicated that Richard had not been responsible for the murder of the princes in the Tower, this would not undermine the power or interest of the play as a work of literature. Similarly, Muslim readers of *The Satanic Verses* who condemn it for its representation of the Prophet are like those who would condemn *Richard III* because they regard it as presenting a historically false picture of Richard. Both sets of readers are guilty of a category mistake: they respond inappropriately to literary discourse. As Rushdie himself writes:

> Fiction uses facts as a starting-place and then spirals away to explore its real concerns, which are only tangentially historical. Not to see this, to treat fiction as if it were fact, is to make a serious mistake of categories. The case of *The Satanic Verses* may be one of the biggest category mistakes in history! (p. 409)

However, it is too early to conclude that literary theory will help Rushdie win the conflict with his Muslim opponents, for his strategy of claiming literary status for his text is not without its dangers. A Muslim opponent familiar with literary theory might question whether Rushdie has the right to claim that his text is a work of art or literature and in consequence exists beyond the scope of grammatical readings. Can Rushdie as author unilaterally consign his text to the category of art or literature? John M. Ellis in his book *The Theory of Literary Criticism* argues that the term 'literature' denotes a special group of texts which are open to a distinctive form of reading: 'Literary texts are not treated as part of the normal flow of speech, which has a purpose in its original context and is then discarded after that purpose is achieved, and they are not judged according to such limited purposes'.[6] In practical terms this means that the figurative dimension assumes predominance in texts categorised as literary, enabling such texts to break with grammatical or literal signification. But Ellis also claims that the most that the author of a text that aspires to be literature can do is to offer it to the community as a literary text. It is up to the community to decide whether or not the text in question deserves to have this privileged status. The author has no power to make the community accept a particular text as literature. Until such acceptance is accorded by the community at large, it could be persuasively argued, it is legitimate to deny that the figurative dimension of the text has an intrinsic priority over the grammatical dimension.

Furthermore, even if a consensus of non-Muslims emerges which claims that the novel deserves to be categorised as a work of literature, it is still doubtful whether Rushdie's Muslim opponents would accept that such a judgement was made in good faith and not mere special pleading. Non-Muslims, it could be reasonably claimed, who support Rushdie in asserting that the text has to be accorded literary status are not expressing a disinterested literary judgement but are ideologically motivated by their desire to protect Western values of free speech and free expression from attack. But more interestingly, Muslims might also argue with some justification that the main reason that non-Muslim readers may find no difficulty in going beyond the grammatical aspect of the text to the figurative is simply a consequence of the fact that they don't care whether or not its representation of the life of the Prophet is an insult to the Muslim religion. If they did care might they not be less ready to accord the text the privileged status of art or literature? When Rolf Hochhuth's play *The Soldiers*, which depicts Churchill as being responsible for the murder of a Polish politician, was first produced in London and was attacked as libellous, Kenneth Tynan defended the play by arguing that it was no different from *Richard III*. Tynan asserted that since theatre-goers did not reject the latter because it presented Richard as a criminal psychopath even though the historical evidence suggests that he was not, why should they refuse to accept Hochhuth's representation of Churchill as murderer? Both plays belonged to the category of art, Tynan implied, and therefore the figurative had priority over the literal or grammatical. But clearly the difference was that whereas in the case of Richard audiences had ceased to care about the historical figure, with Churchill they still did care and this made it difficult for audiences to respond to the play as a figurative representation, as they could with regard to Richard. The grammatical or literal thus had the greater power with the result that the play had to be taken off. Muslim opponents of Rushdie could exploit such cases in order to claim that the only difference between them and non-Muslim readers of *The Satanic Verses* is that they cannot be indifferent to Rushdie's depiction of the Prophet; the literal force of the text is too strong for them to set it aside in favour of the figurative.

It seems to me, therefore, that though it is understandable that Rushdie should attempt to counter Muslim attacks on the novel by claiming that it has to be interpreted as a work of art or literature in which the figurative has priority, this strategy will not be successful and indeed it may be counter-productive since Muslim readers, as I have suggested, have reasonable grounds for rejecting such a claim. However, even more worrying for defenders of Rushdie is the fact that contemporary critical theory casts doubt on the view that even in literary texts the figurative or rhetorical should have priority over the grammatical or literal.

J. Hillis Miller, in his discussion of the relation between grammar and rhetoric in literature, has almost certainly been influenced by Paul de Man's essay on this subject, 'Semiology and Rhetoric'. De Man, like Miller, sees rhetoric as crucial to any understanding of literature and states that he 'would not hesitate to equate the rhetorical, figural potentiality of language with literature itself'.[7] Yet there is a difference in emphasis between their views. Whereas for Miller the grammar and rhetoric of a text must be read together, with rhetoric having priority in literary texts at least, de Man rather places the greatest emphasis on the fact that neither the grammatical nor the rhetorical has intrinsic priority in either literary or non-literary texts. Indeed, he states that even in literary texts, literal meaning cannot be effaced by figurative meaning, as he shows in an analysis of Yeats's line from 'Among School Children', 'How can we know the dancer from the dance?' In de Man's view the meaning generated by neither the grammatical nor the rhetorical can totally prevail since the line can be read either as an ordinary question inviting an answer or as a rhetorical question, and this creates an undecidability of meaning which for him is characteristic of texts that deserve to be called literary. De Man thus stresses the irreconcilability of grammar and rhetoric, not, like Miller, the necessity of reading them together.

It would seem to follow from the de Man essay that the literal dimension even of literary texts cannot be set aside in favour of the figurative. If he is right then clearly the Muslim literal reading of *The Satanic Verses* cannot merely be dismissed as the consequence of a category mistake. And further, if one denies that *The Satanic Verses* is a work of literature or believes that it is too early to assign it such a status why should the figurative be accorded the greater force than the literal? Why should one accept the author's view that the text has to be read figuratively? Thus de Man's treatment of the grammar-rhetoric relation offers little protection to Rushdie in his conflict with Muslim readers.

One can also argue from a different point of view that it is impossible with any text, literary or non-literary, to assign priority either to the figurative or the literal. To claim intrinsic superiority for one method of reading is to essentialise reading since no account is taken of the social and cultural factors that necessarily have a determining influence on the construction of the reader and the reading process. The reader is not an abstract entity but a social and cultural product, and the particular methods of reading that are practised at a particular period cannot be seen in isolation from social, cultural and political forces. This is true both for methods of reading that are predominantly grammatical or rhetorical and also for de Manian deconstructive methods which play off the grammatical and the rhetorical. It would be easy, for example, to construct a social explanation as to why deconstruction was such a force during the 1970s and similarly explain why its power has greatly diminished in the past decade. Since social or cultural factors will have a determining influence on whether the grammatical, the figurative, or the deconstructive will tend to have greater force as a reading method at any particular historical moment, one cannot therefore categorically state that one method of reading is intrinsically superior to another. To adopt such a view is to assume that reading can be abstracted from the cultural situation within which all reading must take place.

Clearly, for devout Muslims it is virtually impossible for a text such as *The Satanic Verses* to be read in such a way that figurative meanings stand in place of the literal meaning of the text; the text is so offensive to them that the figurative dimension has little if any force. But there have been circumstances in which the rhetorical has seemed to dominate the grammatical with a similar degree of power for readers at particular periods. For example, for people under occupation or living in totalitarian states it is well known that certain literary texts when taken figuratively have such relevance to their cultural situation that the literal force of the language of the text is virtually abolished in favour of meanings produced by metaphorical or allegorical forms of reading. Modern productions of classic drama have tended similarly to exploit the figural in an effort to make such texts as directly meaningful as possible to a twentieth-century audience. There seems to me to be no justification for judging modes of reading that emphasise either the grammatical or the figurative as invalid in an intrinsic sense, as critics such as Abrams and Miller seem inclined to do. One cannot separate reading from the interests which govern it and from the cultural situations which shape those interests.

But perhaps what makes Rushdie's defence of *The Satanic Verses* as a literary text that must be read figuratively particularly problematic at the present time is that recent literary theory has seen a decided shift from the view that the figurative should be predominant in the reading of literary texts. The Rushdie position relies implicitly on a critical ideology which the most influential contemporary critical theory has rejected. The major tendency of critical theory over the last ten years or so has favoured a theorised and politicised historical criticism which contends that literature is not a discourse in which the figurative has an independent force that has priority over the grammatical but that even the works of a writer as canonic as Shakespeare must be read contextually and politically in a very specific sense. John M. Ellis's view that literary texts 'are defined as those that outgrow the original context of their utterance' and 'are not dependent on that context for meaning'[8] is rejected. For example, Jean E. Howard and Marion F. O'Connor describe as follows how such a critical approach deals with Shakespeare:

> By a political analysis we mean one which examines how Shakespearean texts have functioned to produce, reproduce, or contest historically specific relations of power ... [The text] lives

in history, with history itself understood as a field of contestation …
[T]o posit a category of self-evidently literary works, somehow
above ideology, is to ignore the historicity of the very category of
the literary …[9]

Rushdie, in contrast, views literature as anti-ideological:

If religion is an answer, if political ideology is an answer, then
literature is an inquiry; great literature, by asking extraordinary
questions, opens doors in our minds …
… literature is, of all the arts, the one best suited to challenging
absolutes of all kinds. (pp. 423-4)

It would be a distortion to say that this new historical criticism rejects
the rhetorical meaning of texts in favour of their grammatical meaning. In
many respects this form of criticism is highly rhetorical in that it introduces
into criticism a complex intertextuality founded on the belief that texts do
not exist in isolation. As Stephen Greenblatt has put it, the aim of new
historical criticism is to investigate 'both the social presence to the world of
the literary text and the social presence of the world in the literary text'.[10]
But one can argue that the aim of situating literary texts in their historical
contexts is fundamentally grammatical in that their contemporary meaning
is recovered and interpretations which exploit the figurative language of texts
in order to read them in a more universal human context are attacked. Thus
a critic such as Jonathan Dollimore, in discussing *King Lear*, rejects
interpretations of the play which read it metaphorically as being about
human nature or the human condition and insists on reading the play in
relation to ideological issues in the Jacobean period. He dismisses readings
which emphasise general humanist themes in favour of a reading which
emphasises power and property within specific material conditions.[11]

Earlier I used *Richard III* as an example in discussing the view that a text
had to be divorced from questions of historical fact, or the grammatical, in
order to function as a literary text, so that those who attacked or condemned
it on the grounds of perpetrating lies about Richard would not be treating it
as a literary text but merely as an ordinary speech act. New historical
criticism would take a different view. If there existed contemporary attacks
on the play—for being, for example, a blatant piece of Tudor propaganda
which employed lies and character assassination for political purposes—these
could not be dismissed, new historical critics would surely argue, as anti-
literary for they would show that literature does not exist outside of ideology

but rather that the text lives in history as a 'field of contestation', as Howard and O'Connor put it. Critics who would take such a view can hardly therefore deny the legitimacy of the Muslim response to *The Satanic Verses*. Indeed from such a critical perspective is the Muslim way of reading the text not preferable to attempts to defend the text as a work of literature whose metaphorical force enables it to communicate in a more universal human context since the Muslim response in effect refuses to accept that the novel is a text which is beyond ideology?

If one were discussing a classic literary text, such as a play by Shakespeare, there would be no difficulty in accepting that the text can be read in different ways, depending on the interests and critical outlook of the reader or interpreter of the text, even though there may be great debate as to which critical approach is most valid. Such literary texts can be read figuratively, that is as texts which have transcended their originating contexts, grammatically as texts which participate in the ideological struggles of their historical moment, hermeneutically as texts in which there is a 'fusion of horizons' between the originating context and the situation of the modern reader, or deconstructively as texts in which there is an undecidable play of meaning between the rhetorical and the grammatical. But when it comes to discussing contemporary works such as *The Satanic Verses*, a novel whose literary status is still undecided, the grammatical critical perspective is surely the most powerful. In a hundred years time, if the work has been accorded literary status, it will no doubt be possible to read it figuratively or outside of any specific ideological or political context but such a reading hardly seems possible at present. The Muslim literal reading of the text refuses to accept figurative meanings that allow it to communicate in a wider human context and is therefore a form of grammatical reading, and in the present critical climate how can it be said to be illegitimate?

In a recent essay Alan Sinfield writes:

> The traditional goal of literary study assumed an essential humanity, informing both text and critic ... It is now easy to see that this reading position was in fact that of the discourse of literary criticism, and that teaching amounted to persuading people who were attached to other discourses to abandon them and adopt ours. If a lower-class person, woman, student, person of colour, lesbian or gay man did not 'respond' to 'the text', we thought it was because they were reading partially, wrongly ... We believed they—we—became fuller human beings. Perhaps we did; but it was at the expense of abandoning subcultural

allegiances. The profession requires you to read not as a homosexual or a Black, but in accordance with its established criteria.[12]

Sinfield goes on to urge that academics 'should seek ways to break out of the professional subculture and work intellectually in dissident subcultures'.[13] This view has a powerful appeal but one should face the fact that there is no logical reason why 'Muslim fundamentalist' should not be added to Sinfield's list of 'lower-class person, woman, student, person of colour, lesbian or gay man'. Probably a majority of contemporary literary theorists would accept Sinfield's position, but how can they then avoid, as a consequence, supporting the Muslim point of view in *The Satanic Verses* debate?

If, as I have suggested, one can defend the Muslim reaction to *The Satanic Verses* by using arguments derived from de Manian deconstruction or new historical criticism, why then have contemporary theorists not registered their support of the right of Muslims to respond to the text in the way they do or indicated their disagreement with Rushdie's claim that the text's literary aspirations render such a reading invalid? Obviously literary theorists must sympathise with Rushdie's situation and do not therefore wish to be seen as offering support to his enemies. But though it is understandable that literary theorists do not want to make Rushdie's situation any worse than it is, it seems to me to be a mistake for literary theory to keep silent on this subject. Not only would it be morally wrong to withhold support from the Muslim manner of reading *The Satanic Verses* if it is more defensible than the claim that it has a protected literary status but, even more important, non-Muslims' untheorised partiality for the Rushdie case may have made matters worse. Not only do non-Muslim supporters of Rushdie proclaim that Muslims are wrong in seeking to have a book banned, a view I share, but more significantly they also appear to suggest that Muslims have no right even to find the book offensive since they are reading the text in an improper fashion. Thus Malise Ruthven in his book *A Satanic Affair* has no sympathy with a Muslim, who believes in regard to *The Satanic Verses* that 'certain words have a certain plain meaning' and who is offended 'that lies should be propagated' because 'Islam stands for the propagation of truth'. For Ruthven this Muslim 'had a naive, unscientific view of what was essentially a literary question' and he goes on to assert that

fundamentalism ... is hard, factualistic and philistine, impervious to the multi-layered nuances of meaning that reside in texts, in

fictions, in music and iconographies, in the cells of art and culture
where modernity—that universal modernity created by a vibrant,
still dynamic 'West'—stores its spiritual wealth.[14]

Literary critics and theorists would, I believe, make a positive
contribution to the Rushdie affair if they openly admitted that Muslim
readers are justified in finding *The Satanic Verses* offensive. To argue that the
novel is a work of literature and therefore incapable of giving offence is not
a view that it is reasonable to expect Muslim readers of the work to accept
and, as I have suggested above, it is a view that many contemporary literary
theorists would also, rightly I believe, reject. Instead of being urged to
tolerate *The Satanic Verses* or to accord it the privileged status of literature,
Muslim readers should rather be encouraged by literary critics and theorists
to enter into debate with the book, to answer back as vigorously as they wish.
If literary critics and theorists had adopted this policy from the beginning
then it is possible that Muslim anger with the novel may have taken a
different form. But the lack of sympathy of non-Muslims for Muslim outrage
with the book, together with explicit and implicit accusations that the
Muslim response was primitive and philistine, only served to create a buildup of frustration among Muslims that has led to many British Muslims
supporting the Ayatollah's 'fatwa'. It may be too late to do anything to defuse
the situation. Nevertheless I think critics and theorists, however late in the
day, should make an effort to redress this situation by acknowledging that the
Muslim response to the text is, from the standpoint of contemporary literary
theory, legitimate even if *The Satanic Verses* is a text which aspires to be
literature, since literary texts cannot be dissociated from ideological struggles
and conflicts of various sorts and thus necessarily provoke opposition. It
follows from this that literary critics and theorists should offer their support
to Muslims who enter into ideological or political debate with the novel and
consequently go beyond mere attack and condemnation. To be fair to
Rushdie, despite his efforts to have the novel read figuratively in the manner
of literary texts as he conceives them, he accepts that his opponents have the
right to enter into dispute with the novel 'with the utmost passion' (p. 393).

What the Rushdie affair clearly demonstrates is that both Muslims and
those who have inherited Western values need to make an effort to resist
strong forces within their different traditions and should be prepared to
enter into a dialogic relation with difference. This would help promote
compromise rather than intolerance and conflict. Muslims, especially those
who now reside in Western countries, have to strive to come to a *modus
vivendi* with European Enlightenment values, especially the latter's

encouragement of scepticism and critique. But inheritors of Western values should also learn to view works of art in a less idealistic spirit. The Romantic tradition encouraged the tendency to set works of art on a pedestal, as in Keats's 'What the imagination seizes as Beauty must be truth', and this valorisation of the work of art has continued in the twentieth century in such critical movements as the New Criticism and Leavisism. Thus Rushdie's appeal to art tends to have considerable force for the Western consciousness. In the debate over *The Satanic Verses*, however, the pressure has been almost entirely on Muslims to modify their position, but there is much more likelihood of persuading Muslims to do this if there is a corresponding modification in Western attitudes. If both sides could recognise the necessity for such a spirit of compromise then a more positive outcome to an apparently intractable conflict may still be possible.

NOTES

1. See 'Words for Salman Rushdie', *New Statesman and Society*, 31 March 1989, p. 25.

2. Salman Rushdie, *Imaginary Homelands: Essays and Criticism 1981-1991* (London: Granta Books in association with Penguin, 1991), p. 393. Page numbers incorporated in text.

3. See M. H. Abrams, *Doing Things with Texts: Essays in Criticism and Critical Theory* (New York: W. W. Norton, 1989), pp. 297-332.

4. J. Hillis Miller, *Theory Now and Then* (Hemel Hempstead: Harvester-Wheatsheaf, 1991), p. 188.

5. Ibid.

6. John M. Ellis, *The Theory of Literary Criticism: A Logical Analysis* (Berkeley: University of California Press, 1974), p. 111.

7. Paul de Man, *Allegories of Reading: Figural Language in Rousseau, Nietzsche, Rilke and Proust* (New Haven: Yale University Press, 1979), p. 10.

8. Ellis, p. 111-2.

9. Jean E. Howard and Marion O'Connor, eds, *Shakespeare Reproduced: The Text in History and Ideology* (New York: Methuen, 1987), pp. 3-5.

10. Stephen Greenblatt, *Renaissance Self-Fashioning: From More to Shakespeare* (Chicago: University of Chicago Press, 1980), p. 5.

11. See Jonathan Dollimore, *Radical Tragedy: Religion, Ideology and Power in the Drama of Shakespeare and his Contemporaries* (Brighton: Harvester Press, 1984), p. 197.

12. Alan Sinfield, 'Englit and Subcultures', *CUE News: The Newsletter of the Council for University English*, 4: No. 1 (1991), p. 8.

13. Ibid., p. 9.

14. Malise Ruthven, *A Satanic Affair: Salman Rushdie and the Rage of Islam* (London: Chatto and Windus, 1990), pp. 138, 139, 142.

NICHOLAS D. ROMBES, JR.

The Satanic Verses
as a Cinematic Narrative

Near the end of *The Satanic Verses*, the narrator suggests that there are "places which the camera cannot see."[1] This statement embodies one of the novel's focal concerns with the differences between how an engaged, omniscient narrator apprehends the novel's events and how the camera eye apprehends them. I will be arguing that Rushdie establishes these opposing constructs in order to highlight this dichotomy of perception as well as to expose the potential danger of relying on the camera as a source of truth. Rushdie juxtaposes a questioning, engaged narrator who is preoccupied with the nature of good and evil, justice and mercy, and revenge and compassion, with a camera whose quest for truth is severely restricted by economic and physical constraints. Not only does the camera flatten events and reduce them to mere facts, but it also invites potential manipulation of those events since the camera's vision is limited by restrictions beyond its control.

Although my primary concern is with how Rushdie presents these two opposing ways of seeing. I will also briefly examine his use of film language within the novel, as well as ways in which he incorporates cinematic techniques into the narratological framework. The novel resonates not only with the "language" of film, but with narratological strategies borrowed from the cinema.[2] Rushdie himself has acknowledged the influence of cinematic technique in his fiction: "The whole experience of montage technique, split

From *Literature/Film Quarterly* 21, no. 1 (1993): 47-53. © 1993 by Salisbury State University.

screens, dissolves, and so on, has become a film language which translates quite easily into fiction and gives you an extra vocabulary that traditionally has not been part of the vocabulary of literature. And I think I used that quite a bit."[3] Rushdie employs various cinematic strategies not only to create "visual" images (frequent aerial or high shots, for instance) but also to shape the narrative, as well (focus-through or racking, dissolves, and crosscutting, for instance). Likewise, Rushdie's prevalent use of "film language" to describe various scenes works to continually reinforce this link between fiction and film.

On one level, Rushdie uses recurring references to film or film industry jargon to remind his readers of the connection between this particular narrative and film. By keeping us in this frame of mind. Rushdie is able to insert narrative techniques of cinema into the novel. For instance, many of the characters are film actors engaged in various film projects: Gibreel himself had been "the biggest star in the history of the Indian movies" (11). Likewise, these references often "link various story lines threading through the novel. S.S. Sisodia, the lecherous movie producer, suggests that Gibreel begin making movies about the archangel Gibreel: "The proposal was for a series of films, both historical and contemporary, each concentrating on one incident from the angel's long and illustrious career: a trilogy at least. 'Don't tell me.' Allie said, mocking the small shining mogul. '*Gibreel in Jahilia, Gibreel Meets the Imam, Gibreel with the Butterfly Girl*'" (345).

Not only does Rushdie use these frequent film references to link the frame story to the separate stories, but also to comment on the nature of film itself:

> And Sisodia's purloining of the dream-narratives he'd heard at Gibreel's bedside could be seen as serendipitous: for once those stories were clearly placed in the artificial, fabricated world of the cinema, it ought to become easier for Gibreel to see them as fantasies, too. That Berlin Wall between the dreaming and waking state might well be more rapidly rebuilt as a result. (347)

Although the transference of dreams into an "artificial" reality via the screen may be therapeutic, it assumes that Gibreel's dreams are in fact just dreams, and that fictionalizing them will somehow help him to overcome them, both of which are highly questionable. The proposed cinematizing of Gibreel's dream-state creates only more confusion about the nature of Gibreel's dreams, as Sisodia's scheme to re-introduce Gibreel to the public at the gala "Filmmela" ends in chaos.

The narrative often adopts the language of film itself in order to remind the readers of the connection between fiction and film. In the "Mahound" chapter, Mahound himself is described in a kind of character sketch frequently found at the beginning of scripts. The description is limited only to the outward, physical characteristics of the man. The language is almost terse, as definite articles and pronouns are dropped from the beginnings of the sentences. Mahound is a businessman who "looks as he should, high forehead, eaglenose, broad in the shoulders, narrow in the hip. Average height, brooding, dressed in two pieces of plain cloth, each four ells in length, one draped around his body, the other over his shoulder. Large eyes: long lashes like a girl's" (93). This is a sketch of how Mahound looks or *should* look, as if he were being cast for a scene. Rushdie uses this technique to explore how the novel might "look" or sound as a movie. He frequently introduces or dismisses characters from scenes with the language of film, as when Miss Pimple Billimoria leaves the set crushed because the scheduled love scene between her and Gibreel was not to be: "Exit Pimple, weeping, censored, a scrap on a cutting-room floor." (13).

Finally, Rushdie imbues the story with obvious references to films, famous names associated with film, and ways in which films are shown. Conflating D. W. Griffith's name with the suffix "Rama" used to suggest extravagance, he introduces a producer named D. W. Rama. During the *Bostan's* ill-fated flight, Gibreel and Chamcha are subjugated to "the inflight inevitability of Walter Matthau" and Goldie Hawn (18). After Gibreel's disappearance, his public "image" begins to rot and deteriorate:

> "Even on the silver screen itself, high above his worshippers in the dark, that supposedly immortal physiognomy began to putrefy, blister and bleach: projectors jammed unaccountably every time he passed through the gate, his films ground to a halt, and the lamp-heat of the malfunctioning projectors burned his celluloid memory away." (16)

Although it is not my intention to explore it, there is much more going on here than random references to cinema or cinematic devices. Rushdie uses scenes such as the aforementioned to explore the modern spectacle of religion and its cinematization. The star is equated God-like status, as his "worshippers" watch his "immortal physiognomy" decay. Gibreel's films cinematize religious stories, moving them from the private to the public. Artificial, gaudy, and over-produced, the stories become commodities in the hands of film industry executives.

The novel opens with Gibreel and Chamcha falling from a very great height, an aerial perspective which will be repeated often throughout the story. Yet the height from which various characters fall, or see, is not always so lofty: that is, the equivalent of the cinematic crane shot is often substituted for the aerial shot:

> Gibreel: the dreamer, whose point of view is sometimes that of the camera and at other moments, spectator. When he's a camera the pee oh vee is always on the move, he hates static shots, so he's floating up on a high crane looking down at the foreshortened figures of the actors....(108)

This perspective, among other things, creates a sense of "flatness"—hence the "foreshortened figures." Alan Spiegel has written, at length, on "depthlessness" in the modern novel, suggesting that "just as the modern cinematized narrative cultivates the raw immediacy of the retinal image, so too does it cultivate this image's flattened-out, two-dimensional structural quality."[4]

Later, as Gibreel "zooms through the night" with the Imam firmly perched upon his shoulders, they fly toward Jerusalem over "the immense landscape, reddish, with flat-topped trees. They fly over mountains that are also flat-topped; even the stones, here, are flattened by the heat" (213). We are impressed with the way in which the image becomes almost photographic, or cinematic. That is, unlike "normal vision," the photo-graphed image is presented on a plane in which the foreground and background tend to gravitate toward each other, reducing three-dimensional images to two-dimensional ones. Rushdie exploits this effect and tries to reproduce it—even though we obviously don't see this scene in the same way we would see a photographed version of it, his language invites us to.

Yet the image is distorted even further, beyond flatness, as the aerial vantage point tends to reduce parts to whole. If anything, these "high shots" reveal the relativism of perspective—what we're shown from up close becomes something else from an aerial view. This perspective dehumanizes or objectifies the action below, removing us, as well as Gibreel and the Imam, from the stark immediacy of the attack upon the Empress's palace: "They are at rooftop-level when Gibreel realizes that the streets are swarming with people. Human beings, packed so densely into those snaking paths that they have blended into a larger, composite entity, relentless, serpentine ... the people are walking up the slope towards the guns: seventy at a time, they come into range: the guns babble, and they die ..." (213). This cinematic "looking down" imbues the narrative with a detached, distant quality that creates for us a different kind of horror. The detailed, precise account of these people marching to their imminent deaths is replaced with an almost statistical account which is horrifying not because of individual destruction, but because of the sheer numbers of individuals destroyed. Our "seeing," although it removes us from the uncomfortable, claustrophobic nearness of "ground level" perception, allows us to witness the sheer magnitude of death. In short, the aerial perspective shows us more by sacrificing intimate proximity.

This sweeping, elevated perspective becomes even more visual when the narrator uses the second person, thus explicitly encouraging the reader to adopt the "eye" of the camera:

> Coney crouches over you like an imaginary beast. You ascend along its spine. Leaving behind the last trees, white-flowered with thick, milky leaves, you climb among the boulders, which get larger as you get higher, until they resemble huge wails and start blotting out the sun. The lizards are blue as shadows. Then you are on the peak. Jahilia behind you, the featureless desert ahead. (109)

Not only does this aerial perspective suggest the flatness of the "featureless" desert, but it also mimics the way in which movement alters our perceptions of objects. The vast boulders *seem* to get larger "as you get higher." although they really do not. The boulders are apprehended purely visually, not abstractly.

Not only does Rushdie use the "high" camera eye as a method for flattening out perceptions of events, but he also uses the technology of cinema or video[5] to suggest another kind of flatness—a type of cultural or artistic flatness. Near the end of the novel, alone and brooding. Chamcha watches television "with half an eye, channel-hopping compulsively," well aware that he is a member of the "remote-control culture" (405). As he manipulates the television with this device, he realizes "what a leveller this remote-control gizmo was, a Procrustean bed for the twentieth century; it chopped down the heavy weight and stretched out the slight until all the set's emissions, commercials, murders, game-shows, the thousand and one varying joys and terrors of the real and the imagined, acquired an equal weight ..." (405). So there is a flatness, a depthlessness of a different sort here, as the banal and the significant become conflated and presented, or packaged, with no distinction. This is not [presented] visually or cinematically to the reader; in other words, the scene is not constructed in any obviously cinematic ways. However, as the scene progresses, the narrative structure begins to imitate the events taking place. The sentences begin to change from long, convoluted cadences to the staccato, abrupt changes suggested by flipping rapidly through the channels with a remote control: "Lycanthropy was on the increase in the Scottish Highlands. The genetic possibility of centaurs was being seriously discussed. A sex-change operation was shown" (405). Although the narrative structure has adopted the spontaneity of the scene, the language itself remains quite passive ("was shown," "was discussed"). Here, Rushdie is using cinematic techniques (such as cutting—from image to image)[6] not as a purely visual device, but as a narratological device to mimic the discontinuity and randomness of video images at the mercy of remote control.

Rushdie borrows even more heavily from the cinema in those scenes in which he uses specific adaptations of the montage technique.[7] In one scene in which Gibreel completes Rosa Diamond's "last revelation," he dreams this sequence: "Now he was by a pond in the infinity of the thistles, allowing his horse to drink, and she came riding up on her mare. Now he was embracing her, loosening her garments and her hair, and now they were making love. Now she was whispering, how can you like me, I am so much older than you ..." (154). The sequence progresses via a series of shots in which the chronology is fragmented—the characters move from their horses to lovemaking in three sentences. The series of shots retains an immediacy not only because of the montage technique used to accelerate time, but also because of the word "now" used to begin each sentence. Again, Rushdie uses cinematic constructs not so much to add a significantly visual dimension, but to shape the narrative.

Rushdie also uses the montage technique to link themes together by bridging them over time, rendering the frequent leaps forward or backward through time less jarring. In one scene, Chamcha successfully manages to eat a bone-filled kipper under the watchful eyes of his British school mates, even though it takes him a full ninety minutes: "The eaten kipper was his first victory, the first step in his conquest of England" (44). The very next scene takes place five years later, in India. Rushdie bridges the gap of time and distance through the montage techniques in which elements of the previous scene recur in this one, both visually and thematically. Chamcha's mother fails to eat fish successfully, "choking on the fishbone of her death" (46).

Rushdie also uses the cinematic equivalent of the dissolve, which serves as a transition shot in which the old shot gradually fades as the new shot appears.[8] As John Harrington has noted, the dissolve is frequently used to suggest either the passage of time or changes in location, which is precisely how Rushdie uses it here.[9] In the "Ayesha" chapter, Gibreel moves from his dream of destruction with the Imam, to "the next narrative" involving Ayesha the prophetess (216). Gibreel's dream with the Imam takes him to Jerusalem while his dream with Ayesha takes him to the village of Titlupur, and Rushdie links these to sequences via the dissolve. While the iconography of the text suggests a scene change (an icon of a curling flower physically divides portions of the text within chapters) the dissolve links the scenes together, slowly introducing the thread of the next section at the very end of the preceding one:

> ... what story is this? Coming right up. To begin at the beginning: On the morning of his fortieth birthday, in a room full of butterflies. Mizra Saeed Akhtar watched his sleeping wife....

*   *   *   *   *

> On the fateful morning of his fortieth birthday, in a room full of butterflies, the zamindar Mizra Saeed Akhtar watched over his sleeping wife.... (216)

While the story of Gibreel and the Imam slowly fades out, a new story begins to appear, finally replacing the old one altogether. The language at the end of one scene and the beginning of the other is strikingly similar, narratologically bridging the abrupt shift in location and story.

Yet my primary purpose is to explore the different ways of "seeing" offered by the novel, suggested by the dichotomy between the narrator's omniscient point of view and the constricted point of view of the "camera eye." Rushdie not only uses film language and technique to imbue the novel with the "feel" of cinema and to shape the novel narratologically, but to raise epistemological questions as well.

Before proceeding, however. I would like to briefly investigate the identity of the narrator himself. At various points throughout the novel, the narrator provides clues as to who he is: either he is God, Satan, or Rushdie.[10] That the narrator may be God is suggested by an incident in which Gibreel sees who he thinks is God on Allie Cone's bed (318-19). Later on, the narrator says that "I sat on Allelulia Cone's bed and spoke to the superstar, Gibreel. *Ooparvala or Neechayvala*, he wanted to know, and I didn't enlighten him" (409). Yet there are also explicit indications that the narrator is Satan himself, and that *The Satanic Verses* are indeed his verses. Speaking about

Chameha's and Gibreel's tremendous "fall," the narrator says: "You think *they* fell a long way? In the matter of tumbles. I yield pride of place to no personage, whether mortal or im—. From clouds to ashes, down the chimney you might say, from heavenlight to hellfire ..." (133). Finally, there are statements whose irony seem to indicate that the narrator is none other than Rushdie himself: "I know the truth, obviously. I watched the whole thing. As to omnipresence and—potence. I'm making no claims at present ..." (10). So while we cannot assuredly claim one of these voices as that of the narrator, we can assume that whoever it is is at least semi-omniscient, in that he is able to freely move from external actions to the inner selves of the characters, as well as periodically comment upon the unfolding action.

This is precisely where the distinction between the "camera eye" and the "narrator eye" becomes important, as the narrator's vision entertains questions about the nature of what he sees, while the camera's vision is so constricting and limited that it can only perceive and record what it sees. From the very beginning of the novel, the narrator frames the story's action with direct questions about the nature of good and evil, justice and mercy, and revenge and compassion. The narrative voice asks, "How does newness come into the world? How is it born? Of what fusions, translations, conjoinings is it made? How does it survive, extreme and dangerous as it is" (8)? The narrator adopts the tone of a curious observer, leading us through the convoluted story via a series of questions which serve as guideposts.

The narrative voice struggles to find meaning in what unfolds during the story, often by exploring different ways of interpreting these various actions:

> A man who sets out to make himself up is taking on the Creator's role, according to one way of seeing things: he's unnatural, a blasphemer, an abomination or abominations. From another angle, you could see pathos in him, heroism in his struggle, in his willingness to risk: not all mutants survive. (49)

The plurality of options suggests an inquisitive narrator who questions the story he is telling at the same time he is telling it. Near the end of the novel, as Gibreel wanders through London struggling to determine exactly what kind of metamorphosis has befallen him, the narrator asks whether Gibreel is to be the agent of God's wrath or of his love: "Is he vengeance or forgiveness? Should the fatal trumpet remain in his pocket, or should he take it out and blow? (I'm giving him no instructions. I, too, am interested in his choices—in the result of his wrestling match)" (457). Questions like this permeate the novel, directly implicating the narrator in the quest for answers to the very questions he raises.

However, this is not the case with the "camera" eye, which sees but is unable to formulate the questions necessary to understand the action unfolding before it. During the raid on Club Hot Wax, television cameras are present: "This is what a television camera sees: less gifted than the human eye, its night vision is limited to what klieg lights will show" (454). Not only is the camera limited by what it is able to do with what it sees, but it is also beholden to the technology available to it. Just because it can only record that which is illuminated by klieg lights does not mean that in the absence of light there is nothing happening. The only reality for the camera is that which it immediately apprehends, while for the narrator reality exists beyond the purely phenomenal.

Rushdie uses this dichotomy between seeing as a method of discovering the truth and seeing as a means of recording to speculate on the dangerous potential for manipulating what we see and how we see it via technology. In the long Club Hot Wax section punctuated with such film language as "cut," we are told:

> And now there's a camera in the sky: a news editor somewhere has sanctioned the cost of aerial photography, and from another helicopter a news team is *shooting down* … the noise of rotor blades drowns the noise of the crowd. In this respect, again, video recording equipment is less sensitive than, in this case, the human ear." (454)

The "depthlessness" which I spoke of earlier takes on new meaning here, as the helicopter which serves as the apparatus for the aerial shot drowns out the noise of the humans below. Yet there is more taking place here, as the entire perspective from which the camera shoots depends upon economic factors, the "cost" of the aerial perspective. So not only are video images potentially dangerous because they provide only one way of seeing things, but also because they are so dependent on factors which are open to manipulation.

This manipulation involves not only economics, but physical force, as well … while the reporter, whose audience is the camera, confines himself to facts rather than meanings (454), "the camera sees what he does not say. A camera is a thing easily broken or purloined: its fragility makes it fastidious. A camera requires law, order, the thin blue line. Seeking to preseve itself, it remains far behind the shielding wall, observing the shadow lands from afar, and of course from above ..." (455). The camera is subject to the force of the police, who are in "riot helmets, carrying shields" during the raid on the Club. Thus, its perception is once again limited by how close it can get to its source, with factors such as sound, lighting, police prevention, and funding standing in its way.

Not only is the camera subject to economic and authoritarian manipulation, but even when these barriers are removed and the subjects of the camera eye are accessible, the camera is unable to make sense out of what it perceives. Whereas the narrator is concerned with truth and meaning, the camera can only record facts, which strip away circumstances and intentions:

> From the air, the camera watches the entrance to Club Hot Wax.... The camera homes in on the arrested persons: a tall albino man; a man in an Armani suit, looking like a dark mirror-image of de Niro; a young girl of—what? —fourteen, fifteen? — a sullen young man of twenty or thereabouts. No names are titled: the camera does not know these faces. Gradually, however, the facts emerge. (456)

The camera knows nothing about these people or their motivations. They are described just as they are seen, as a "tall albino," and "a man in an Armani suit." The camera renders them flat and thus subject to distortion and manipulation, for the "facts" which emerge about them are select and reveal only what the police want them to reveal. Although the narrator himself may be just as unable to understand the events he is observing, he is at least capable of asking questions. The scene ends with an acknowledgement that much happens "in places which the camera cannot see" (457).

Ultimately, *The Satanic Verses* is an attempt not only to structure parts of a fictional narrative with cinematic devises, but to raise epistemological questions about the ways in which we perceive events. The narrator's overt preoccupation with dilemmas such as the nature and source of good and evil are explicitly contrasted with the camera's inability not only to access such events, but to understand them. I do not mean to suggest that the narrator finally finds answers to his persistent questions, but that his attempt to do so is sharply contrasted with the flat and factual world conveyed by the camera. Rushdie continually uses a metaphor of flatness or depthlessness via aerial camera shots to represent the camera's limited capability for understanding. I believe Rushdie highlights this dichotomy in order to explore the potential danger of "one way of seeing" suggested by the camera perspective, as well as to raise questions about how all of the ways in which to manipulate the camera render it a possible tool for exploitation. Since "it cannot understand, or demonstrate" the causes or reasons for any actions it may record, others must do that for it (455). Rushdie's ironic achievement is that he has exposed the camera's potential shortcomings via the very language and structure of cinema itself. The novel is, finally, less a condemnation of cinema and more a cautious affirmation of our curiosity—our desire to ask important questions despite what we "see."

NOTES

1. All quotations and line numbers are from *The Satanic Verses* (New York: Viking. 1988) 457. I would like to thank Kit Hume for her helpful comments and suggestions on this essay.

2. For a concise yet well-documented analysis of the relationship between fiction and film, see the introduction to Harris Ross. *Film as Literature, Literature as Film: An Introduction to and Bibliography of Film's Relationship to Literature* (Westport, Connecticut: Greenwood P. 1987) 1–57. Ross surveys many of the various arguments for and against critical approaches which assume a relationship between fiction and film.

3. Salman Rushdie, interviewed by Jean W. Ross, *Contemporary Authors* 111 (1983): 414-17.

4. Alan Spiegel, *Fiction and the Camera Eye Visual Consciousness in Film and the Modern Novel* (Charlottesville: UP of Virginia, 1976) 134. Many consider this study as important in terms of developing a common language by which to discuss or compare the relationship between fiction and film.

5. I realize there is of course a distinction between video and film, especially in terms of how they are perceived by the human eye. Yet my concern here is not so much with how video is apprehended, but with how it shares certain basic features with film in regard to its voyeuristic characteristics. Rushdie himself moves between discussions of film and video with no distinction between them.

6. Although the meaning of the term "cut" is not the object of as much debate as the meaning of the term "montage," there is, nonetheless, some disagreement as to how at should be used. For my purposes. I refer to it to indicate the switch from one image to another, generally within the same scene, or series of shots, which occur in the same locate and are part of the same general action.

7. There is a theoretical debate about the precise meaning of the word montage as well as how it should be applied, not only to literature, but to film

as well. Although I cannot review the entire history of this debate here. I will attempt to briefly justify my use of the word. I am not using it in the same sense that Eisenstein used it, that is, to refer to the principle of conflict between elements of shots to create a sense of dissonance. I use it to refer to a process in which a number of short shots are woven together in such a way as to manipulate time.

8. The dissolve is actually the superimposition of a fade out over a fade in, and is sometimes referred to as a lap dissolve. The spatialized nature of cinema allows us to perceive the two images simultaneously as one fades out and the other fades in, whereas literature can only approximate the technique, not replicate it exactly.

9. In *The Rhetoric of Film* (New York: Holt, Rinehart and Winston, 1973) Harrington suggests that "like a paragraph or chapter division, a dissolve provides a viewer with a momentary break and a chance to collect his thoughts before going on. The break in continuity is not complete, however, since a dissolve links rather than separates like a jump cut. A dissolve may represent the passage of time, a change in location, or a psychological shift such as a flashback" (135).

10. I am working with two assumptions here: that the narrator of this novel is in fact a character, based on his frequent explicit intrusions into the text, and that Rushdie is of course the ultimate source of the book itself, though not necessarily the "character" of the narrator.

VIJAY MISHRA

Postcolonial Differend: Diasporic Narratives of Salman Rushdie

"Home" has become such a scattered, damaged, various concept
in our present travails.

—Salman Rushdie (*East, West* 93)

For large groups of people around the world—Cubans and Mexicans in
the US, Indians and Pakistanis in Britain, Canada, and the US, Meghrebis in
France, Turks in Germany, Chinese in Southeast Asia, Greeks, Polish, and
Armenians in various parts of the world, Chinese and Vietnamese in
Australia, Canada, and the US, Indians in Mauritius, Fiji, the Caribbean (the
list can go on and on) —the idea of "home" has indeed become a "damaged"
concept. The word "damaged" forces us to face up to the scars and fractures,
to the blisters and sores, to the psychic traumas of bodies on the move.
Indeed, "home" (the *heimlich*) is the new epistemological logic of (post)
modernity as the condition of "living here and belonging elsewhere" begins
to affect people in an unprecedented fashion (Clifford 311). No longer is
exile rendered simply through an essentially aesthetic formulation (note the
geographical breaks, the "damaged" hyphens of Joyce [Dublin-Trieste],
Pound [London-Paris-Rome], or Eliot [New England-London], for
instance); on the contrary, it is a travail/travel to which we are becoming
inextricably linked as we are progressively dragged into a global village.

From *ARIEL: A Review of International English Literature* 26, no. 3 (July 1995): 7-45. © 1995 by
The Board of Governors, The University of Calgary.

"Home" now signals a shift away from homogeneous nation-states based on the ideology of assimilation to a much more fluid and contradictory definition of nations as a multiplicity of diasporic identities. The Indian shopkeeper in Vancouver who comes to Canada via Fiji already has held two previous passports; his (for he is a man) third, the Canadian passport, is one that gives him the greatest difficulty in reconciling his body with the idea of Canadian citizenry. He remains a negative yet to be processed, a penumbra in the new nation-state of Canada, his privileges as a Canadian citizen most obvious only when he is travelling overseas. Back at home his condition remains hyphenated because in Canada (as in Australia, Britain, and Europe, but not to the same degree in the US), "home" is only available to those passport holders, those citizens whose bodies signify an unproblematic identity of selves with the nation-state. For Indian shopkeepers who are outside of this identity politics, whose corporealities fissure the logic of unproblematic identity of bodies with citizens, the new dogma of multiculturalism constructs the subject-in-hyphen forever negotiating and fashioning selves at once Indian and Canadian: *Canadian* Indian *and* Canadian *Indian*.[1]

It is becoming increasingly obvious that the narrative of the "damaged" home thus takes its exemplary form in what may be called diasporas, and especially in diasporas of colour, those migrant communities that do not quite fit into the nation-state's barely concealed preference for the narrative of assimilation. Diasporas of colour, however, are a relatively recent phenomenon in the West and, as I have already suggested, perhaps the most important marker of late modernity. In the larger narrative of postcolonialism (which has been informed implicitly by a theory of diasporic identifications), the story of diasporas is both its cause and its effect. In the politics of transfer and migration, postcolonialism recovers its own justification as an academic site or as a legitimate object of knowledge. To write about damaged homes, to re-image the impact of migration in the age of late capital, requires us to enter into debates about diasporic theory. This is not my primary concern here, but a few words about it will not be out of place. One of the overriding characteristics of diasporas is that they do not, as a general rule, return. This is not to be confused with the symbols of return or the invocations, largely through the sacred, of the homeland or the home-idea. The trouble with diasporas is that while the reference point is in the past, unreal as it may be, there is, in fact, no future, no sense of a teleological end. Diasporas cannot conceptualize the point towards which the community, the nation within a nation, is heading. The absence of teleologies in the diaspora is also linked to Walter Benjamin's understanding of the ever-present time of historical (messianic) redemption. In this lateral argument, an eventual homecoming is not projected into the future but introjected into the present, thereby both interrupting it and multiplying it. Diasporic history thus contests both the utopic and irreversible causality of history through heterotopic (Foucault) or subversive (Benjamin) readings. In these readings, time is turned back against itself in order that alternative readings, alternative histories, may be released. In this "diverse scansion of temporality,"[2] in this active re-membering (as opposed to the mere recalling) of traces and fragments, a new space in language and time is opened up, and historical moments are sundered to reveal heterotopic paths not taken. The absence of teleologies, this intense meditation on synchronicity, thus opposes the tyranny of linear time and blasts open the continuum of history to reveal moments, fragments, traces that can be re-captured and transformed into another history. As Salman Rushdie has written:

> It may be that writers in my position, exiles or emigrants or expatriates, are haunted by some sense of loss, some urge to reclaim, to look back, even at the risk of being mutated into pillars of salt. But if we do look back, we must also do so in the knowledge—which gives rise to profound uncertainties—that our physical alienation from India almost inevitably means that we will not be capable of reclaiming precisely the thing that was lost; that we will, in short, create fictions, not actual cities or villages, but invisible ones, imaginary homelands, Indias of the mind. (*Imaginary Homelands* 10)

We cannot trace the growth of diasporas in any systematic form here. All we can do is refer very schematically to one particular diasporic development that has a direct bearing on the texts discussed in this paper. 1963, the year the Beatles exploded on the world scene, may also be chosen as the watershed year in global migration. Demand for labour in Western Europe and Britain and the collapse of the colonial empires of Britain, France, and Holland meant that millions of non-white migrants from the outposts of the Empire, as well as guest workers from Turkey, began to enter the European city on a scale unprecedented since the Moorish invasions. The contemporary European city, for instance, is now a very different demographic fact. It is no longer the centre out of which radiates imperial activity. Instead, European cities (there are 16 million non-Europeans who live and work in them; there are a million people of colour in Australian cities, and probably twice that number in Canadian cities) are no longer controlled by the logic of centre and periphery (the metaphor of the Empire). Instead, what we get, in Iain Chambers's words, is a new kind of demographic redistribution "along the spatio-temporal-information axes of a world economy" (*Migrancy, Culture, Identity* 108). He continues, "the national, unilateral colonial model has been interrupted by the emergence of a transversal world that occupies a 'third space' (Bateson, Bhabha), a 'third culture' (Featherstone) beyond the confines of the nation state" (108). It is symptomatic of a greater awareness of the transnational nature of nation-states and the presence within them of degrees of difference that led Khachig Tölölyan, editor of the new journal *Diaspora*, to maintain that struggles from the margins for the centre and for definitions of the "national" subject are equally legitimate concerns for the constructions of identity or selfhood. Nevertheless, Tölölyan's cautious remarks towards the end of his editorial warn us of the difficult space occupied by diasporas and the dangers of displacing the centre (made up of the vast majority of citizens that do not define themselves in diasporic terms) totally by the margins. Tölölyan writes: "To affirm that diasporas are the exemplary communities of the transnational moment is not to write the premature obituary of the nation state, which remains a privileged form of polity" (5). This proviso is important.

Elsewhere I have spoken about this condition as the indeterminate, the contaminated condition of diaspora (Mishra, "The Diasporic Imaginary"). Here I want to do something slightly different, something at once bold and fraught with difficulties. I want to examine the literary production of an author—Salman Rushdie—whose works exemplify the blasting open of agonistic politics in embattled ethnicities within nation-states that can no longer construct their nationalisms through a homogeneous and synchronous imagining of a collective body consensually reading its newspapers or responding to global events as a totality. Indeed, if we are to follow the hidden text of the previous sentence—Benedict Anderson's influential *Imagined Communities*—we begin to detect not so much the logic of capitalism at work here but the religious, millenarian dogma of an earlier age in which the issues were not necessarily that of imagining national identities but of participating, through sacred languages (Latin, Sanskrit, Pali, or Arabic), with communities across "nations." There is, then, a reverse scansion of history at work here, a desire for a lost unity within the ethnicized state that minorities continue to inhabit. In the cultural sphere, this leads to the end of consensual politics, the end of a community of speakers/thinkers that could be relied upon to arbitrate for the national good. In short, what is emerging is "the postcolonial differend." What I would like to offer in the following pages is an instance of this postcolonial differend with reference to the Indian-Pakistani diaspora in Britain.

The diaspora, however, stages a "difference" that can be accommodated only if consensual politics also takes into account the possibility of the diasporic subject itself initiating the consensus. In other words, the majority population has to concede that the diaspora's ground rules (what constitutes belief, what is a work of art, what is literary freedom) may be different from its own. It is here that postcolonial theory, through a careful study of diasporic archive(s), could address what Lyotard has called the differend. This is to anticipate my concluding remarks, however. What I would like to continue here is an examination of key texts of an author whose works have something of an exemplary status as proof-texts of diaspora as an intermediate, increasingly mobile idea. In the works of Salman Rushdie, the Indian-Pakistani diaspora in Britain is seen as a powerful source for the hermeneutics of the liminal, the borders of culture, the unassimilable, the margins, and so on. The critique of the centre through the kinds of hybrid, hyphenated identities occupied by this diaspora has been one of the more exciting and original theorizations of the project of modernity itself. As an ideological critique of, as well as a corrective to, established working-class British social histories, the pay-off has been considerable: one remembers how historians of the working class consistently overlooked the diaspora as a significant formation in class histories. There are no people of colour in E. P. Thompson.

THE TEXTS OF SALMAN RUSHDIE

Few works of fiction have been the subject of debates as intense as those that have surrounded *The Satanic Verses* since its publication in 1988. Books have now been written on the Rushdie Affair, a film made on the author's death (much-deserved, as it turns out in the film) by the Pakistani film industry, and Tehran continues to re-emphasize Khomeini's *fatwa* on any staged denunciation of the West. The author's life, meanwhile, is one of double exile in the company of his "protectors" in the Welsh countryside of "unafraid lambs," country houses, and farmers from whom he must "hide [his] face," as Rushdie describes it in his poem "Crusoe."[3] However, he still hankers after travel, the diasporic condition, even though this travel, like V. S. Naipaul's "arrival," is towards the Arthurian "once and future Avalon." The cause of Rushdie's second exile, of course, was a book about migrancy, dispossession, cultural hybridity, and the absence of centres in diasporic lives. To give these

themes an intertext, a frame, or a narrative template, they were hoisted on
another moment in history when "newness" entered the world. The entry of
strange people into so many parts of the globe presents the older inhabitants
with precisely the threat of the new, the threat of "ideas" no longer
commensurable with pre-existing epistemologies. In this retelling, Indian
Islam (always contaminated by autochthonous gods, dervishes, the figure of
the ascetic, and other borrowings from Hinduism) is seen as a hybrid,
contradictory phenomenon that conjures strange dreams about the founding
text and prophet of that religion. Indian Islam thus has a polytheistic splinter
in the side of its monotheism in which the intercession of female gods in any
act of worship is not excluded outright. Moreover, this kind of syncretism is
truer still of Bombay, Rushdie's magical metropolis, *the* postcolonial city, that
challenges the erstwhile metropolises of London and Paris. What is true of
Indian Islam is also true of Indian narrative forms and culture generally. The
Aryans, the Moguls, the British have all been invaders, leaving their traces
behind as the nation gradually reabsorbs multiplicity into a totality. Thus the
central themes of the book—how "newness" enters the world, how the many
coexists within the one, and why love remains the only organizing principle
of our lives—get written in a hybrid discourse that is borrowed from the
Bombay film industry, the idioms of Hobson-Jobson,[4] a colonial English
curriculum, the *Katha-Sarit-Sagar* (342), the nativist jokes on the *ooparvala-
neechayvala* (he who lives upstairs, he who lives downstairs), the narrative of
the epic recast as the battle for the Mahavilayat (283), the populist narratives
of Phoolan Devi,[5] the female dacoit, the fundamentalist world of the post-
Ayodhya Hindus, the references to the Indian Penal Code section 420
(Gibreel sings Raj Kapoor's well-known song from *Shree 420*), as well as the
Indian Civic Code, section 125, and many more. *The Satanic Verses* situates
itself in the midst of these heterogeneous discourses. It is from the space of
hybridity, of multiplicity, that many of the characters speak. Mimi
Mamoulian, for instance, knows very well the meaning of the world as
"pastiche: a 'flattened' world" (261), and the author's own, very postmodern
intervention makes this clearer still:

> Gibreel ... has wished to remain, to a large degree, *continuous*—
> that is joined to and arising from his past; ... whereas Saladin
> Chamcha is a creature of *selected* discontinuities, a *willing* re-
> invention; his *preferred* revolt against history being what makes
> him, in our chosen idiom, "false"? [Where Chamcha is therefore
> perceived as "evil"] Gibreel, to follow the logic of our established
> terminology, is to be considered "good" by virtue of *wishing to*

remain, for all his vicissitudes, at bottom an untranslated man.

—But, and again but: this sounds, does it not, dangerously like an intentionalist fallacy?—Such distinctions, resting as they must on an idea of the self as being (ideally) homogeneous, non-hybrid, "pure,"—an utterly fantastic notion—cannot, must not, suffice. (427)

Rushdie begins by offering the usual binary between the continuous and the discontinuous, between tradition and modernity, between good and evil, only to undercut it through the intervention of the hybrid. Indeed, what this extended statement about the construction of the self indicates, in the context of the diaspora and margins, is that subjectivity is now formed through modes of translation and encoding because erstwhile distinctions "cannot, must not suffice." This last phrase, in fact, sums up the agenda of the book as a whole: distinctions made through established cultural epistemologies (including the ubiquitous self-other distinction) will always fail. Yet, even as hybridity is celebrated, one gets the feeling that the disavowed leaves its traces behind because, as we shall see, *The Satanic Verses* itself failed to convince the diaspora that there is no such thing as an "untranslated man": large sections of the diaspora wish to retain this nostalgic definition of the self and cling to "millenarian" narratives of self-empowerment in which only the untranslated can recapture a lost harmony but, paradoxically, the desire to retain a pristine sense of the past is only possible through the technologies of mechanical reproduction such as cassette tapes, films, and so on.[6] Since historical reconstructions through these apparatuses introduce the heterotopic into the utopian or the linear, what we get here is precisely a heterogeneous, contradictory rendition of history by making memory and cultural fragments metonymic representations of the whole. While cassette culture reconstructs the past as a synchronic moment (old Indian films can be viewed endlessly), it also contaminates the diasporic idea of culture as belonging to the homeland alone. As Paul Gilroy has argued so persuasively in *The Black Atlantic: Modernity and Double Consciousness*, the newer technologies of cultural transmission accentuate the fact that cultural commodities travel swiftly, criss-crossing geographical boundaries, creating new and vibrant forms. The Bhojpuri-Hindi songs of the Indian singers Babla and Kanchan, for instance, combine Hindi film music with calypso/hip hop, while in Britain, Asian Bhangra and Indian groups such as Loop Guru (post-Ravi Shankar music crossed with cyber-religion) show obvious influences of reggae and soul music of Black Africa. In this respect, *The Satanic Verses* affirms the impossibility of millenarian diasporic narratives while at the same time stressing that these narratives invariably will be the starting point of any radical re-theorizing of the diasporic imaginary, which, for Rushdie, is identical with modernism itself and may be read as a "metaphor for all humanity":

> If *The Satanic Verses* is anything, it is a migrant's-eye view of the world. It is written from the very experience of uprooting, disjuncture and metamorphosis ... that is the migrant condition, and from which, I believe, can be derived a metaphor for all humanity.
>
>   (*Imaginary Homelands* 394)

Rushdie goes on to state:

> *The Satanic Verses* celebrates hybridity, impurity, intermingling, the transformation that comes of new and unexpected combinations of human beings, cultures, ideas, politics, movies, songs. It rejoices in mongrelization and fears the absolutism of the Pure. *Mélange*, hotchpotch, a bit of this and a bit of that is *how newness enters the world*. It is the great possibility that mass migration gives the world, and I have tried to embrace it. *The Satanic Verses* is for change-by-fusion, change-by-conjoining. It is a love-song to our mongrel selves. (394)

The celebration of the hybrid—"the process of hybridization which is the novel's most crucial dynamic means that its ideas derive from many sources other than Islamic ones," writes Rushdie (403) —however, also leads to the endowing of the fiction itself with what Gilroy has called "an absolute and non-negotiable privilege" ("Cultural Studies" 190). The aesthetic order as somehow immune to a counter-attack through a non-aesthetic reading of the text has dominated much of the criticism that has been directed against Rushdie in the wake of Khomeini's *fatwa*. We shall return to the question of aesthetic privilege.

THE DIASPORIC AVANT-GARDE

The story of "migration, its stresses and transformations, from the point of view of migrants from the Indian subcontinent,"[7] nevertheless drops the old realist modes of writing and embraces the European avant-garde. Yet it also keeps its realist nose sharply in focus. This is partly because the book is as much about South Asians in a racialized Britain as it is an avant-gardist break in the history of "English" fiction.[8] Rushdie, in fact, is quite explicit about this dual agenda:

> [*The Satanic Verses*] begins in a pyrotechnic high-surrealist vein and moves towards a much more emotional, inner writing. That process of putting away the magic noses and cloven hoofs is one the novel itself goes through: *it tells itself*, and by the end it doesn't need the apparatus any more. (Interview with Blake Morrison 120)

It is, however, the use of non-European narrative forms, summed up in the Arabic narrator's correction of the reader's processes of naturalization through a phrase such as "it was so, it was not," that led Gayatri Spivak to remark that while *The Satanic Verses* was not part of the linear narrative of the European avant-garde, "the successes and failures of the European avant-garde is available to it" ("Reading" 41). Let us accept Spivak's proposition but give the text a further twist. Instead of using the term "European avant-garde," let us use the term "diasporic avant-garde" to mark out a generic space for a variety of literary texts that would use the European avant-garde to interrogate subject positions excluded or silenced by modernism by constructing allegorical or counter-hegemonic subaltern renditions of the geopolitical imaginary of South Asians in Britain.

At the risk of repetition, let me underline once again that *The Satanic Verses* is *the* text about migration, about the varieties of religious, sexual, and social filiations of the diaspora.[9] The work is the millenarian routed through the space of travel (the aeroplane replaces the ship) and then problematically rooted in the new space of the diaspora. In this respect the text's primary narrative is a tale of migrancy and the ambiguities of being an Indian (or Pakistani) in Britain. In the process, the work explores the disavowal of so many fundamental assumptions and values because of a massive epistemic violence to the intellect. The narrative, in fact, begins with people who have already lost their faith in religion and who now have a truly diasporic relationship with India. As Rushdie has explained, these people are the new travellers across the planet; having lost their faith, they have to rethink what death means to the living and how desire can find expression when people cannot love (Interview with Blake Morrison 120-21). One of the key phrases that recurs deals with being born again (to be born again, you have to die, says Gibreel to Saladin), and the diasporic world is very much the world in which one undergoes a rebirthing. In the case of Gibreel and Saladin, the context in which this occurs combines the fantastic free-fall from an exploding plane (AI 420 from the height of Mt. Everest, a full 29,002 feet[10]) with the realistic narrative of terrorism and hijacking. The combination of these two generic modes is striking, since it forecloses the possibility of naturalistic readings because the work reveals a kind of simultaneous *karma* and reincarnation: two people die and are immediately reborn as they were at the moment of their deaths. The rebirthing of Gibreel and Saladin, then, parallels, say, the rebirth of Amba as Shikhandin in the *Mahabharata*, the founding Indian text that is simultaneously diachronic and synchronic: it happened then, it happens now. One becomes someone else but keeps the earlier history/biography intact. The relationship between Rushdie's writings and the Indian epic tradition of generic mixing is a narrative we cannot go into here, but it is nevertheless important to refer to it, if only because it reminds us of the fictiveness of the text and its relationship to the "eclectic, hybridized nature of the Indian artistic tradition" (*The Satanic Verses* 70). Moreover, as Gibreel's song (from the film *Shree 420*) shows, the dominant cultural form of modern India, the Bombay film, the successor to the encyclopaedic pan-Indian epic tradition, constantly adapts itself to and indigenizes all global cultural forms, from Hollywood to Middle Eastern dance and music.

The "emigration" of Salahuddin Chamchawala from Bombay has close parallels with Salman Rushdie's own pattern of emigration. From the insertion of the well-known autobiographical "kipper story" (the young Rushdie was not allowed to get up from the dining table until he had finished his kipper, which he didn't know how to eat!) to his own uneasy relationship with his father, there are striking parallels between Saladin and his creator. It is not Gibreel but Saladin who is reborn and who accepts the need for change: the nostalgia for the past (a house, one's ancestral religion, and so on) is not something one can live by but something to which, in an act of both homage and acceptance of his father Changez Chamchawala, Saladin returns. The use of a fused sign—Salman and Saladin—allows Rushdie to enter into those areas, notably the body and the religious body-politic, that accentuate the diasporic condition. Relationships with women—Pamela Lovelace (wife), Mimi Mamoulian (professional partner), and Zeeny Vakil (mistress)—raise the interesting question of diasporic sexuality and gender relations. At the same time, the other autobiographical figure around "Salman"—Salman from Persia in the Mahound and Jahilia sections of the book—is also diasporic and connects with Islam as a political as well as religious revolution staged by "water-carriers, immigrants and slaves" (101). Even the radical Iranian cultural critic suppressed under the Shah's regime, and for many the harbinger of Khomeini's revolution, Jalal Al-e Ahmad (1923-1969), refers to one Salman-e Faresi (Salman the Persian) who "found refuge in Medina with the Muslims and played such an important role in the development of Islam" (16). This Salman-e Faresi may not have been the prophet's contemporary, but the connection between Iran (through the figure of Salman) and the advent of Islam underscores the strength of the Iranian furore against Rushdie. In Al-e Ahmad's reading of the Islamization of Iran, what is emphasized, perhaps too simplistically, is the idea of Islam being invited into Iran. Unlike earlier Western incursions, Islam, another Western ideology, is not an invasion but a response to Iran's own need to embrace the austere harmony of the "one."

It is through Saladin/Salman (Rushdie) that the new themes of diasporic interaction are explored. Saladin sees in the relics of Empire in the heart of London, "attractively faded grandeur." Gibreel, on his part, only sees a "wreck, a Crusoe-city, marooned on the island of its past." When asked about his favourite films, Saladin offers a cosmopolitan list: "*Potemkin, Kane, Otto e Mezzo, The Seven Samurai, Alphaville, El Angel Exterminador*" (439), whereas Gibreel (the larger-than-life Bombay film actor modelled on Amitabh Bachchan and N. T. Rama Rao, the latter a hero-god in countless mythological films turned politician) offers a list of successful commercial Hindi films: "*Mother India, Mr India, Shree Charsawbees*: no Ray, no Mrinal Sen, no Aravindan, or Ghatak" (440). The lists, the choices made, the implied discriminations, the negotiations with the migrant's new land, all indicate the complex ways in which two diaspora discourses (the millenarian and the diasporic) work. Gibreel, for his part, does not undergo mutation but remains locked in the worlds of memory and fantasy. Saladin thus becomes the figure that is both here and elsewhere, and his return to the Motherland to be at his father's deathbed is perhaps the more cogent statement about the diasporic condition. Gibreel, on the other hand, acts out his actor's fantasies and becomes the conduit through whom (in his imagination) the Prophet receives the *Quran*. Blasphemy, therefore, falls not to the hybrid mutant but to the nostalgia-ridden Gibreel. Further, the mutant condition of Saladin (names in the diaspora are similarly mutated, a Hobson-Jobson discourse gets replayed) is both linguistic as well as physical: the he-goat with an erratic pair of horns and the owner of a name that moves between the Indian Chamchawala to the trans-Indian Spoono (English for *chamcha*, "spoon," though in Hindi/Urdu a *chamcha* is a sycophant gleefully doing his/her master's work). In all this, two ideas—the idea of newness and that of love—

keep cropping up. For Dr Uhuru Simba, "newness will enter this society by collective, not individual actions" (415). As for love, the combinations it takes—Gibreel/Rekha Merchant/Allie Cone; Saladin/Pamela Lovelace/ Zeeny Vakil/Mimi Mamoulian—get complicated by other alignments: Jumpy Joshi/Pamela; Saladin/Allie Cone; Billy Battuta/Mimi; Hanif Johnson/Mishal Sufyan. All these relationships are part of the new diasporic combinations, a kind of necessary re-programming of the mind in the wake of the diasporic newness. At the point of interaction where the old and the new come together—as is the case with the diaspora's encounter with the vibrant politics of the metropolitan centre—new social meanings get constructed, especially in the domain of psycho-sexual politics. Thus the capacious Hind and not the bookish Muhammad effectively runs the Shaandaar cafe: her great cooking is what improves the material condition of the family rather than Muhammad's Virgilian rhetoric, which has no use value in Britain. Gender relations therefore get repositioned in the diaspora, and women begin to occupy a different, though not necessarily more equitable, kind of space. The manner in which a diasporic restaurant culture in Britain is actually based on wives as cooks is quite staggering. In another world, in the world of Jahilia, however, it is Hind, the powerful wife of the patriarch Abu Simbel, who has to battle with another new idea: "What kind of an idea are you?" (335), is the question asked of the Prophet. Yet the idea of the "new" (the idea of the "post" in any modernity) also has a tendency to get fossilized, which is where another narrative of the diaspora, the millenarian, becomes the attractive, and easy, alternative. As a heterogeneous, "unread" text, *The Satanic Verses* has been appropriated, positively and negatively, towards both diasporic (hybrid) and essentialist ends. I will return to the latter in the context of Rushdie and the sacred. For the moment, I want to explore further the question of racial politics and diasporic identity.

RACE, IDENTITY, AND BRITISHNESS

The late 1960s saw the emergence of a new racism in Britain for which Enoch Powell was the best-known, but not the only, spokesperson. In what seemed like a remarkable reversal of old Eurocentric and imperialist readings of the black colonized as racially inferior, the new racists began to recast races on the model of linguistic difference. This "difference," however, had to be anchored somewhere, and the easiest means of doing this was by stipulating that nations were not imagined communities constructed historically but racial enclaves marked by high levels of homogeneity. Thus a race had a nation to which it belonged. The British had their nation and belonged to an island off the coast of Europe, and so on. In the name of racial respect and racial equality, this version in fact gave repatriation theorists such as Enoch Powell a high level of respectability in that, it was argued, what Powell stood for was not racism but a nationalism that the immigrants themselves upheld. What the argument simplified was the history of imperialism itself and the massive displacement of races that had taken place in the name of Empire. Nowhere was this more marked than in the Indian, African, and Chinese diasporas of the Empire. More importantly, however, the new racism was used to defend Britishness itself, to argue that multiculturalism was a travesty of the British way of life, which was now becoming extremely vulnerable. The only good immigrant was one that was totally assimilable, just as the only good gay or lesbian was someone who led a closet life. Writes Anna Marie Smith:

> Only the thin veneer of deracializing euphemisms has shifted over this period, with blatantly racist discourse on immigration being recoded in discourse on criminality, inner-cities' decay and unrest, anti-Western terrorism, and multiculturalism. Indeed, the fundamentally *cultural* definition of race in the new racism allows for this mobile relocation of the racial-national borders to any number of sociopolitical sites. (62)

In *The Satanic Verses*, it is by way of the Sufyan family (Muhammad, the Bangladeshi schoolmaster with a weakness for European classics, his wife, Hind, and their daughters Mishal and Anahita) that we enter into changing demographic patterns and race relations in Britain, as well as see how homeland family norms negotiate the new gender politics of diasporas. The Sufyan family lives in Brickhall Street, the old Jewish enclave of tailors and small-time shopkeepers. Now it is the street of Bangladeshi migrants or Packies/Pakis ("brown Jews" [300]) who are least equipped for metropolitan life. Thus, in Brickhall, synagogues and kosher food have given way to mosques and halal restaurants. Yet nothing is as simple as it seems in this world of the diaspora. The space of the Shaandaar Cafe B&B becomes the space of new labour relations between husband and wife but also of new forms of sexuality. Mishal becomes pregnant by the second-generation diaspora Hanif Johnson, while Jumpy Joshi has sex with Pamela, even as her husband Saladin sleeps under the same roof. The diaspora here finally crumbles and falls apart because the pressures come not only from the newly acquired socio-sexual field of the participants in the diasporic drama but also because that drama has to contend with racist hooliganism as the diaspora becomes progressively an object of derision to be represented through the discourse of monsterism. It is through this brand of fascism that death finally comes to the diaspora and to those associated with it. Both the café and the community centre are burned down. Hind, Muhammad, as well as Pamela, die, and suddenly there is no room for nostalgia, no room for the discourse of mysticism (469) that had sustained the discourses of the homeland. Instead, the imperative is to transform one's memory into modes of political action because the world is far too Real (469). It is at this point in the narrative that diasporic identities become complicated by the presence in Britain of people who have already gone through the diasporic experience in other parts of the world. Having co-existed with Afro-West Indians, the Indian diaspora of the West Indies, for instance, is already a hybrid form. Thus Sewsunker Ram (Pinkwalla), the DJ, and John Maslama, the club proprietor, have political and cultural orientations that bring them close to the kinds of diasporic politics endorsed by a Dr. Uhuru Simba. The alignments at work here—Bengali, Afro-Caribbean, East Indian Caribbean, East African Indian, Sikh, Indian, Pakistani, Bangladeshi, and so on—gesture towards new forms of diasporic awareness and coalitional politics. From the Africanist ideal of Dr. Uhuru Simba to the multifaceted, decentred, simulative worlds of the Sufyan girls, Jumpy Joshi and Hanif Johnson, one now begins to see not one legitimation narrative of the diaspora but many.

"The trouble with the Engenglish is that their hiss hiss history happened overseas, so they dodo don't know what it means," stutters S. S. Sisodia (343). When those who were instrumental in creating that history (as subject peoples on whose behest the Empire believed it was acting) are within the metropolitan centres of the Empire itself, the idea of Britishness is threatened. Both the challenge and the threat are summarized elegantly by Iain Chambers, who writes:

> It is the dispersal attendant on migrancy that disrupts and interrogates the overarching themes of modernity: the nation and its literature, language and sense of identity; the metropolis; the sense of centre; the sense of psychic and cultural homogeneity. In the recognition of the other, of radical alterity, lies the acknowledgement that we are no longer at the centre of the world.
>
> (*Migrancy, Culture, Identity* 23-24)

Chambers's "we" here is British, but the definition that he gives of the British is very much an intermediate one. It is a definition in which the subjects of the centre—the British as an ethnic entity—also begin to find that subjectivity is "interactively" constructed, on the move, so to speak. The cultural imperative that underlies Chambers's move is that the diaspora now invades the centre and makes prior, essentialist definitions of nation-states based on notions of racial purity (Enoch Powell), a historical relic of imperialism itself. It is the privileged site of that imperialist history and its constructions of Britishness that get replayed in the doctrines of purity in postcolonial Britain. Yet, as I say this I think what is implicit in the Chambers thesis—the need for a radical pedagogy about ethnic identities—is precisely what needs underlining. How does one make decisive interventions in the curriculum so that Britishness itself is opened up for debate? It is the agenda of the agents who would transform the apparatuses of control through which the idea of the self is constructed that requires further examination.

A "post-diaspora community" in Britain, to use Rushdie's own phrase (*Imaginary Homelands* 40), now becomes a site from which a critique of Britishness itself (and the imperial relationship between the British and Indians that has a 300-year long history) is now being mounted. The migrant living here and elsewhere would find it difficult to fit into, say, Margaret Thatcher's imperious definition of a Briton during the Falklands War. As Chambers again has stressed, any attempt to decipher this appeal to "Britishness" necessarily draws us to a complex, contradictory, and even treacherous terrain, in which the most varied elements "entwine, coexist and contaminate one another" (*Border Dialogues* 15). For the Indian diaspora, this trope of "Britishness" has multiple identities and can be expressed in a variety of ways. To be British in a post-diaspora Britain is to be conscious of multiple heritages and peoples' conflicting participation in the long history of Britain. For many, an easy, unproblematic re-insertion into a utopic or linear narrative of the British nation is impossible. In *The Satanic Verses*, we get a strong affirmation of the undesirability of this version of linear history.

We are therefore faced with "the possibility of two perspectives and two versions of Britishness" (Chambers, *Border Dialogues* 27). One is Anglocentric, frequently conservative, backward-looking, and increasingly located in a frozen and largely stereotyped idea of the national, that is, English, culture. The other is excentric, open-ended, and multi-ethnic. The first is based on a homogeneous "unity" in which history, tradition, and individual biographies and roles, including ethnic and sexual ones, are fundamentally fixed and embalmed in the national epic, in the mere fact of being "English." The other perspective suggests an overlapping network of histories and traditions, a heterogeneous complexity in which positions and identities, including those relating to the idea of the "citizen," cannot be taken for granted and are not "interminably fixed but tend towards flux" (Chambers, *Border Dialogues* 27).

The peculiar irony of Rushdie's own anti-racist rhetoric is that he has been used to fuel racism: the Muslim threat against Rushdie's life is used by the white majority to portray all Muslims as fundamentalists. As Rushdie himself has pointed out, "[t]he idea that the National Front could use my name as a way of taunting Asians is so horrifying and obscene to my mind that I wanted to make it clear: that's not my team, they're not my supporters, they're simply exploiting the situation to their own ends" (Interview with Blake Morrison 115). The uses made of Rushdie in defence of "Britishness" imply a problematic incorporation of the name "Rushdie" into British citizenry. The appropriation of Rushdie by British writers in the name of the autonomy of the aesthetic order again has a similar agenda. Rushdie, the politically correct defender of the diaspora, is now the equally correct "British" citizen under the protection of Scotland Yard and defended by Harold Pinter.

THE DIASPORA, THE SACRED, AND SALMAN RUSHDIE

The Satanic Verses is one radical instance of diasporic recollection or rememoration. The questions that any such rememoration asks of the diasporic subject are: what is the status of its past, of its myths, of its own certainties? How has it constructed these certainties? Does anything or anybody have a hegemonic status within the diaspora itself? Or, do we read diasporas, as I have suggested, through the Gramscian definition of the subaltern? Do the Imams of Islam (in Bradford or in Tehran or in Bombay) constitute a ruling group within the subaltern?

Can one re-invigorate one's myths? One kind of re-invigoration was endorsed by Indian diasporas created in the wake of the British indenture system. In these nineteenth-century diasporas, loss was rewritten as a totality through the principle of a reverse millenarianism. There was a golden age back there that we have forfeited through our banishment. Let us imaginatively re-create this golden age, which would leap over the great chasm created in our history through indenture. One of the grand templates of Indian diasporic millenarianism was the myth of Rama and his banishment. The alternative to this millenarian ethos is a version of rememoration in which the continuum of imperial history is blasted through a radical mediation on the conditions of migrancy and displacement. The recapitulation of one's history (and not just the re-invigoration of myth) leads to a confrontation with the narratives of imperialism itself. Where the old diaspora's myths were, after all, commensurate with the imperial narratives of totality (insofar as these myths were considered to be equally forceful from the subject's point of view), the new diaspora attempts to penetrate the history of the centre through multiple secularisms. When, however, the interventions into secularity threaten an earlier memory, diasporas turn to versions of millenarian rememoration and retreat into an essentialist discourse, even though they know full well that the past can no longer redeem.

It is in this context that I would like to explore the intersection of the radical agenda of diasporas and the idea of the sacred. No reading of *The Satanic Verses* can be complete without considering the reception of the text in terms of the sacred. The sacred, in this instance, refuses to accept the aesthetic autonomy of the text and connects the narrator's voice unprob-lematically with that of the author. In his defence—and in the defence mounted on his behalf by the world literati—it is really the relative autonomy of art that has been emphasized. What this defence raises is a very serious question about whether a diasporic text that celebrates hybridity and rootlessness can be defended with reference purely to the privileged status of the aesthetic order. In the ensuing debates, the British South Asian diaspora has been read as a group that does not quite understand the values of a civic society and has the capacity to relapse into barbarism, precisely the condition that gave the Empire its humanist apology. If I return to the saturated discourses surrounding the Rushdie Affair, it is because the discourse reminds us of yet another kind of privilege, and one that questions the non-negotiable primacy of modernity itself.

Now here comes the difficult part of the presentation in the context of *The Satanic Verses* as a commodity with quite specific effects. The British Muslim response to *The Satanic Verses* has not been through the narratives of hybridity nor through an interventionist politics that would use Rushdie's book to point out the massive contradictions between the diaspora and the ideology of "Britishness"; rather, it has been through a re-appropriation of the myths of totality, of millenarianism, that was the survival mechanism of the old diaspora. In other words, the defence has been mounted not through a constantly re-validating and contingent subjectivity *in medias res* but through an unreal resistance based on the discourse of a prior diasporic mode of narrativization. *The Satanic Verses* as an intervention into the project of modernity now faces modernity itself as an unnecessary formation in diasporic culture. Clearly, the Bradford Imams cannot be both modern and anti-modern, but such indeed is the complex/contradictory narrative that is being articulated. Thus what we get is the second diaspora trying to cling to totalities, to the unreal completedness of the first, where, even for a Naipaul, there was never an unproblematic totality to aspire to in the first instance. The old diaspora, in spite of its ideologies of totality, could not have responded to *The Satanic Verses* with the same sense of unqualified rejection. The *fatwa* against Rushdie originated in the diaspora—in Bradford—and not in Iran.

From the borders, from the interstices of existence, from the liminal, the diasporic subject uses, in Rukmini Nair's and Rimli Bhattacharya's words,

> fragments of religious faith ... [to] "shore" up his existence, give him much needed stability in a hostile environment. When that stability is blown to bits by an author as well ensconced and integrated as Rushdie, panic results. The neurosis of *nemesis* replaces the certainties of *nostalgia*. (28-29)

One may disagree with Nair's and Bhattacharya's use of "certainties," but the point is valid. What is missing from diasporic theory is a theory of the sacred based not on the idea of the sacred as a pathological instance of the secular in itself defined along purely modernist lines but as a point from which interventions can take place. In short, as Al-e Ahmad pointed out, the sacred is a source of metaphors of empowerment easily available for ethnic mobilization. In all our debates about the diaspora, the sacred is missing. I return to *The Satanic Verses*, which, by its very title, foregrounds something highly contentious in Islam and in Islamic definitions of the sacred. Racialized politics meets its sacralized other here. To emphasize this, to find how Rushdie reads the sacred and how the unified discourse of the sacred is used by the diaspora to defend a lost purity from within the hybrid, the hyphen, is not to say that *The Satanic Verses* is best read along these lines. What I am doing is selectively using *The Satanic Verses* to underline the dual narrative of the diaspora: the hyphen and the total, the fracture and the whole. Clearly, both have different historical antecedents for the diaspora: the hyphen is the presencing of the boundary where the politics of epistemic violence and a self-conscious re-definition of the project of modernity are located firmly within the global politics of migrancy (which also affects the construction of the non-diasporic subject); the "sacred" is a function of narratives that the almost self-contained diasporic communities constructed out of a finite set of memories. They gave permanence to mobility (the mothered space is always mobile—the child in the womb moves) by creating a fixed point of origin when none existed. The sacred refuses to be pushed to the liminal, to the boundary. It wants to totalize by centring all boundaries: the many and the one cease to be two dialectical poles. Since its narratives are transhistorical, the absurdity of the move for a disempowered diasporic community is overtaken completely by the illusory power of the act itself, from which the colonizer is excluded. This is true of all religious attitudes in the diaspora. As Ashis Nandy writes: "Hinduism in the diaspora, for example, is much more exclusive and homogenic. Out of feelings of inferiority, many Hindus have tried to redefine Hinduism according to the dominant concept of religion" (104).

In *The Satanic Verses*, Rushdie, in fact, connects the moment of newness itself with the diasporic performance in the sense that the Prophet's intervention into the staid politics and religion of Jahilia is made possible only through people who are always on the margins of society, "water-carrier immigrant slave" (104). The sacred is thus a means of radical self-empowerment, especially for those who work under the tyranny of the merchant classes of the Arab world. In that sacred discourse, the language, however, was not of the many, of the hybrid, but of the one. The radical, in other words, was not the idea of multiple narratives and contingency or coalitional politics, it was not the affirmation of the hyphen, but the starkness of the total, of the one:

> Why do I fear Mahound? [thinks the Grandee of Jahilia Abu Simbel]. For that: one one one, his terrifying singularity. Whereas I am always divided, always two or three or fifteen.... This is the world into which Mahound has brought his message; one one one. Amid such multiplicity, it sounds like a dangerous word. (102-03)

The radical one, however, also carried a dangerous principle of female exclusion. Where the many had always found space for female goddesses, the Prophet, finally, excludes them from the position of divine intermediaries, though not before toying with the idea of their symbolic incorporation into the "new":

> "Messenger, what are you saying? Lat, Manat, Uzza—they're all *females*!
> For pity's sake! Are we to have goddesses now? Those old cranes, herons, hags?" (107)

In the deserts of Arabia and at a particular historical moment, the radical, the new, could be conceived of only as an austere unity around the mathematical one. In the version of radical alterity that defines the modern diaspora, it is the many that must now splinter the impregnable fortresses of the one. This is the monumental irony of the debates around the book. The trouble is that the nation-state has never acknowledged the diasporic contribution to modernity, always reading diasporas as the "one," always regarding them as a dangerous presence in the West. At the height of the controversy surrounding the burning of the book, the British Home Minister responsible for Race Relations, John Patten, issued a news release entitled "On Being British" (18 July 1989), in which the ideology of the one is used to berate the excesses of another ideology of oneness. It can be seen that race relations in Britain itself produced a desire to return to the security of the past: both whites and Muslims in Britain return to their own essentialisms in moments of (perceived) crisis. Have the efforts of those who have struggled for a multiply centred nation-state therefore collapsed because the state itself created an environment in which a historical moment (that of the Prophet) would be de-historicized, reshaped, and used as a defence of the diaspora itself? Homi Bhabha confronts these questions in *The Location of Culture*:

> The conflict of cultures and community around *The Satanic Verses* has been mainly represented in spatial terms and binary geopolitical polarities—Islamic fundamentalists vs. Western literary modernists, the quarrel of the ancient (ascriptive) migrants and modern (ironic) metropolitans. This obscures the anxiety of the irresolvable, borderline culture of hybridity that articulates its problems of identification and its diasporic aesthetic in an uncanny, disjunctive temporality that is, at once, the *time* of cultural displacement, and the *space* of the "untranslatable." (225)

Bhabha's examination of the politics of *The Satanic Verses* very quickly becomes a kind of an aestheticization of the diaspora. The dominant semantics of this aesthetics may be stated through one of Bhabha's favourite metaphors, the metaphor of the "trans-." Applied to the diaspora, it means that a double time-frame, a double space, is always, everywhere, present. This is a good point, since the disjunctive temporality (both here and elsewhere; the space of present location and the rememoration of the past) is the diasporic condition. To ask the diaspora to function from one space, from one time, is to create what William Godwin in *Political Justice* (1793) called "impostures." Yet the decisive question remains: what political articulations indeed can be made from the position of a disjunctive temporality? And if this is also the condition of hybridity (the term goes back to the nineteenth-century botanists), then what hope is there for hybrids to become agents of change and not just positions that one may occupy for purposes of critique?

Clearly, Bhabha's reading of the diasporic subject within the European, nation-state is more or less identical with the non-hegemonic or pre-hegemonic Gramscian subaltern whose histories are fragmented and episodic. In the context of the Rushdie Affair, the question that we may ask is, "Does hegemony always suppress difference?" Or does it entertain and even encourage difference provided that it is a "difference" that can be footnoted adequately in the grand history of Empire, which Sir Ernest Baker once referred to as a "mission of culture—and of something higher than culture" (qtd. in Asad 250)? When the hegemonic power loses its clarity of vision in terms of its own definition of unity, then a crisis erupts—and both Salman Rushdie and Homi Bhabha believe that post-imperial British society is in crisis. Terms such as cultural minorities, ethnics, blacks, New Commonwealth immigrants, multiculturalism, are all used by a hysterical centre that no longer knows how to normalize the other in the nation within. It is then the celebration of difference by Rushdie that is endorsed by Bhabha:

> It has achieved this by suggesting that there is no such whole as the nation, the culture or even the self. Such holism is a version of reality that is most often used to assert cultural or political supremacy and seeks to obliterate the relations of difference that constitute the language of history and culture.... Salman Rushdie sees the emergence of doubt, questioning and even confusion as being part of that cultural "excess" that facilitates the formation of new social identities that do not appeal to a pure and settled past, or to a unicultural present, in order to authenticate themselves. The authority lies in the attempt to articulate emergent, hybrid forms of cultural identity.
>
> (qtd. in Asad 262-63)[11]

It goes without saying that social identities do need authenticating (Asad), but their authentication, according to both Rushdie and Bhabha, derives from our ability continuously to re-invent ourselves out of our hybrid cultural condition (Asad 263).[12] The sacred asks different questions. Hybridity for whom? Does the state apparatus always want homogeneity? Is it in its interest to pursue this? Or is difference (but difference within a panoptical power) the desired aim of the nation-state? At one level, how is postcolonial difference (as hybrid) to be re-theorized as postcolonial hybridity? Is hybridity the desirable aim or a fact of life? Does the sacred reject the aestheticization of culture? Is the sacred point of view homogeneous to begin with? The debates surrounding the aesthetic order, the diaspora, and the sacred reached a point of extreme dissonance once Khomeini invoked the *fatwa* against Rushdie. What the debates also underlined, in the general context of the relationship between diasporas and the nation-state, is that often the ground rules that govern the nation itself may not be applied uncritically to inhabitants who fashion themselves in ways that are not identical with those of the majority of the citizens of the state. By way of a lengthy conclusion, I want to examine the Rushdie Affair and its (mis)readings on the assumption that what we have in a diaspora's relationship to the nation is a case of what Lyotard referred to as the differend.

THE RUSHDIE AFFAIR AND THE POSTCOLONIAL DIFFEREND

The Rushdie Affair draws us towards what Jean-François Lyotard has referred to as the case of the differend, in which the aesthetic and the sacred are so opposed to one another that there is no equitable resolution of the differences. Indeed, I would be even more forthright. *The Satanic Verses* has generated a number of discourses that quite simply are incommensurable with each other on any count. If one were to use Lyotard's legal terminology, we have a case of litigation in which there are no ground rules acceptable to all the parties concerned. At the extreme end is a position theorized by the Iranian intellectual Jalal Al-e Ahmad. In his intriguing book, *Plagued by the West*, Al-e Ahmad calls Westernization a pathology (*Gharbzadegi* or "western strickedness"), by which he means the manner in which Westernization functioning as a cosmetic ideal in the Orient effectively destroys the Iranian's understanding of his or her own culture. There is no room here for any kind of hybridity. Indeed, Al-e Ahmad writes,

> The west-stricken man has no personality. He is a creature
> lacking in originality. He, his house, and his speech are colorless,
> representative of everything and everybody. Not "cosmopolitan."
> Never! Rather he is a nowhere man, not at home anywhere. He
> is an amalgam of individuals without personality and personality

without specificity. Since he has no self-reliance, he puts on an act. Although he is a master of politesse and charm, he never trusts those to whom he speaks. And, since mistrust is a watchword of our times, he never reveals his true feelings. The only thing which might give him away and is visible is his fear. Whereas in the West the individual's personality is sacrificed to the requirements of specialization, in Iran the west-stricken man has neither personality nor speciality. Only fear. Fear of tomorrow. Fear of dismissal. Fear of anonymity and oblivion. Fear that he will be discovered for what he is, a blockhead. (70)[13]

Clearly, Al-e Ahmad's pathologization of the hybrid would sit uncomfortably with hybridity as an essential component of the diasporic aesthetic—not simply uncomfortably, in fact, but in an incommensurable manner, because between Al-e Ahmad and Rushdie we see a clear instance of the differend at play. In the aesthetic domain, *The Satanic Verses* bears witness to differends by finding idioms for them. Yet in the political domain the reaction to the text has been articulated through conflicting discourses that cannot lead to equitable resolution because the discourses presuppose rules of judgment that are totally at variance with each other. There is not an effective law that could accommodate these two competing positions because there is nothing in law that relates, with equal detachment and validity, to both. It is here that the Rushdie Affair itself becomes modernity's test case for the differend, and one, I would argue, that is more interesting than other literary debates such as those over *Lady Chatterley's Lover* or *Lolita* or *Power Without Glory*. To pursue the differend here, I will limit myself to a handful of statements made both for and against Rushdie.

The Satanic Verses had a dual audience: English readers in the West and people from the Indian subcontinent, whether in India, Pakistan, and Bangladesh or the eight-million strong "Indian" diaspora overseas. The fantasies recounted in the book are those of people who are Indian (especially Bombaywallahs), and much of the humour in the book is also very distinctly Indian, as are innumerable allusions that are readily accessible only to the ideal Indian reader. Rushdie's Islam, too, is Indian Islam with its mixture of strong Hindu elements. Not surprisingly, among non-white readers the book has been discussed most intensely by British Asians (largely British Muslims) and by Indians in India. In Pakistan and in Bangladesh, the critical reception has not been as great. For Indian Muslims its publication could not have come at a worse time. Already on the defensive in the wake of Hindu revivalism, the last thing the Muslims in India wanted to see was a book that

exploded (or attempted to explode) Islam's non-negotiable position about
Muhammad and the text of Gib-reel's revelation. As the Persian saying goes,
Ba khuda diwana bashad/Ba Muhammad hoshiyar ("Take liberties with Allah,
but be careful with Muhammad" [Naqvi 179]). Yet the Indian audience must
have been of special significance to Rushdie because the first review of the
book, by Madhu Jain (even before the book was launched in Britain), and
interview with the author appeared in *India Today* on 15 September 1988.
This was followed immediately by another interview with Shrabani Basu in
Sunday (18-24 September). The *India Today* issue also carried excerpts from
the Mahound section of the book, clearly with the author's permission. The
cynic could argue that this was a calculated risk by both Rushdie and
Viking/Penguin, his publishers, and was aimed at creating vigorous but
critical debates among the Indian intelligentsia.[14] However, politicians, too,
read the review, and the Muslim Opposition MP Syed Shahabuddin, eager to
fill the Muslim leadership vacuum in India, immediately asked the
Government of India to ban the book.[15] Whether it was out of political
expediency (the Muslim vote bank in India is huge) or out of a genuine worry
that the book was indeed blasphemous, one does not know, but the book was
banned within a month of the publication of Madhu Jain's review. Because
the book was not officially launched until 26 September, it is unlikely that
many people had seen the book before it was banned in India. In fact, the
excerpts published in *India Today* were probably the only sections of the book
that people had read. Before looking at Shahabuddin's own "reading" of the
book, I want to go back very briefly to Jalal Al-e Ahmad's critique of
Westernization in his remarkable *Plagued by the West*, because Al-e Ahmad
positions the differend as the failure on the part of the Iranian Westernised
bourgeoisie to understand and transform Iran's real, democratic concerns in
the postwar period. Whether in regard to oil or to the dissemination of
knowledge, Iran functioned under the Shah as an imperial outpost of the
West. The Iranians themselves—at least those who belonged to the
establishment—had acquired Western habits (through mimicry) but had lost
their own much longer traditions of social concern and equity. Yet Al-e
Ahmad also notes the crucial differend at the level of disputation when he
writes, "whereas at one time a verse from the Koran or one of the traditions
[hadiths] of the Prophet was enough to win an argument and put an
opponent in his place, today quoting some foreigner on any subject silences
all critics" (72). The other fear that Al-e Ahmad has is that Western
liberalism contains within itself the seeds of fascism.[16] More precisely, and
Al-e Ahmad returns to this point over and over again, he fears the manner in
which an instrumental reason at the core of nineteenth-century Western

liberalism transforms the self-reflexive and self-critical reason of the Enlightenment into an instrument of coercion that reduces the Orient to a collective body of superstitions from which Oriental subjects can be saved only if they can be made to think like Europeans. The massive investment in Oriental archives in the West, to which imperialists sent their Oriental students, is symbolic of a belief that only when the Orient can be archived in the West, and Orientals exposed to research principles based on Western bibliographic practices, will they be able to study their own cultures. Reformulated, the Western Orientalist argument goes something like this: Orientals cannot understand themselves because they have no theory of research. Nor do they have a systematic archive collected in one place that they can use as their data. They must either learn from the West or use the work of Western scholars who have had the benefit of years of training in analytical techniques. The Oriental replies, but you plundered our resources, and you never allowed us to develop research skills in languages that came naturally to us, because you connected research with the acquisition of a Western language.

If we return to Syed Shahabuddin's argument in the context of the foregoing, it soon becomes clear that he continues to read imperialism's instrumental reason as if this were the same reason as the Enlightenment (and certainly Kant) interpreted the term. It is also of some concern that in defending "Islam" from a perceived threat, he played into the hands of the Hindu fundamentalists for whom Shahabuddin's ire confirmed Islam's perceived (and erroneous) inflexibility and totally closed world view. In this version, Shahabuddin made a religiously correct statement but a politically naive one. Let us explore the case a bit more. Shahabuddin's essay appeared in *The Times of India* on 13 October 1988. It is important to realize that by 1988 the right-wing Hindu fundamentalist Bharatiya Janata Party (BJP) had become an extremely powerful political party with strong grass-root support, especially in North India. The Ayodhya Affair had reached a point of no return, and, looking back, one can see that the destruction of the mosque was simply a matter of time. It is important for us to invoke Ayodhya here because what Shahabuddin is really speaking about is the feeling of the average Muslim in India who is now being told about this unpardonable affront to the prophet on the part of a renegade Muslim. This information was not available to the average Indian Muslim before Shahabuddin politicized Rushdie. In the same essay, Shahabuddin then becomes a defender of the many avatars, *rishis* ("our religious personalities"), for which the Quran has no place at all. In making this naive political remark, he in fact begins to speak precisely like the devil who can entertain a multiplicity of gods in the pantheon for the sake of civic harmony. In short, Shahabuddin speaks less like a Muslim and more like Rushdie at this point and fails to appease precisely the electorate he is in most need to convince—the vast Hindu electorate. This kind of counter-reading is possible because even Shahabuddin's non-fictional prose has another agenda: to speak of national harmony, even as he invokes a fundamental fact of Indian life, which is that there is precious little intellectual dialogue between Hindus and Muslims in India precisely because Islam cannot countenance idolatry. The Hindu, on the other hand, cannot live without it. As an instance of the differend at play, Shahabuddin's rhetoric exposes the differend within India, and the need, in that country, too, to discover other means by which dialogue can take place. The Hindu intellectual speaks with ease with the Marxist Aijaz Ahmad, but has great difficulty following Shahabuddin. There are, then, three levels at which Shahabuddin operates. At the level of the Islamic defender of the faith, the claim is a simple one of Rushdie giving offence to Muslims who revere the Prophet as the perfect man and whose name the devout Muslim chants five times a day. The connection between Mahound and the Prophet is made explicitly in *The Satanic Verses*, which, of course, suggests that the book was written to offend.

The second text of Shahabuddin is different. It is based on Indian legal codes that explicitly state (Article 295A of the Indian Penal Code) that offence to anyone's religion in India is punishable by fine and/or imprisonment (not by death, let us add). Shahabuddin here invokes a variant of a law that exists, in different forms, in the West. In this instance, it is a case of litigation that can be mounted and/or defended successfully. However, it is the third text of Shahabuddin, the use of the Affair to underline Islam's own respect for other religions (even those that are not religions of the Book and condemned in the *Quran*), that is interesting. *The Satanic Verses* thus becomes a means by which Indian Islam distances itself from one of the fundamental characteristics of Islam (that the Hindu is essentially a Kafir). In 1989 this was an important move on the part of thinking Muslims in India who saw Hindu fundamentalism as their greatest threat. How to appease the Hindu, how to emphasize that Islam never condoned the destruction of temples, how to use *The Satanic Verses* to become a defender not only of Islam but of the multitude of religions within India? Indeed, how to be another Rushdie and yet uncompromisingly anti-Rushdie? These are the texts that have emerged from the debates thus far, as they touch on Indian social and political life. And the strategy backfired. The vernacular press did not support Shahabuddin, and Rajiv Gandhi's banning of the novel was seen as another act of appeasement of the Muslims not long after the Shah Bano case, in which Muslim Sharia laws were allowed to override Indian secular law. In Britain, where the protest began with the Islamic Foundation in Leicester's director Faiyazuddin Ahmad and where Muslims did read the book closely, the protests were directed not so much against the author as against his publisher, Viking/Penguin Books, which was asked to withdraw the book and pay compensation to the Muslim community for sacrilege. It was also in Britain that pan-Islamic support was mustered and, finally, if we are to believe one version of the events, a request made to Khomeini to act on behalf of all aggrieved Muslims. The request, however, seems to have been anticipated in remarks made by a number of British Muslims, one of whom, M. H. Faruqi, in fact, wrote, "[p]erhaps it would be more salutary if the author is allowed to enter into Islamic jurisdiction and prosecuted under relevant law" (qtd. in Appignanesi and Maitland 61). It hardly needs to be added that this "relevant law" condemns the offenders of Islam to death. Two points to Rushdie, two points to Islam, one to Hinduism (unwittingly).

It was against this furore that one would like to read Rushdie's most important defence, which was published on 22 January 1989. It is an interesting defence because it is straight out of the project of modernity that began, as many would argue, and persuasively I believe, with the Enlightenment. The key to Rushdie's argument is to be found in his carefully written sentences against what he sees as the essentialist Islam of the "tribe of clerics," a "contemporary Thought Police" (qtd. in Appignanesi and Maitland 74-75). The "Thought Police" have established the ground rules for the discussion of Islam, not Islam itself. Rushdie writes:

> They have turned Muhammad into a perfect being, his life into a perfect life, his revelation into the unambiguous, clear event it originally was not. Powerful taboos have been erected. One may not discuss Muhammad as if he were human, with human virtues and weaknesses. One may not discuss the growth of Islam as a historical phenomenon, as an ideology born out of its time.
>
> (qtd. in Appignanesi and Maitland 74-75)

These are perfectly reasonable arguments, and not at all unusual among liberal intellectuals in the West, or, for that matter, in other parts of the world as well. However, in presenting the argument in these terms, Rushdie implicitly accepts that the book is a critique of Islam and, furthermore, assumes, against the evidence, that any religion can survive the kind of historicization that he has in mind. Since the spheres of religion and the state are not at all clearly demarcated in Islam, Rushdie's case makes sense only if the two spheres indeed were separate. The choice for civilization, as Rushdie argues, is simple: one has to choose between Enlightenment and barbarism. However, is the choice so straightforward that one can state quite simply, "It is time for us to choose"? Choose what? A secular sphere from which the Muslims are excluded and a religious sphere in which the laws of blasphemy do not apply? Diasporic ideology, as we have argued, resists the historical in favour of the mystical and universal. No matter how powerfully the argument is presented, it cuts no ice, even with British Muslims, as may be seen from Michael Foot's elegant defence of Rushdie. Foot's target text is Dr. Shabbir Akhtar's defence of the burning of the book in Bradford: "Any faith which compromises its internal temper of militant wrath is destined for the dustbin of history, for it can no longer preserve its faithful heritage in the face of corrosive influences," wrote Akhtar (*Agenda*, 27 February 1989; qtd. in Foot 243). The point that Akhtar misses is that if all religions were similarly militant against each other, especially in those nation-states in which one of the religious groups has been defined traditionally as the outsider, we would all be in a dreadful mess. What is there in Islam that needs the temper of militancy and what is the political and social payoff of underlining this militancy? Foot's counter-argument is that the retreat from militancy has been Christianity's new-found strength, an argument with which Akhtar would not agree, or refuses to see. Clearly, the force of the argument (and Foot scores strongly against Akhtar here) is not at issue. What is at issue is whether Foot (and Rushdie) can see Akhtar's argument. Millions of Muslims can, just as many Westerners cannot. Two points to Rushdie here, two to Islam.

We can, of course, go through any number of defences of Rushdie. One, however, that is of some importance is Carlos Fuentes's essay "Words Apart," which appeared in the *Guardian* on 24 February 1989, just more than a week after the proclamation of the *fatwa*. Fuentes invokes Mikhail Bakhtin to make the case that the novel is *the* form of modernity, in which a multiplicity of languages and voices can expose the folly of a world view that locks itself into meaning. Such a world view—where "reality is dogmatically defined" —is that of the Ayatollahs of this world. For them, the source of all meaning is a closed sacred text that allows for no disagreement. Fuentes then goes on to counterpoint absolute truth against the idea of constantly searching for the truth. He affirms Luis Buñuel's position: "I would give my life for a man who is looking for the truth. But I would gladly kill a man who thinks that he has found the truth" (246). The statement exaggerates, in a surrealist sort of way, but the point comes across clearly. It is this position that is reversed for those who have condemned Rushdie. They would gladly give their lives away for those who claim to have found the truth and would murder the unbelievers or those incapable of living with absolutes.

We can cite many more instances of the debates surrounding the Rushdie affair, but the lines of the differend return to a simple opposition. Rushdie views the case as one in which justice can be meted out provided all parties concerned can talk about the issues, but within an Enlightenment framework in which the aesthetic object has a special place. As the Affair dragged on, Rushdie began to repeat the aesthetic argument. The book is fiction, a work of art, and therefore not subject to absolutely realist readings. In *Imaginary Homelands*, this position is extensively and monotonously argued. In a recent interview (October 1994), Rushdie states that the work of art is essentially an aesthetic object and should be read through aesthetic categories (sensibility, organization, design, etc.); its politics is only of secondary significance (Interview with Kerry O'Brien).

CONCLUSION: THE POSTCOLONIAL DIFFEREND

Can one theorize the Rushdie Affair and make an intervention into diasporic aesthetics without repeating the rhetoric of intractability? I have suggested in the second half of this paper that the Rushdie Affair dramatically draws our attention to diasporic politics within a nation-state as an instance of the differend. Through the use of the term "the postcolonial differend," I now want to make some (in) conclusive remarks about the uses of the differend as a mode of analysis that goes beyond consensual politics.

This is how Lyotard defines differend in the opening page of his book *The Differend*:

> As distinguished from litigation, a differend [*différend*] would be a case of conflict, between (at least) two parties, that cannot be equitably resolved for lack of a rule of judgment applicable to both arguments. One side's legitimacy does not imply the other's lack of legitimacy. However, applying a single rule of judgment to both in order to settle their differend as though it were merely a litigation would wrong (at least) one of them (and both of them if neither side admits this rule). (xi)

The most obvious modern instance of the differend is the claim on the part of certain revisionist historians such as Robert Faurisson and David Irving that the Holocaust needs to be rethought and the "facts" modified.[17]

Faurisson, for example, goes on to dispute the very existence of gas chambers because he could not find a single individual who had actually seen a gas chamber with his own eyes. What is at issue here is the nature of the referent. Since reality is not "what is 'given' to this or that 'subject'" but a "state of the referent (that about which one speaks) which results from the effectuation of establishment procedures defined by a unanimously agreed-upon protocol" (Lyotard 4), it follows that any object of analysis or knowledge comes into being only insofar as it "require[s] that establishment procedures be effectuated in regard to it" (Lyotard 9). When the establishment procedures unproblematically link up diverging phrase regimens within discursive laws that are fixed, laws such as dialogue, consensus, and so, on, the matter is resolved. However, when the linkages cannot be effectuated by virtue of a radical heterogeneity of the items—by virtue of their intrinsic incommensurability—then we begin "to bear witness to the different." Lyotard continues: "A case of differend between two parties takes place when the 'regulation' of the conflict that opposes them is done in the idiom of one of the parties while the wrong suffered by the other is not signified in that idiom" (9). To give the differend any real presence or effectiveness, to make it legitimate in spite of the absence of assimilative linkages between the phrase regimens of the competing ideas, one needs to recast the phrases themselves through new idioms in order that the elements that make up a phrase—its referent (what it is about, the case), its sense (what the case signifies), the person to whom it is addressed (the addressee), the person through whom the case is made (the addressor) —can be given new meaning. Lyotard speaks of silence, a negative phrase, as an example of something that has yet to be phrased: since it cannot be staged, it has no effectiveness.

The claim here is not that every dispute must be resolved but "how to argue for a nonresolvable heterogeneity (the basis for all true discussion) that is not a simple pluralism" (Carroll 80). What the Rushdie Affair dramatizes so forcefully is that the diasporic imaginary and the postcolonial are phrases in dispute because in moments of crisis the parties concerned present their case in a language and through sets of manoeuvres unacceptable to the other in a court of law. The conflict is not a simple opposition between us and them, the postcolonial and the nation-state, or the colonizer and the colonized; rather, it is a consequence of phrase regimens endemic to the worlds engendered by these terms.

It seems that Rushdie's works confirm the radical practice of heterogeneity where the differend is affirmed and not "suppressed or resolved" (Carroll 75). The subjects in his works do not exist outside or prior to the phrases through which they are constituted. There is, then, no supra real or a real outside the subject positions so constructed through which arbitration can take place. This does not mean that there is no room for correct or proper political action from a position of consensus or detachment (the image of the law); rather, the flight from spurious ground rules (the "authentic base," as some would say) draws attention to the problematic nature of the subjects in these works. A refusal to grant objective history (the real) priority and, furthermore, to see this reality as an instrument of totalitarianism and injustice because the victim's testimony is considered to be without authority leads Lyotard to claim that history (rationality) is really unjust in cases of the differend. One has to return to disarticulations, to silence, to feelings, to the corporeal, and not simply to the mental, for counter-hegemonic positions.

In this respect, the aesthetic order especially signals the possibility of alternative worlds that do not seek legitimation purely through facts. The aesthetic then contains unresolvable "heterogeneities" —Keats came close to it with his phrase "negative capability" —because unbridgeable gaps are left in "dispute." Lyotard sees this in Kant's own claim that the ethical, for instance, could not be deduced from the cognitive. The aesthetic, too, cannot be demonstrated through recourse to the cognitive and hence to reality. The Kantian sublime is thus a celebration of heterogeneity because, while it demands a certain universality, it does not assume that the universal is a given. The sublime celebrates antinomy as the mind stretches it as far as it can. The mind embraces the sublime as if this were desirable and necessary and would continue to do so if reason were not to reestablish its law. Yet in that moment of celebration, in that dispute between faculties, in that incommensurable differend, no object can be represented that equals the idea of the totality.

In all this the urgent demand is that the differend should be listened to. The diasporic imaginary, as the littoral, is that which defies social assimilation with ease. If and when that assimilation occurs, diasporas disappear. Until then what we have to address—as a matter of justice—is the radical politics of heterogeneity. Since the differend ultimately is unresolvable, and phrases cannot be linked unproblematically, the differend, as David Carroll explains, "proposes strategies ... of resisting ... homogenization by all political, aesthetic, philosophical means possible" (87) —except, of course, for a genre of discourse such as the novel, which does link the various phrase regimens together. These phrase regimens, such as the cognitive, the prescriptive, the performative, the exclamatory, the interrogative, in themselves represent mutually exclusive modes of representing the universe (Lyotard 128). The aesthetic then becomes a site for the differend to be presented even as the phrase regimens themselves remain incommensurable.

Ultimately, of course, Rushdie is speaking about justice for the diaspora. Is the concept of justice (not just the legal bourgeois term surrounding specific legal codes and acts) equally available to all citizens or is it that justice is the prerogative of only those citizens who are part of a homogeneous British family that includes not only white Britons but also the assimilable black? What I have done is think through some of the radical incommensurabilities in the texts of Rushdie from the perspective of what Lyotard has called the differend, as both the staging of and engagement with difference as dispute. In the politics of the Rushdie Affair, we encounter phrase regimes that are in conflict. So firmly grounded are the opposing views in a particular ideological and epistemological formation that either, from the point of view of the given epistemology or truth conditions, is equally true and valid. Given such a persuasive rhetoric, even the question of a communicative community capable of arbitrating, consensually, is out of the question. In the case of the Rushdie Affair, compromise or justice is not possible because the grounds of the arguments are incommensurable. There are no winners and losers in the Rushdie Affair, only the presencing of the differend through agonistic discourses and politics. What must be recognized is that in this presencing there is no possibility of a recourse to the grand narratives of the centre or the nation-state (recall both Powell and Thatcher here). The grand narrative therefore is replaced by the local and by the differend, which, as I read it, is a phrase that designates precisely those conditions such as Rushdie's, where the rupture, the drift, the inconclusive, begin to designate the diasporic condition itself. In diasporic theory we must bear witness to the differend.

NOTES

1. My thanks to Jim Clifford, Iain Chambers, Christopher Connery, Stephen Slemon, Brett Nicholls, Maria Degabriele, Abdollah Zahiri, and Horst Ruthrof for their help in writing this paper.

2. I owe this phrase to Iain Chambers.

3. The poem reads:

> Let me tell you, boyo, bach: I love this place,
> where green hills shelter me from fear,
> jet fighters dance like dragonflies

mating over unsteady, unafraid lambs,
and in the pub a divorcée, made needy
by the Spring, talks rugby and holidays
with my protectors, drinks, and grows
more lovely with each glass. So, too, do they.
As for me, I must hide my face
from farmers mending fences, runners, ponied girls;
must frame it in these whitewashed, thickstoned walls
while the great canvas of the universe
shrinks to a thumbnail sketch. And yet
I love the place. It remembers, so it says, a time
older than chapel, druid, mistletoe and god,
and journeys still, across enchanted pools,
towards that once and future Avalon. (128)

4. See Rushdie, "*Hobson-Jobson*," in *Imaginary Homelands* (81-83).

5. Phoolan Devi was released on 19 February 1994 after spending 11 years in prison. She was imprisoned on charges of murdering 18 upper-caste landowners. She turned a dacoit after she was gang-raped in her village of low-caste Hindus. Wanted in 55 criminal cases on charges including murder, kidnapping, and robbery, she gave herself up in February 1983. Her story already has been made into films and books. It is very likely that Devi will now enter politics. See *San Jose Mercury News* 20 February 1994; Sen; and Shekhar Kapur's film *Bandit Queen* (1994).

6. Millenarian narratives are an integral part of diasporic recollections and may be designated, for their respective diasporas, through terms such as the Indological, the Africological, and the Zionist.

7. *Observer*, 22 January 1989 (qtd. in Appignanesi and Maitland, 75).

8. Two of the novels that Rushdie admires most are *Moby Dick* and *Ulysses*.

9. "[T]he book isn't actually about Islam, but about migration, metamorphosis, divided selves, love, death, London and Bombay," wrote Rushdie to the Indian Prime Minister Rajiv Gandhi (qtd. in Appignanesi and Maitland 44).

10. Air India Flight 182 exploded in 1985, one of the more audacious acts of Sikh terrorism that actually originated, it seems, in the Canadian Indian diaspora. 29,002 feet was compulsory knowledge for geography students in the colonies.

11. Asad asks in footnote 21:

> Does Bhabha mean (a) that it is not worth appealing to the
> past as a way of authenticating social identities because the
> act of articulating emergent identities authenticates itself or
> (b) that the past, albeit unsettled, is not worth contesting
> because it is merely an aesthetic resource for inventing new
> narratives of the self? (263)

12. Asad notes that to speak of cultural syncretism or cultural hybrids presupposes a conceptual distinction between pre-existing ("pure") cultures. Of course, all apparent cultural unities are the outcomes of diverse origins, and it is misleading to think of an identifiable cultural unity as having neutrally traceable boundaries. (262)

13. Note that on his visit to an Islamic seminary in Qom, Naipaul chanced upon a book with a sepia-coloured cover that had been written by an Iranian who, the director of the seminary said, "had spent an apparently shattering year in England. This book was called *The West Is Sick*" (Naipaul 50).

14. See Naqvi, 166-69.

15. Unless otherwise stated, my source for the debates surrounding *The Satanic Verses* and the *fatwa* against Rushdie's life is *The Rushdie File*, edited by Appignanesi and Maitland. See also Fischer and Abedi, Chapter 7.

16. "One of the basic problems of western civilization (in the Western countries themselves) is the constant threat of the seeds of fascism within the body of 19th century liberalism" (97).

17. See Lipstadt.

Works Cited

Al-e Ahmad, Jalal. *Plagued by the West (Gharbzadegi)*. Trans. Paul Sprachman. New York: Caravan Books, 1982.

Anderson, Benedict. *Imagined Communities: Reflections on the Origin and Spread of Nationalism*. London: Verso, 1991.

Appignanesi, Lisa, and Sara Maitland, eds. *The Rushdie File*. London: Fourth Estate, 1989.

Asad, Talal. *Genealogies of Religion*. Baltimore: Johns Hopkins UP, 1993.

Bhabha, Homi. *The Location of Culture*. London: Routledge, 1994.

Carroll, David. "Rephrasing the Political with Kant and Lyotard: From Aesthetic to Political Judgements." *Diacritics* 14.3 (Fall 1984): 74-88.

Chambers, Iain. *Border Dialogues: Journeys in Postmodernity*. London: Routledge, 1990.

———. *Migrancy, Culture, Identity*. London: Routledge, 1994.

Clifford, James. "Diasporas." *Cultural Anthropology* 9.3 (1994): 302-38.

Faruqi, M. H. "Publishing Sacrilege is not Acceptable." Appignanesi and Maitland 60-61.

Fischer, Michael M. J., and Mehdi Abedi, *Debating Muslims. Cultural Dialogues in Postmodernity and Tradition*. Madison: U of Wisconsin P, 1990.

Foot, Michael. "Historical Rushdie." Appignanesi and Maitland 242-44.

Fuentes, Carlos. "Words Apart." *The Guardian* 24 February 1989. Appignanesi and Maitland 245-49.

Gilroy, Paul. *The Black Atlantic: Modernity and Double Consciousness*. Cambridge, MA: Harvard UP, 1993.

———. "Cultural Studies and Ethnic Absolutism." *Cultural Studies*. Ed. Lawrence Grossberg, Cary Nelson, Paula A. Treichler. New York: Routledge, 1992. 187-98.

Lipstadt, Deborah. *Denying the Holocaust*. New York: The Free Press, 1993.

Lyotard, Jean-François. *The Differend: Phrases in Dispute*. Trans. Georges Van Den Abbeele. Manchester: Manchester UP, 1988.

Mahood, M. M. *The Colonial Encounter: A Reading of Six Novels*. London: Rex Collings, 1977.

Mishra, Vijay. "The Diasporic Imaginary." Paper presented at the Feminist Studies/Cultural Studies Colloquium Series, University of California, Santa Cruz, 2 February 1994.

Naipaul, V. S. *Among the Believers. An Islamic Journey*. London: André Deutsch, 1981.

Nair, Rukmini Bhaya, and Rimli Bhattacharya. "Salman Rushdie: The Migrant in the Metropolis." *Third Text* 11 (Summer 1990): 17-30.

Nandy, Ashis. "Dialogue and the Diaspora: Conversation with Nikos Papastergiadis." *Third Text* 11 (Summer 1990): 99-108.

Naqvi, Saeed. *Reflections of an Indian Muslim*. Delhi: Har-Anand Publications, 1993.

Rushdie, Salman. "Crusoe." *Granta* 31 (Spring 1991): 128.

———. *East, West*. London: Jonathan Cape, 1994.

————. "*Hobson-Jobson.*" *Imaginary Homelands: Essays and Criticism 1981-1991*. London: Granta/Viking, 1991. 81-83.

————. *Imaginary Homelands: Essays and Criticism 1981-1991*. London: Granta/Viking, 1991.

————. Interview with Blake Morrison. *Granta* 31 (Spring 1991): 113-25.

————. Interview with Kerry O'Brien. "Lateline." Australian Broadcasting Corporation Television. 4 October 1994.

————. *The Satanic Verses*. London: Viking, 1988.

Sen, Mala. *India's Bandit Queen: The True Story of Phoolan Devi*. Delhi: Indus/Harper-Collins, 1993.

Smith, Anna Marie. "The Imaginary Inclusion of the Assimilable 'Good Homosexual': The British New Right's Representations of Sexuality and Race." *Diacritics* 24.2-3 (Summer-Fall 1994): 58-70.

Shahabuddin, Syed. "You Did This With Satanic Forethought, Mr. Rushdie." *The Times of India* 13 October 1988. Appignanesi and Maitland 45-49.

Spivak, Gayatri Chakravorty. "Reading *The Satanic Verses*." *Third Text* 11 (Summer 1990): 41-60.

Tölölyan, Khachig. "The Nation State and Its Others: In Lieu of a Preface." *Diaspora* 1.1 (Spring 1991): 3-7.

ELENI COUNDOURIOTIS

Materialism, the Uncanny, and History in Toni Morrison and Salman Rushdie

"Unreality is the only weapon with which reality can be smashed, so that it may subsequently be reconstructed."

—Salman Rushdie, from
"The Location of *Brazil*" in *Imaginary Homelands*, 122.

Can "unreality" be construed as a problem of history? Salman Rushdie proposes that historical conditions can be changed by an act of violent misrepresentation. Unreality—the *not* real—destroys; it unravels a given set of representations while it sets in motion a new act of representation. The unreal is productive; it generates new historical conditions.

Rushdie's *Shame* and Toni Morrison's *Beloved* are novels which present two monstrous (unreal) women—Sufiya and Beloved—as the transformative agents of history. In both novels, the unreal is a manifestation of the repressed. The other side of history reveals itself in a violent disruption which recasts history as a series of incommensurable actions which cannot be accommodated in narratives of causality. Both novels, moreover, create incongruous and competing historical spaces: they refer to a recognizable place, community, or nation by means of its fictive, uncanny re-rendering which claims, through the fiction, to be historical. Sufiya's violent outbursts in *Shame* recreate the landscape of the nation in a manner which remains

From *Literature Interpretation Theory* 8, no. 2 (1997): 207-225. © 1997 by Overseas Publishers Association. Reprinted by permission of the Taylor and Francis Group.

incommensurate with the actual nation of Pakistan. The fictional Peccavistan has its only reality in the novel and the historical claim of the novel is that Peccavistan is the truth about Pakistan. Readings of *Beloved* reenact the remembrance of slavery that the novel sets in motion and rehearse in its proper chronology Sethe's biography culminating in her reunion with the ghost of her daughter and the communal cleansing of the shame of her murder. Yet the novel also achieves a very different historical focus, evident in Morrison's concluding remarks on communal forgetfulness —(274–5): the unreal space of 124 Bluestone Rd., the actuality of Beloved's ghost are incommensurate with the hard, unbearable reality of Sethe's sufferings as a slave, her escape from slavery, and the price paid (as Sethe asserts) for her escape. But this incommensurability (the fantasy of forgiveness, reunion, and even denial) speaks in itself of a different and more urgent historical problem, the consequences of slavery.[1] Addressing the novel's present, the difficult space and time of the uncanny events at 124, we discover a different historiographical project which addresses the construction of identity after slavery.

But why Rushdie and Morrison? What can we gain through this kind of comparative reading? Discussions of postcolonial and ethnic literatures have taken place largely as separate academic discourses even when thematically and historically these works are very closely linked.[2] While Rushdie has a prominent place in the canon of postcolonial writers, his status as an ethnic writer in Britain has been overlooked. *Shame*, although a novel about Pakistan, is explicitly contextualized within the narrator's autobiographical explanations of his experience as an emigre in London. The history of Pakistan (a place remembered from the other side of an absolute historical divide not unlike Morrison's distance from a place like Sweet Home) is explored to explain the emigre's identity in London in the 1980s. Remembrance is about constructing identity in a present marked by dislocation.[3] While the comparison to Morrison helps us relocate Rushdie as an ethnic writer, the themes of postcolonial discourse help refocus the discussion of Morrison on history after slavery. Indeed by drawing into the discussion *Sula*, a novel which anticipates many of the problems of historical memory that Morrison explored at length in *Beloved* and which proffers a heroine who is similar to Rushdie's heroine, Sufiya, the repression of historical memory emerges as a theme central to postcolonial and ethnic literatures.

Because *Beloved* has an actual historical source (the life of Margaret Garner), readers have not hesitated to read Morrison's narrative experiments as a historiographical project. Both *Shame* and *Beloved* resort to the uncanny

to do history and the comparison is particularly useful because it can help us recognize the historiographical intent of the earlier Morrison novel, *Sula*. Like Sufiya, Sula is marginal to the historical contextualization of the novel. Historical context is elaborated in *Sula* as the background for the experiences of the protagonist but seems fundamentally disconnected from these experiences. *Sula* sets up a divided historical space: the unrealities and psychological complexities of Sula's experience that produce uncanny effects on the one hand, and actual history, the realm of wars and political change on the other. These function as markers of realism in the novel. While Sufiya, like Beloved, represents the return of the repressed, unlike *Beloved* (and like *Sula*) she is in no direct way anchored to historical fact but is instead Rushdie's vehicle for a fictive enactment of what is left out of history. *Beloved*, however ghostly, is anchored in the real life of Margaret Garner, and Morrison's historical novel is legitimated as history through its connection to a real life character. In *Sula* and *Shame* the historicity which interests the authors relies less on a mimetic correspondence to verifiable events. The result is that to read *Sula* historically can help refocus a reading of *Beloved* on the possibilities of African-American history after slavery: how do you create historical space and possibility when the present is completely overshadowed by the past, whether it is your own memory or a cultural memory? How do you remember and still invent a future and possibilities for your people?[4]

I

According to Tzvetan Todorov, the fantastic is a function of the reader's hesitation between two distinct possibilities offered but not resolved by the narrative: either there is a plausible explanation for events that appear supernatural, or there is no explanation. "The fantastic occupies the duration of this uncertainty," Todorov argues (25). Furthermore, he distinguishes the marvellous and the uncanny from the fantastic; in the marvellous, the reader learns and must accept the "fact" that the events are indeed supernatural. In the uncanny, strangeness is distanced in the past. *Shame* conforms to Todorov's definition of the marvellous, but *Beloved*, where explanations are provided but events retain their unfamiliar quality all the same, remains *uncanny*.[5]

If the function of the fantastic (as defined by Todorov) hinges on prolonging the reader's uncertainty, then the fantastic cannot readily engage with problems of historical knowledge. The fantastic explores the reader's

experience as a reader and not the reader's experience of the empirical world. By contrast, Todorov's definitions of the marvellous and the uncanny offer two distinct possibilities of historiographic emplotment:

> the marvellous corresponds to an unknown phenomenon, never seen as yet, still to come—hence to a future; in the uncanny, on the other hand, we refer the inexplicable to known facts, to a previous experience, and thereby to the past. (42)

The identification of the marvellous with the future and the uncanny with the past corresponds to the different orientations of *Shame* and *Beloved* respectively. Rushdie posits *Shame* as a historical novel about the future; he uses the Hegiran calendar and thus dates the events in Peccavistan after the events in London.[6] The reader of course recognizes the outlines of recent Pakistani history in the fictional Peccavistan, but Sufiya's violent vengeance is posited as an unrealized possibility. Beloved on the other hand manifests herself as a realized impossibility. Although the ghost mediates historical consciousness and remembrance in the novel, it remains unassimilable, strange, despite the explanation.

In *Shame*, Sufiya symbolizes the effectiveness of historical determinations on individuals. Yet her violence also speaks to the limits of such determinations. Like the excess that Beloved represents according to Caroline Rody (93, 109), Sufiya transgresses the historical determinants of her circumstances. Her real meaning lies in the excessive gestures of her violence. While her idiocy has come about as a result of harms done to her and registered on her person (actions which are explicitly historicized and located by Rushdie), Sufiya is not a mere tabula rasa to be written over but an agent who reacts to the harms done to her. Rushdie describes Sufiya's agency in a paradoxical sentence:

> What seems certain is that Sufiya Zinobia, for so long burdened with being a miracle-gone-wrong, a family's shame made flesh, had discovered in the labyrinths of her unconscious self the hidden path that links **sharam** to—violence ... (150–1)

Sufiya, "a family's shame made flesh" and thus not her own person, is capable however of making discoveries in her unconscious. Sufiya's unconscious is the location of the other side of history, the location of the repressed. Rendered conscious in this fashion by Rushdie, Sufiya is not only a receptor of actions done to her but an agent in her own right. Rushdie transforms

Sufiya into a symbol of resistance to historical determinations.[7] Her bursts of violence—her unreality in fact—have a magical transformative power which can release (at least fictively) a momentum toward revolutionary change.[8]

Not only is Beloved also unreal precisely in the same terms—she escapes the determinations of history and is reborn—but she recalls Sula. Like Beloved, Sula is a potential agent of liberation, a person who seems unreal because she is unaffected by the usual determinants. Although more realistically drawn than Beloved, Sula is inescapably uncanny. Her unreality results from her ability to escape her community's determining influence. Morrison presents Sula as a character who lacks an ego:

> She had no center, no speck around which to grow.... She was completely free of ambition, with no affection for money, property or things, no greed, no desire to command attention or compliments—no ego. For that reason she felt no compulsion to verify herself—be consistent with herself. (119)

Through her use of the word "ego," Morrison seems to invite a psychoanalytic interpretation of Sula. Yet the above can be read also as a historical evaluation of Sula. She is a character whose unreality is a result of her *difference* from others (118), a miraculous escape (however partial) from the social mores which defined her community. Not bound to be consistent, or to "verify herself" to herself, Sula is curiously unmarked by the community in which she lives. However, Sula is also the other against whom the community of the Bottom defines itself. It is only against Sula's difference, her monstrosity as a "witch" (150), that the Bottom sustains its sense of community.[9] Sula's otherness echoes Beloved's. The communal expurgation of Beloved's ghost comes as a confrontation with the otherness of shame denied through the tendency to forgetfulness.

Drawing from the theoretical contributions on historical materialism by Raymond Williams and Walter Benjamin, I find in the unreality of Rushdie's and Morrison's heroines the traces of a concrete materiality. The subversion of causal narratives attempted by Rushdie and Morrison attests to their shared belief that the meaning of the past lies in its uses in the present, a key tenet of historical materialism. Personal experience is recorded in these novels not as a result of history, or deterministic reflection, but as a continuous dialogue with the past which shapes the direction of new narratives. The stress is on the emergence of the new out of a constant engagement with the past.

In his analysis of historical materialism, Raymond Williams argues that despite the effectiveness of incorporative pressures, domination can never be absolute. Domination, by its very selectivity, always leaves out certain areas of experience which can then gather into oppositional forms:

> no mode of production and therefore no dominant social order and therefore no dominant culture ever in reality includes or exhausts all human practice, human energy, and human intention. This is not merely a negative proposition, allowing us to account for significant things which happen outside or against the dominant mode. On the contrary it is a fact about the modes of domination, that they select from and consequently exclude the full range of human practice. What they exclude may often be seen as the *personal or the private*, or as the natural or even the metaphysical. Indeed it is usually in one or other of these terms that the excluded area is expressed, since *what the dominant has effectively seized is indeed the ruling definition of the social* (*Marxism* 125, emphasis added)

Williams's opposition of the personal and the social shows how this division actually serves to disguise the social significance of the realm of personal experience. The novel as a genre has sought to reappropriate the personal as the social.[10]

The central importance of sexual experience in *Sula*, for example, demolishes the distinctions between personal and social experience. The World Wars—the history the reader readily recognizes as history in the novel—take place somewhere outside the fictional world that Morrison creates. Yet Morrison clearly treats sex as that realm of experience left over from the overdetermining incursions of the dominant culture. From that space outside the "ruling definition of the social," sex is at the core of Sula's disruptive energy; it is where the implications of her lack of selfhood affect the community most deeply. Through her promiscuity, she wreaks havoc on her community. Out of these disruptions rises the only possibility of a conscious community and thus quite explicitly an awareness of the social and historical.

In order to signal the socially disruptive potential of private experience ignored by the social, Rushdie exploits the Victorian literary convention of demonic women (a convention, moreover, which is entirely foreign to his subject matter).[11] He exploits Sufiya's ambiguous status as *really* supernatural: "Sufiya Zinobia turned out to be, in reality, one of those supernatural beings ... about whom we are happy to read in stories..." (216). Sufiya escapes from her safe assignation in the private experience of reading because she is linked to two of the author's real life experiences in London: his sister's attack in the London subway and the murder of a young Pakistani girl by her father.

The historical method of these two novelists is a type of historical materialism which can be located theoretically in Walter Benjamin's "Theses on the Philosophy of History." Historical materialism in its classic Marxist sense posits a correspondence between material conditions and human thought and culture which is also operative in the act of writing fiction. Fiction realistically (and in various degrees mimetically) seeks to reflect the world. Yet instead of relying on a simplistic notion of direct correspondence in mimetic representation, historical materialists draw attention to the mediations of, and even deviations from determinism, which locate the meaning of determination in the differences and not the correspondences between reality and its representation.

In his "Theses on the Philosophy of History," Benjamin conceives the function of the historical materialist as the disruption of narrative. He dismisses the usefulness of any narrativization of time as progress or development. Repeatedly resorting to the image of explosions, Benjamin describes the analysis of a historical materialist as an explosion. The historical materialist aims to "blast open the continuum of history" (262). The moment of the blast is both the historian's return to the past but also a moment which belongs historically to the present of the historian's writing. Anchored in two moments, the historian writes about the dialectical relationship between two specific situations, a relationship which once elaborated explains less about continuities and development than it does about the simultaneity of the past in the present, the presence of historical memory as a shaping force in everyday experience and the need to render this presence conscious.

To blast continuity, to arrest the flow of time and bring to the fore the actuality of a repressed past which has maintained itself in the present—these are the revolutionary tasks of the historical materialist, and they are carried out significantly first on the level of representations. Here, in fact, Rushdie follows closely on Benjamin's imagery: his characters blast into history. Bilquis emerges from the explosion of her father's movie theater naked and placeless, a metaphor for the birth of Pakistan from an abrupt severance of ties with the past. As a result of the explosion, however, Bilquis ends up in the care of a man who as a future leader of this new country will determine history. So while the explosion is a severance of ties to the past, it also places Bilquis in a new position where history holds the promise of the future.

"Thinking," Benjamin tells us, "involves not only the flow of thoughts but their arrest as well" (262). Balancing the imagery of explosions with the arrest of time, Benjamin describes the task of the historical materialist as the articulation of a repressed history. To quote Benjamin once again:

> Where thinking suddenly stops in a configuration pregnant with tensions, it gives that configuration a shock, by which it crystalizes into a monad. A historical materialist approaches a historical subject only where he encounters it as a monad. In this structure he recognizes the sign of a Messianic cessation of happening, or put differently, a revolutionary chance in the fight for the oppressed past. He takes cognizance of it in order to blast a specific era out of the homogeneous course of history—blasting a specific life out of the era or a specific work out of the lifework. (262–3)

Turning to Morrison, the materiality of her uncanny characters can be found in their Benjaminian sense of the arrest of time. Beloved arrives on the scene as an interruption of time which affords the return to the past and retrieval of memory. Her insatiable appetite for listening to stories of the past caters to Sethe's and Denver's need to talk and remember, a need which leads the three women eventually to form a carefully demarcated space apart. In the suspended time of this separate space, they can integrate their identity with the collective memory of their family's and race's traumatic history. The word, stories, memory emerge out of the dissolution of the normal strictures of coping and keeping up appearances that life goes on, an effort to which Baby Sugs was committed but to which Sethe cannot adhere. The banishment of Paul D. from 124 frees the women from their domestic roles and precipitates the integration of their identities.

Sula also fits Benjamin's paradigm. Not a fictional character in the traditional sense of an individualized, psychologically layered person, Sula is instead a point of orientation, Benjamin's "monad." This entity is organized around the culturally identifiable unit of an individual but functions in the novel as an energy and a prism through which Morrison articulates her historical understanding.

Sula's monstrosity is established in the novel through a number of incidents in which she fails to act appropriately or to act at all and instead watches something happen. Her voyeurism is described in the novel as an arrest of time, and I would argue that incidents of her voyeuristic absorption draw the reader's attention to historical truths that are revealed by the text.

The most shocking example of Sula's voyeurism is her passive observation of her mother's death. As Hannah burns, Sula stands by. Late in the novel, Sula provides us with a retrospective account of that event which seems at first to resist interpretation. Sula denies that her passivity had meaning:

> "That's the same sun I looked at when I was twelve, the same pear trees. If I live a hundred years my urine will flow the same way, my armpits and breath will smell the same. My hair will grow from the same holes. I didn't mean anything. I never meant anything. I stood there watching her burn and was thrilled. I wanted her to keep on jerking like that, to keep on dancing."

The seemingly endless continuum of time that Sula desires here is a denial of history. The natural world remains the same and unchanging. There are no "events," no history, in the natural world. But, of course, Hannah did not "keep on jerking like that"; she died. Sula's dumbness, her denial of meaning, is a recognition of her own and her people's status as historically marginalized—a marginalization that Morrison, as author, resists. Sula's desire to suspend time, to disconnect the event from its spectacle—what Johnson called "affective discontinuity" (168)—disturbs us and solicits explanation. It creates a narrative space, her own presence in language, which records a broader cultural sensibility of marginalization that has led to Sula's monstrosity. Like Sufiya, Sula is defined by her historical placement and her rejection of it.

II

While the distinctions between fictional and nonfictional historical narratives have gradually been eroded, I would like to propose an examination of the historicity of fictional narratives which reestablishes a meaningful difference between fictional and nonfictional discourses.[12] Historians and novelists may both deploy similar narrative techniques, but in most instances they construct their object of knowledge differently. The evocation of place and memory as a function of dislocation is particular to the ways in which fictions address problems of history. The difficulties with memory in *Beloved* stem from its associations with a place called Sweet Home, which is horrific because of slavery but also inevitably a home lost to Sethe who remembers its physical beauty, for example, with longing. It is a place or landscape from which she has been violently dislocated. Indeed

Morrison's idiosyncratic substitution of rememory for remembrance could be construed as a way to draw attention to the difficulties of remembrance rather than as a sign for its inevitability and force. The "re" in rememory signals a barrier, an acknowledgement of distance and difficulty.[13] In *Sula* where Morrison is more concerned to show the effects of forgetfulnes she describes at the end of *Beloved*, she invents a place and tells of a culturally specific memory of loss which is operative in that community but has no viable narrative. Her subject is broadly the history of African-American experience from 1919 until 1941. To conclude her novel, Morrison then skips ahead to 1965. The fictional place is demarcated by these historical markers.

Morrison's need to invent a place in *Sula* is consonant with the history she tells. It is a history of the loss of a sense of place and thus a history which can be retrieved only through the invention of the place that is lost. Morrison in fact specifically addresses the relation between a notion of place and the viability of a community. At the end of her retrospective account of the Bottom's disappearance, Morrison's narrator can ask whether the Bottom was a place or a community:

> The black people, for all their new look, seemed awfully anxious to get to the valley, or leave town, and abandon the hills to whoever was interested. It was sad, because the Bottom had been a real place. These young ones kept talking about the community, but they left the hills to the poor, the old, the stubborn—and the rich white folks. Maybe it hadn't been a community, but it had been a place. Now there weren't any places left. (166)

Morrison's story has rendered the Bottom into a community which is no longer dependent on a physical location in space but to its rhetorical location in a narrative of history. By positing the Bottom as a lost place which may never have been a community, Morrison sets up a myth of its dialectical opposite—a myth of real community.[14]

Shame also illustrates how novelists construct the object of historical knowledge differently from historians. Rushdie assumes we already have a substantial factual knowledge about Pakistani history. His tale does not provide facts but tries to explain how the facts (whose knowledge he shares with his reader) were constructed, in what cultural milieu they developed, and by what ethos they were motivated. Whereas Morrison invents a place but relies on an identifiable historical period, Rushdie barely fictionalizes a real place and invents an anachronistic time frame. He posits the experience of Pakistani emigres as anterior to the political history of the creation of Pakistan. Rushdie dislocates cause and effect from chronology, thematizing memory negatively as the loss of memory. Emigres, the narrator of *Shame* tells us, are people without a history, people whose ties have been severed by an act of physical dislocation to a new place (64). By positing the past as future, Rushdie demonstrates that historical memory is a constant process of becoming. To reimagine one's past is also to project one's future.

Rushdie thus dislocates the historian: he writes in London through the imagery and fiction of the East, a consciousness of place which he tells us is carried as a passive memory by migrants. A migrant's consciousness testifies to the disruptive presence of the past in our everyday lives. There is no such thing as a past neatly contained in a chronologically other time from our own, but only a presently unfolding sense of the past which is shaped by and also determines in its own turn our experience in the present.

Rushdie gives testimony to this present sense of the past when he names the fictional Pakistan, Peccavistan. This act of naming establishes continuities with the past while also registering the instability of the past which is constantly being rediscovered from shifting moments in the present:

> My story's palimpsest-country has, I repeat, no name of its own. The exiled Czech writer Kundera once wrote: "A name means continuity with the past and people without a name." But I am dealing with a past that refuses to be suppressed, that is doing battle with the present; so it is perhaps unduly harsh of me to deny my fairyland a title.
>
> There's an apocryphal story that Napier, after a successful campaign in what is now the south of Pakistan, sent back to England the guilty, one-word message, "Peccavi." **I have Sind**. I am tempted to name my looking-glass Pakistan in honour of this bilingual (and fictional, because never really uttered) pun. Let it be **Peccavistan**. (92–93)

The name "Peccavistan," as it is used by Rushdie, is an accusation against the imperialist Napier.[15] But at the same time, it functions as the heritage ("'the continuity with the past'") of the subject peoples. The *palimpsest* country is a country written over, one which hides and erases one version of its history with another.

Historical fictions occupy a persistently secondary status in regards to proper histories no matter how far we go in recognizing the fictionality of histories. With Hayden White leading the way, theorists of the narrativity of historical accounts have aimed primarily at persuading us of the fictionality of history.[16] Yet the historicity of fictional narratives always remains dubious because of what is perceived as their method of indirection. If historical fictions recount *what was*, they do so by a circuitous method.[17] They posit invented stories as allegories for real circumstances whose facts can be verified by referring outside the fictional text. But the secondary status of historical novels can be theorized in an entirely different way if fictions are viewed as critical investigations of a historical consciousness that is already widely disseminated. Rushdie and Morrison both recognize that their historical novels are parts of larger historical narratives which have been extensively disseminated in their respective cultures.

Thus secondariness is not a result of indirection. It is not the avoidance of fact, or a deliberate casting of truths as metaphors which could presumably also be represented without recourse to such literary devices. I would propose instead that postmodern historical fiction in particular is history's metalanguage. This secondariness is what Paul Ricoeur calls history's "second-order discourse," a discourse which responds to and thus comes after (or second to) an existing narrative but is not lesser than the first. Ricoeur does not distinguish between fiction and history when he refers to second-order discourse. Instead he refers to his own task as a philosopher who wishes to analyze not the narrative method of historians but the ways in which they construct their object of knowledge. Thus his subject matter in *The Contribution of French Historiography to the Theory of History* is "the second-order discourse of the historian on the nature of historical knowledge" (1).

Ricoeur draws from the structuralist vocabulary of the early Roland Barthes who in *Elements of Semiology* defines semiology as a *metalanguage* or second order discourse. A *metalanguage* is any discourse which sets out to describe ("operate on") another discourse. Thus semiology, "is a metalanguage, since as a second-order system it takes over a first language (or language-object) which is the system under scrutiny; and this system-object is *signified* through the metalanguage of semiology." Thus in metalanguage, "the signifieds of the second system are constituted by the signs of the first" (Barthes 92).[18]

Shame dramatizes its own second order discourse. To represent the way meaning is made, Rushdie deploys a metalanguage, an explicatory discourse about his own story. In a novel that is not a simple reflection of its epoch but a highly conscious effort to change the way in which this epoch sees itself, he transforms the peripheral stories of women in a repressive society into the privileged "angle to reality" of the novel. The most privileged of all such moments is the description of Rani's embroidered shawls. Rani's embroidered shawls are proof of how "the women seem to have taken over" (189), and by this Rushdie intends that women have taken over the making of meaning in his fiction. They have clearly not taken the world over politically.

The "unspeakable things," which Rani's "sorceress's art" has made visible, have been unspeakable even on the level of the story's rhetoric. Rushdie resorts to the device of Rani's shawls in order to tell more fully. As a moment of narrative explication, Rani's testimony, in fact, not only supplements but contradicts the general impression given by the narrator's own testimony. In some instances, the additional, incriminatory information which Rani provides about Iskander closely echoes previous passages in the story which seem, in retrospect, to have silenced these particular incriminatory facts. For example, when the narrator explains to us why the people loved Iskander, a mere twelve pages before the description of the first shawl depicting Iskander's philanderings with the "pink-skinned concubines" (210), the narrator elaborates on Iskander's vow to give up women, Pinkie in particular. We are told that he transposed that erotic energy onto his political image and projected eros as love for the people:

> People could see it in Isky, he was plainly full of the stuff, up to the brim, it spilled out of him and washed them clean.—Where did it come from?—Arjumand knows; so does her mother. It was a diverted torrent. He had built a dam between the river and its destination. Between himself and Pinkie Aurangzeb. (198)

While it is true that Isky gave up Pinkie, "the diverted torrent" had other "destination(s)" not mentioned here. More importantly, however, the reader finds out from the "badminton" shawl that Rani and Arjumand do not "know" the same things. The badminton shawl, like the others, teaches us that "no two sets of memories ever match" (209), something which the above passage obscures because it deliberately asserts the coincidence of both the daughter's and the mother's views.

Retrospectively, we understand that Arjumand's belief in her father's political image is inadequate while Rani's superior insight ("you swallowed everything he dished out, ... he hid nothing from me," 210) explains the political lie of Iskander's cavorting. By her act of representation, Rani changes the personal context of a betrayal of the wife by a husband into a political context. At the time that Iskander was engineering his political rise, Rani was isolated at Mohenjo. At this time we know that "her love for

(Iskander) had refused to die, but had become, instead, a thing of quietness and strength ... Rani subsided into a sanity which made her a powerful, and later on dangerous, human being" (165). The danger she poses is unlike Sufiya's, but equally subversive because it proposes a new way of seeing. In her later period of isolation in Mohenjo, Rani creates her shawls and signs them in her maiden name. The realism of her embroidered visions empowers Rani with a clear moral authority over her husband whom she rejects and accuses in her work. In this instance, Rani and more specifically the history which she inscribes in her embroidery are emblematic of the people (absent from the novel itself) and their accusations against Iskander.

Shame is undoubtedly a moral tale. But more than simply stating its moral, *Shame* explores the ways in which the moral can be legitimized and thus find an audience that will see it. In the instance of the shawls, the narrator describes a supposedly real series of perfectly executed representations. At the same time, he is creating a fiction about such shawls, a fiction in which his reader is necessarily a co-creator. Rushdie dramatizes one of his central beliefs in the way representations are established. To see and recognize is to legitimate.

The virtuosity of the shawls' execution and their aesthetic brilliance (literally breathtaking) arrest the narrative; they pause time. But this moment of wondrous seeing is also a powerful interpretation of the story itself. Rushdie here subverts the usual mechanism of spectacle and quite clearly politicizes our aesthetic sensibility.[19] In fact the thematization of reading as seeing in *Shame* is largely concerned with demystifying the spectacularization of politics and creating a method of seeing which helps narrativize one's history.[20] *Shame*'s method is distinctly anti-spectacular.

The shawls that "said unspeakable things" (210) are doubly important to the story. "An act of accusation on the grandest conceivable scale" (212), the shawls are first a moment of narrative explication from which the reader learns the full extent of Iskander's corruption. Second, "leaving out nothing" (214), the shawls propose the fiction of a perfect representation. The total representation achieved by Rani's shawls invites comparison with Rushdie's own magical realism. Rani is called an "artist" and her embroidery is a "sorceress's art" (209). In a similar fashion, Morrison presents Sula as an artist:

> In a way her strangeness, her naivete, her craving for the other half of her equation was the consequence of an idle imagination. Had she paints, or clay, or knew the discipline of the dance, or strings, had she anything to engage her tremendous curiosity and

her gift for metaphor, she might have exchanged the restlessness and preoccupation with whim for an activity that provided her with all she yearned for. And like any artist with no art form, she became dangerous. (121)

Sula's lack of a form leads to a fundamental doubleness in the novel's structure whereby Morrison posits Sula as the central organizing consciousness and the narrator as the consciousness from which meaning can be made. This doubleness of muteness and articulateness is clearly at play in the episode of Chicken Little's death where the actual words exchanged between Sula and Nel about the incident are evidence of an empty, contrived language that operates under the suspicion of external controls. This language in which Nel tells Sula, "you didn't mean it" —(62–63), is curiously mute and even outright false. Of course this denial of meaning is analogous to Sula's own denial later in the novel which I have cited already—"I never meant anything."

While Morrison's characters in *Sula* consciously disengage with language and choose to uninhabit it (a function of their historical forgetfulness), her narrator finds language to describe their silence. The extremely rich emotional lives of Morrison's characters and their complex communication with each other take place outside of language and are then placed in language by Morrison herself. The intensity of this nonverbal communication is established in the scene which precedes Chicken Little's murder.[21] As Sula and Nel lie together in the sand digging their twin holes, Morrison tells us, "Neither one had spoken a word" (59), but their actions were entirely in sync and the meaning of these actions entirely obscured from the reader except that they lead directly into the teasing carelessness which results in Chicken Little's death. Sula's action is a defiance of the laws of nature; she spins Chicken Little without regard for the force that the accumulated action creates. Moreover, she does it for the pleasure of the moment and as an assertion that she exists despite the internalization of her own marginalization—that she never meant anything.

By contrast, in *Beloved* the characters talk obsessively and find their own salvation in recognizing and sharing their stories.[22] In a novel which tries to solve the problem of silence marginalizing African-Americans in the period examined in *Sula*, Morrison performs an archaeology, a historical and fantastic retrieval of the moment in which remembrance and telling could have been most productive. She describes Paul D's desire to stay with Sethe at the end of the novel in terms of congruent stories: "He wants to put his story next to hers" (273). Paul D pleads with Sethe, "me and you, we got more yesterday than anybody. We need some kind of tomorrow" (273). Tomorrow arises as a possibility only in the recognition of a common history, the shared and lost place of Sweet Home. *Beloved* prepares the ground for becoming.

By being committed to the repressed side of history, both Rushdie and Morrison are interested in the disruption and suspension of narratives of becoming. Their narratives reveal instead certain consciousnesses or sensibilities normally censored or unarticulated at play in an identifiable historical context. Just as Nel's grief at the end of *Sula* "had no bottom and it had no top, just circles and circles of sorrow" (174), so does postmodern historical fiction construct itself on this image of infinitely expanding circles in which the reader reinhabits a time in the past which he/she remembers—not personally necessarily, but culturally. The novel provides what Rushdie claims repeatedly is a "new angle to reality."

Fictional historical narratives do not aim only to question historical truths which are established outside of their own discursive parameters. Rushdie and Morrison tell a particular history primarily by establishing the historical validity of their subject matter (an idiot girl, a ghost). If historical knowledge has been questioned by raising the issue of the narrativity of historical accounts, then paradoxically these and other historical fictions reassert the possibility of historical knowledge through their wildly fantastic characters and places.

NOTES

1. Although the appearance of Beloved manifests the overcoming of repression, it is paradoxical. The fantasy of a reunion of mother and daughter depends on the manifestation of a denial of the consequences of past actions, a denial which facilitates the confrontation with the past. Without this illusion (however temporary and ultimately maddening) the retrieval of the past is impossible.

2. Sally Keenan diagnoses the same division of academic discourses and tries to redress it in her reading of *Beloved* as a postcolonial text.

3. The impact of memory on identity has been the focus of much recent criticism. Walter Benn Michaels has described "the transformation of history into memory" in *Beloved* as "the deployment of history in the constitution of identity." In his comparison of *Beloved* and Holocaust literature (memory and testimony), Michaels argues convincingly that "it is only when it's reimagined as the fabric of our own experience that the past

can become the key to our own identity" (7). The function of the ghost in Morrison's novel is to dramatize this process for the reader.

4. For a discussion of the desire for and the resistance to the memory of slavery see Ashraf Rushdy who characterizes *Beloved* as "a requiem that is a resurrection" (568).

5. For a discussion of the uncanny in *Sula* see Barbara Johnson, "'Aesthetic' and 'rapport' in Toni Morrison's *Sula*."

6. "All this happened in the fourteenth century. I'm using the Hegiran calendar, naturally: don't imagine that stories of this type always take place longlong ago" (6). By using the Hegiran calendar, Rushdie can appear to be talking about the distant past while the knowledgeable reader knows that this fourteenth century is in the future.

7. My argument here runs counter to Aijaz Ahmad's critique of Rushdie's portrayal of Sufiya's negativity in *In Theory* (150). Ahmad sees Sufiya as an unfortunate portrayal of the revolutionary as monstrous and thus never truly redemptive. By being attentive to Rushdie's historical argument, however, I hope to establish that Sufiya's energies are a symbol of what has been done as well as of the impossibility of containing her.

8. Before the final explosion with which the novel ends, Omar senses the apocalyptic violence that Sufiya is releasing: "He persisted in his belief that the world was changing outside, old orders were passing, great structures were being cast down while others rose up in their place" (303). The promise of a new world remains unspecific, but it is held out as a possibility to the reader.

9. Morrison gives a telling negative example of how Sula gave the Bottom a sense of identity. Sula had the following effect on other blacks: "even those Negroes who had moved down from Canada to Medallion, who remarked every chance they got that they had never been slaves, felt a loosening of the reactionary compassion for Southern-born blacks which Sula had inspired in them." After Sula's death, however, "they returned to their original claims of superiority." The vision of a broad African-American community which Sula could inspire held a revolutionary historical potential that was unrealized.

10. In a related point, Geoffrey Hartman (using *Beloved* as his example) has described how literature personalizes memory and thus renders cultural, social, memory meaningful to individual lives: "One reason literature remains important is that it counteracts, on the one hand, the impersonality and instability of public memory and, on the other, the determinism and fundamentalism of a collective memory based on identity politics. Literature creates an institution of its own, more personal and focused than public

memory yet less monologic than the memorializing fables common to ethnic or nationalist affirmation" (85).

11. Sufiya has features of various of the demonic types identified by Nina Auerbach in *Woman and the Demon: The Life of a Victorian Myth*. Most tellingly Sufiya appropriates the repressive powers of society on her self and turns herself into an agent of destruction. Thus Sufiya conforms to a pattern identified by Auerbach in gender terms where the social is the male realm and the private is the female realm. Sufiya transgresses with her female, private monstrosity into the male world of political and social organization. In Auerbach's description of the type, the "slain heroine [slain in Sufiya's case by the brain fever that turns her into an idiot] restores herself to appropriate the powers of the destroying male" (15).

12. In "The Fictions of Factual Representation" Hayden White distinguishes between history and fiction by claiming that each discourse deals with a different order of event. History harks back to real events— "events which can be assigned to specific time-space locations" (121)—while fictions mix references to actual events with invented events. Yet White quickly backs away from the significance of this distinction. He stresses instead the dependence of both discourses on fictional devices for their strategies of representation. Thus proper history fictionalizes the events it accounts for. In a gesture which devalorizes the scientific authority of historical accounts, White focuses persistently on history's dependence on language, its complicity in invention and artificial emplotment.

13. Caroline Rody finds in rememory a tension between the author's desire to remember and recount and her characters' tendency to want to forget —(101–2). The critical consensus on the meaning of Morrison's term, however, has learned the other way. Rememory has been interpreted as stressing the forcefulness and inevitability of memory, that, whether you want to or not, you will confront memory as concretely as a physical presence you bump into. See, for example, Ashraf Rushdy.

14. Barbara Johnson makes a related point: "Morrison's novel conveys a sense of what she calls 'rootedness' precisely by writing under the sign of uprootedness" (166).

15. The British annexed Sind in 1843. After his participation in several imperial campaigns (in Africa as well as India), Robert Cornelis Napier served as commander in chief in India from —1870–1876.

16. In *Mclahistory* (1973). Hayden White set out to demonstrate the inevitable narrativity of all historical accounts. Historians, according to White, use literary techniques such as *prefiguration* and *emplotment* to shape the facts of history and make them meaningful. Ricoeur also uses the

vocabulary of *prefiguration* and *emplotment* in *Time and Narrative*. For an overview of the reaction against narrative history in the work of the Annales historians, see Peter Burke, *The French Historical Revolution*. Finally Ricoeur has argued in *Time and Narrative* that even Braudel, despite his denial, wrote narrative history.

17. The secondariness of fiction arises from the perception that fiction and history have the same intention. For White, both discourses of fiction and history share a fundamentally similar conception of their own historicity. Both posit themselves as a retrospective account of the "'way things really were'" ("Fictions" 122). This stems from their fundamentally mimetic narrative structure whereby history and the novel both compete as versions of realistic representation. I would argue, however, that deliberately fictional engagements with history do not narrate *what was*. They need not be substitutes for fully elaborated histories. Instead they offer self-reflexive statements about what it means to write history and to think historically. They engage directly with the problem of the nature of historical knowledge.

18. For the sake of clarity, I have reversed the order of Barthes's statements in my explanation of his definition.

19. Dana Polan quotes Benjamin to make his point about spectacle as an "aestheticizing activity." He says "fiction here is a practice by which a society engages in an 'aestheticization of politics'" ("Above All Else to Make You See" 56).

20. Iskander, who is an apt image-maker, instinctively spectacularizes himself: "Iskander Harappa tore off his shirt and ripped it in half; he bared his hairless breast to the cheering, weeping crowd. (The young Richard Burton once did the same thing, in the film *Alexander the Great*. The soldiers loved Alexander because he showed them his battle scars)" (197).

21. Jane Bakerman reads this scene as a failed initiation which leaves both women "incomplete—and isolated—for life" (552). Bakerman problematizes the silence, the girls' mutual repression of their murder of Chicken Little, as the cause of their failures as adults.

22. For a narratological analysis of story telline by various characters in *Beloved* see Shlomith Rimmon-Kenan.

Works Cited

Ahmad, Aijaz. *In Theory*. London: Verso, 1992.

Auerbach, Nina. *The Woman and the Demon: The Life of a Victorian Myth*. Cambridge, Mass.: Harvard UP, 1982.

Bakerman, Jane S. "Failures of Love: Female Initiation in the Novels of Toni Morrison." *American Literature* 52.4 (1981): —541–563.

Barthes, Roland. *Elements of Semiology*. 1964. Trans. Annette Lavers and Colin Smith. Boston: Beacon Press, 1967.

Benjamin, Walter. *Illuminations*. Trans. Harry Zohn. New York: Schocken Books, 1969.

Burke, Peter. *The French Historical Revolution: The—Annalcs School 1929–1989*. Stanford, CA: Stanford UP, 1990.

Hartmann, Geoffrey II. "Public Memory and Its Discontents." *The Uses of Literary History*. Ed. Marshall Brown. Durham and London: Duke UP, —1995, 73–91.

Johnson, Barbara. "'Aesthetic' and 'rapport' in Toni Morrison's *Sula*." *Textual Practice* 7.2 (1993): —165–172.

Keenan, Sally. "Four Hundred Years of Silence': Myth, History, and Motherhood in Toni Morrison's *Beloved*." *Recasting the Word: Writing after Colonialism*. Ed. Jonathan White. Baltimore and London: The Johns Hopkins UP, —1993, 45–81.

Michaels, Walter Benn. "'You who never was here': Slavery and the New Historicism, Deconstruction and the Holocaust." *Narrative* 4.1 (1996): —1–16.

Morrison, Toni. *Beloved*. 1987, New York: Plume, 1988.

———. *Sula*. 1973. New York: Plume, 1982.

Polan, Dana B. "'Above All Else to Make You See': Cinema and the Ideology of Spectacle." *Postmodernism and Politics*. Ed. Jonathan Arac. Minneapolis: U of Minnesota —P, 1986, 55–69.

Ricoeur, Paul. *The Contribution of French Histeriography to the Theory of History*. Oxford: Clarendon Press, 1980.

———. *Time and Narrative: Volume 1*. Trans. Kathleen McLaughlin and David Pellauer. Chicago: U of Chicago P, 1984.

Rimmon-Kenan, Shlomith. "Narration, Doubt, Retrieval: Toni Morrison's *Beloved*." *Narrative* 4.2 (1996): —109–123.

Rody, Caroline. "Toni Morrison's *Beloved*: History, 'Rememory,' and a 'Clamor for a Kiss." *American Literary History*. 7.1 (1995): —92–119.

Rushdie, Salman. *Imaginary Homelands: Essays and Criticism —1981–1991*. London: Granta Books, 1991.

———. *Shame*. New York: Alfred A. Knopf, 1983.

Rushdy, Ashraf H. A. "Daughters Signifyin(g) History: The Example of Toni Morrison's *Beloved*." *American Literature* 64.3 (1992): —567–97.

Todorov, Tzvetan. *The Fantastic*. 1970. Trans. Richard Howard. Ithaca: Cornell UP, 1975.

White, Hayden. *Metahistory: The Historical Imagination in Nineteenth-Century Europe*. Baltimore: The Johns Hopkins UP, 1973.

———. "The Fictions of Factual Representation." 1976. In *Tropics of Discourse*. Baltimore: The Johns Hopkins UP, 1978, —121–134.

Williams, Raymond. *Marxism and Literature*. New York and Oxford: Oxford UP, 1977.]

PAUL A. CANTOR

Tales of the Alhambra: Rushdie's Use of Spanish History in The Moor's Last Sigh

> If history creates complexities, let us not try to simplify them.
> –Salman Rushdie, *Imaginary Homelands*

I

Salman Rushdie's *The Moor's Last Sigh* tells the complicated story of four generations of a Christian-Jewish family involved in the spice trade in India.[1] The political, financial, romantic, sexual, and emotional entanglements of the da Gama-Zogoiby family easily fill the 400 or so pages of the novel. But as if the Indian narrative were not complex enough, Rushdie creates a frame tale for the novel. The narrator and central character, Moraes Zogoiby, has composed most of the story while imprisoned by a madman named Vasco Miranda in a mock-up of the Alhambra Palace built in a remote village in Spain called Benengeli. The name of the village, of course, alludes to the fictional Arabic narrator of Cervantes' *Don Quixote*, Cide Hamete Benengeli. Rushdie refers to the great Spanish novel several times in *The Moor's Last Sigh*,[2] and indeed as a narrative involving Christians, Moors, and Jews, it serves as a literary precursor of his work.

In general, Spanish history hovers in the background of *The Moor's Last Sigh*. The Moor of the title is Boabdil the last Moorish monarch of Granada,

---

From *Studies in the Novel* 29, no. 3 (Fall 1997): 323-341. © 1997 by the University of North Texas.

itself the last stronghold of Moorish rule in Spain. The last sigh refers to Boabdil's reaction when in 1492 he was forced to leave the seat of his power, the Alhambra, by the conquering armies of the Catholic monarchs, Ferdinand and Isabella. "The Moor's Last Sigh" is not simply the title of Rushdie's novel; it is also the title of a painting that plays a crucial role in the narrative, or rather two paintings with the same name, one done by Vasco Miranda and the other by Moraes' mother, Aurora da Gama Zogoiby. From the first page to the last of *The Moor's Last Sigh* Rushdie interweaves Indian and Spanish history. Moraes' grandmother Isabella Souza is nicknamed Queen Isabella and even credited with her own form of "*reconquista*" (pp. 43-44). The Jewish ancestors of the businessman Abraham Zogoiby are said to have come to India as a result of the same Christianization of Spain that led to the expulsion of the Moors, and, according to family legend, the Indian Zogoibys are descended from Boabdil himself, who, after his loss of Granada, purportedly had an interracial romance with a Spanish Jewess (pp. 82-83).

Why this new fascination with Spain and Spanish history in Rushdie's latest novel?[3] He seems to be turning to Moorish Spain as a model of a multicultural society—"the fabulous multiple culture of ancient al-Andalus" (p. —398)—a world in which the tolerance of the Muslim rulers for Christian and Jewish citizens led to the flourishing of a highly complex and productive culture.[4] Rushdie provides a clue to his own project when he describes a series of so-called Moor paintings by Aurora as "an attempt to create a romantic myth of the plural, hybrid nation; she was using Arab Spain to re-imagine India" (p. 227). Rushdie's emphasis fails on the particular issue of religious toleration: "Aurora Zogoiby was seeking to paint a golden age. Jews, Christians, Muslims, Parsis, Sikhs, Buddhists, Jains crowded into her paint-Boabdil's fancy-dress balls" (p. 227). Indeed Aurora tries to create a superhybrid of Moorish Spain and Mughal India, as the architectural styles of the two cultures fuse in her artistic vision:

> The Alhambra quickly became a not-quite-Alhambra; elements
> of India's own red forts, the Mughal palace-fortresses in Delhi
> and Agra, blended Mughal splendours with the Spanish building's
> Moorish grace. (P. 226)

In this dream of different cultures merging into a larger unity, one can see what attracts Rushdie to Spanish history. Moorish Spain appears to have solved the problem that has figuratively and literally torn India apart in the twentieth century. Religious conflicts between Hindus and Muslims led to the division of the subcontinent into India and Pakistan (and later to the splitting off of Bangladesh), but even within contemporary India profound tensions remain between the Hindu majority and the Muslim minority, tensions that periodically erupt into murderous violence. Rushdie has devoted much of his career to chronicling the catastrophic effects of religious fanaticism and intolerance, particularly in India (*Midnight's Children*) and Pakistan (*Shame*), but also throughout the Islamic world (*The Satanic Verses*). He returns to this subject again and again in *The Moor's Last Sigh*, detailing the latest incidents in the ongoing sectarian conflicts in India:

> Violence was violence, murder was murder, two wrongs did not make a right.... In the days after the destruction of the Babri Masjid, 'justly enraged Muslims'/'fanatical killers' (... use your blue pencil as your heart dictates) smashed up Hindu temples, and killed Hindus, across India and in Pakistan as well.... They surge among us.... Hindu and Muslim, knife and pistol, killing, burning, looting. (P. 365)

For Rushdie, Moorish Spain offers an historical alternative to this sad spectacle of religious violence. In one form or another. Moorish rule lasted nearly eight centuries in Spain, and during much of that period, Muslims, Christians, and Jews were able to live together in relative peace and harmony and to spur each other on to ever greater cultural achievements. In such diverse areas as architecture, astronomy, medicine, mathematics, music, literature, and philosophy Moorish Spain equalled and frequently surpassed contemporaneous cultural developments across the Pyrenees in Christian Europe. One need only look to the complex interaction of Islamic and Jewish philosophers in Moorish Spain to see how fruitful the hybrid nature of the culture proved to be. Some classics of Islamic philosophy have come down to us only in Hebrew translations.[5] The rich diversity of culture in Moorish Spain came to an end only when Catholic forces succeeded in reconquering the whole of the Iberian peninsula and expelling the last of the Moorish rulers. The aim of the Catholic monarchs was to impose a uniformly Christian culture on Spain, a policy that sooner or later left Muslims and Jews with the equally unpleasant alternatives of converting to Christianity or leaving the country. Though the results may not have been immediately apparent, the loss of both Muslims and Jews in Spain was to impoverish the country and make its period of imperial glory in the sixteenth century evanescent and ultimately hollow.[6]

Rushdie's use of Spanish history in *The Moor's Last Sigh* thus seems at first relatively straightforward and evidently places him squarely in the camp of the contemporary ideology of multiculturalism. He condemns efforts to impose a uniform culture on a nation and celebrates instead cultural hybridity. Rushdie's multiculturalism seems in perfect harmony with his status as one of the most important postcolonial authors in the contemporary world. Multiculturalism would seem to go hand-in-hand with anti-imperialism, and indeed in *The Moor's Last Sigh*, as elsewhere, Rushdie is highly critical of the British colonial presence in India, precisely because of the ways in which their rule tried to impose an alien culture upon a subject people. Rushdie's version of Spanish history thus appears to be a kind of postcolonial rewriting, in which the heroes traditionally celebrated by Spanish historians—*los reyes Católicos*, Ferdinand and Isabella—become Rushdie's villains, presented as the destroyers of the golden age of multicultural toleration under Moorish rule.

But even though Rushdie's Spanish history seems to be deliberately written from a non-European or even anti-Western perspective, let us not forget that we are still talking about *Moorish rule* here. Whatever the precise nature of the Moorish regime in Spain, it was not an example of the kind of multiculturalism ordinarily praised today, namely *democratic* multi-culturalism. The great cultural synthesis of Moorish Spain was itself the product of an imperialist venture, the conquest of Christian communities in the Iberian peninsula by Muslims from North Africa (both Berbers and Arabs). This fact calls into question any simple equation one might be tempted to make between imperialism and monoculturalism on the one hand or between anti-imperialism and multiculturalism on the other. As Rushdie's example of Spanish history suggests, imperialism may at times be linked to multiculturalism and, as we shall see in *The Moor's Last Sigh*, Rushdie shows how monoculturalism may in turn be linked to postcolonial nationalist movements. It is a tribute to Rushdie's integrity that he cuts through all narrowly ideological positions to present the full complexity of the issues he raises. His use of Spanish history turns out to be part of a larger project of rethinking imperial history in general.

II

Imperialism is commonly viewed today as a one-way street, running, as it were, from West to East, with all the attention centered on the way Europe has dominated non-European territories. As much as this view is rooted in sympathy with non-European peoples, it actually underestimates and underrates the active role that they have played in world history, treating them as merely the passive victims of European expansionism. The Ottoman Empire, for example, is a rather large and long-lived phenomenon to omit from any history of imperialism. Awareness of the very active role of Islam in world history breaks down the neat polarities people like to draw in theorizing colonialism. In Moorish Spain, a power ultimately derived from the East conquered a Western nation and ruled it for many centuries. With his interest in Indian history, Rushdie is particularly alert to Islamic expansionism, since centuries before the British took control of India, the land was invaded by Muslim conquerors, who founded the Mughal Dynasty. The historical background of *The Moor's Last Sigh* seems to be generated by Rushdie's fascination with the parallels between Moorish Spain and Mughal India. In both cases a complex hybrid culture resulted from the encounter between invading Muslim forces and the local populace.

In the standard paradigm of imperialism, a European power invades a hitherto untouched non-European country and imposes an alien culture on one that until that point had been pure, unadulterated, and perfectly unified. In the case Rushdie knows best, India, this model is completely misleading.[7] When the British came to the Indian subcontinent, they found a country with a fabulously complicated history and an extraordinarily complex culture. One cannot say that the British presence in India introduced an unprecedented element of heterogeneity into an otherwise homogeneous culture. In Rushdie's view, India is, as it were, always already invaded. Its culture is highly sedimented, the product of layer upon cultural layer deposited by successive invaders, each of whom had something to contribute to the vast synthesis that constitutes Indian civilization.[8]

Rushdie develops this view of the cultural history of India throughout *The Satanic Verses*, especially in the ideas of a character named Zeenat Vakil:

> She was an art critic whose book on the confining myth of authenticity, that folkloristic straitjacket which she sought to replace by an ethic of historically validated eclecticism, for was not the entire national culture based on the principle of bor-rowing whatever clothes seemed to fit, Aryan, Mughal, British, take-the-best-and-leave-the-rest?—had created a predictable stink. (P. 52)[9]

Vakil suggests that, in building a national culture, India was able to take something valuable from each of its invaders. Rushdie realizes how controversial this position is, since it runs afoul, in this case of "Hindu fundamentalism" (p. 52), but more generally of what he calls "the confining myth of authenticity," an ideology frequently promoted in postcolonial regimes.[10] Many have argued that a newly independent nation seeking to decolonize fully must reject all foreign influences, especially those from its former colonial master, and embrace a pure native culture. But Rushdie views the very notion of a pure native culture as a chimera. For the glory of Indian culture is its complexity, not its purity. Vakil's history of Indian painting dwells on the ways in which the Mughal invaders enriched the native artistic traditions:

> The pictures also provided eloquent proof of Zeeny Vakil's thesis about the eclectic, hybridized nature of the Indian artistic tradition. The Mughals had brought artists from every part of India to work on the paintings: individual identity was submerged to create a many-headed, many-brushed Overartist who, literally, *was* Indian painting.... In the *Hamza-nama* you could see the Persian miniature fusing with Kannada and Keralan painting styles, you could see Hindu and Muslim philosophy forming their characteristically late-Mughal synthesis. (P. 70)

Zeenat Vakil provides an important link between *The Satanic Verses* and *The Moor's Last Sigh*. She re-appears in the later novel, where, based on her earlier "influential study of the Mughal *Hamza-nama* cloths" (p. 324), she becomes the curator of a retrospective of Aurora Zogoiby's paintings.

Aurora's career as a painter illustrates the difficulty of pursuing the middle course of cultural hybridity in the contemporary world, where aesthetic fashion tries to force artists either to adopt the international style of Western modernism or to remain true to the well-trodden paths of local tradition, in short to choose between nativism and what Rushdie calls "Westoxication." Despite her success, Aurora periodically finds herself subject to contradictory criticisms:

> Those artists who were truly in thrall to the West, and spent their careers imitating, to dreadful effect, the styles of the great figures of the United States and France, now abused her for 'parochialism', while those other artists ... who floundered about in the dead sea of the country's ancient heritage, producing twentieth-century versions of the old miniature art (and often, secretly, making pornographic fakes of Mughal or Kashmiri art

on the side), reviled her just as loudly for 'losing touch with her roots'. (P. 178)

Rushdie is particularly troubled by the kind of criticism that condemns an artist for refusing to remain confined within the narrow limits of native tradition. *The Moor's Last Sigh* continues and deepens his interrogation of the postcolonial myth of cultural authenticity, whose chief representative in the novel is a distasteful character named Raman Fielding. Even his name reflects the underlying hybridity of culture in India; his first name is Indian but his last name is very British, the same as that of a canonical English author and said to be "derived, according to legend, from a cricket-mad father" (p. 230).[11]

Despite his hybrid name (he usually goes under the nickname of Mainduck), Fielding is an ultranationalist, fascistic politician, who campaigns for the restoration of an aboriginal Indian purity:

He spoke of a golden age 'before the invasions' when good Hindu men and women could roam free. 'Now our freedom, our beloved nation, is buried beneath the things the invaders have built. This true nation is what we must reclaim from beneath the layers of alien empires.'... The invaders would have to be repulsed. (P. 299)[12]

Rushdie shows how this kind of cultural chauvinism leads to disastrous religious violence in the incident of the destruction of the Muslim temple at Ayodhya, but even Mainduck himself is of two minds on the issue of Indian culture, as shown by his reaction when his followers take his message too literally:

But when they began, in their guffawing way, to belittle the culture of Indian Islam that lay palimpsest-fashion over the face of Mother India, Mainduck rose to his feet and thundered at them until they shrank back in their seats. Then he would sing ghazals and recite Urdu poetry–Faiz, Josh, Iqbal–from memory and speak of the glories of Fatehpur Sikri and the moonlit splendour of the Taj. (P. 299)

If the Hindu fundamentalist Mainduck can embrace Islamic elements in his view of Indian culture, Rushdie's vision is even more inclusive. That explains his decision in *The Moor's Last Sigh* to tell a story of India, not from

the usual perspective of Hindu and Muslim characters, but from the odd
angle of Christians and Jews, two of the smallest minorities in the nation.[13]
Rushdie has his half-Christian, half-Jewish narrator comment on the
strangeness of this approach:

> Christians, Portuguese and Jews; Chinese tiles promoting godless
> views; pushy ladies, skirts-not-saris. Spanish shenanigans,
> Moorish crowns.... can this really be India? (P. 87)

Even after detailing the seriousness of the issues dividing the Hindu majority
in India from the huge Muslim minority during the period prior to
independence, Moraes passionately defends his right to tell a story of India
centering on Christians and Jews:

> At such a time of upheaval, of the ruinous climax of divide-and-
> rule, is this not the most eccentric of slices to extract from all that
> life—a freak blond hair plucked from a jet-black (and horribly
> unravelling) plait? No, sahibzadas. Madams-O: no way. Majority,
> that mighty elephant, and her sidekick, Major-Minority, will not
> crush my tale beneath her feet. Are not my personages Indian,
> every one? Well, then: this too is an Indian yarn. (P. 87)

Far from simply rejecting European influence in India, Rushdie seems
determined in *The Moor's Last Sigh* to chronicle the contribution seemingly
alien cultural forces have made to Indian civilization. To be sure, Rushdie
makes fun of the tendency of part of the Indian population during the
colonial era always to take the side of their British rulers against their fellow
natives. When Moraes' great-grandfather, Francisco da Gama rebels against
colonial exploitation and announces to his family: "The British must go," his
wife Epifania claims that the British Raj has been purely beneficent,
something for which all Indians should be thankful:

> What are we but Empire's children? British have given us
> everything, isn't it?—Civilization law, order, too much. Even
> your spices that stink up the house they buy out of their
> generosity putting clothes on backs and food on children's plate.
> Then why speakofy such treason? (P. 18)

Like a few other characters in the novel,[14] Epifania clearly goes too far in her
Anglophilia, but Rushdie is equally critical of characters who feel that

Europeans have nothing to contribute to India. He seems particularly disturbed by the way that the heightened nationalism generated by Indira Gandhi's assumption of emergency powers in 1975 led to a new sense of who belongs in India and who does not:

> After the Emergency people started seeing through different eyes. Before the Emergency we were Indians. After it we were Christian Jews. (P. 235)

Rushdie is especially eloquent in lamenting the extinction of any Jewish role or influence in India:

> They have almost all gone now, the Jews of Cochin. Less than fifty of them remaining, and the young departed to Israel.... It is the last generation; arrangements have been made for the synagogue to be taken over by the ... State of Kerala, which will run it as a museum.... This, too, is an extinction to be mourned; not an extermination, such as occurred elsewhere, but the end, nevertheless, of a story that took two thousand years to tell. (P. 119)

III

One particularly rich example of the strange hybridity that results when Eastern and Western traditions meet in India may help us sort out Rushdie's complex understanding of the relation between multiculturalism and imperialism. As Rushdie shows, a solidly European tradition such as Christmas takes on a new meaning in an Indian context,[15] indeed in some ways is brought closer to its original meaning:

> Christmas, that Northern invention, that tale of snow and stockings, of merry fires and reindeer, Latin carols and *O Tannenbaum*, of evergreen trees and Sante Klaas with his little piccanniny 'helpers,' is restored by tropical heat to something like its origins, for whatever else the Infant Jesus may or may not have been, he was a hot-weather babe; however poor his manger, it wasn't *cold*; and if Wise Men came ... they came, let's not forget it, from the East. (P. 62)

Yet this tropical warmth is absent from the Christian celebrations in the English community in India:

> Over in Fort Cochin, English families have put up Christmas trees with cotton wool on the branches; ... and there are mince pies and glasses of milk waiting for Santa, and somehow there will be turkey on the table tomorrow, yes, and two kinds of stuffing, and even brussel sprouts. (P. 62)

Rushdie stresses the artificiality of the English attempt to recreate Christmas in India, symbolized by the cotton wool that simulates snow in this warm climate. Later, the falseness of the British position in India becomes evident even to the very English Reverend Oliver D'Aeth:

> Here at Fort Cochin the English had striven mightily to construct a mirage of Englishness, where English bungalows clustered around an English green, where there were Rotarians and golfers and tea-dances and cricket and a Masonic Lodge. But D'Aeth could not help seeing through the conjuring trick.... And when he looked out to sea the illusion of England vanished entirely; for the harbour could not be disguised, and no matter how Anglicised the land might be, it was contradicted by the water. (P. 95)

We begin to see how Rushdie discriminates between different kinds of imperialism, or, more generally, different forms of European influence in India. In this case, the English do not try to meet the Indians halfway; they insist on striving to recreate a little bit of England in Cochin. Their whole effort is in fact devoted to avoiding any taint of hybridity and maintaining the purity of their English ways. Rushdie contrasts this attitude with that of the Portuguese Catholics in the da Gama household:

> There are no trees here; instead there is a crib. Joseph could be a carpenter from Ernakulam, and Mary a woman from the tea-fields, and the cattle are water-buffalo, and the skin of the Holy Family (gasp!) is rather dark.... Nobody is shinning down a chimney in *this* house. (P. 63)

By contrast to the English Protestant Christmas ceremonies, this Catholic nativity scene is an example of genuine cultural hybridity, as no less than the

Holy Family itself goes native. Going native was the outcome the British authorities in colonial India most feared, and they did everything possible to maintain a way of life separate from that of the local population. In Rushdie's view, the British erred insofar as they failed to seek out ways of amalgamating their traditions and customs with those of India. Perhaps because the Portuguese presence in India was less massive and less powerful than the British, Rushdie portrays the da Gama family as more adaptable to local customs, even in their mode of speech. Rushdie in effect makes a similar distinction in his view of Spanish history. The Moorish conquest of Spain led to the development of a genuinely multicultural community, while the Christian reconquest led to its dissolution and destruction. In short, by looking at a variety of episodes and approaches in colonial history, Rushdie avoids presenting a monolithic view of imperialism.

One cannot even reduce Rushdie's position to a simple formula such as: the Portuguese presence in India was good and the British presence was bad. Though the conscious cultural policies of the British may have been ill-conceived,[16] in some ways they inadvertently left a valuable cultural legacy behind in India. To the extent that Indians were able to appropriate British culture and make it their own, they could overcome their colonial dependency. A number of Rushdie's characters find a way of nourishing themselves on British culture. Francisco da Gama presents the paradox of "a nationalist whose favourite poets were all English" (p. 32), although in the case of his son Aires, Rushdie hints that Anglophilia in India may be a form of escapism:

> Aires da Gama had given up his secret fantasy that the Europeans might one day return to the Malabar Coast, and entered a reclusive retirement during which he set aside his lifelong philistinism to begin a complete reading of the canon of English literature, consoling himself with the best of the old world for the distasteful mutabilities of history. (P. 199).[17]

But Rushdie suggests that the British did make at least one genuine and lasting contribution to Indian culture, namely the English language itself. In the midst of a politically charged linguistic divisiveness, English supplies India with the *lingua franca* it needs, a point made strongly by Aurora Zogoiby:

> It was at this time, when language riots prefigured the division of the state, that she announced that neither Marathi nor Gujarati

would be spoken within her walls; the language of her kingdom was English and nothing but. 'All these different lingos cuttofy us off from one another,' she explained. 'Only English brings us together.' (P. 179)

As early as *Midnight's Children*, Rushdie was concerned with the way that the issue of language has the potential to divide India and provoke conflict:

India had been divided anew, into fourteen states and six centrally-administered "territories". But the boundaries of these states were not formed by rivers, or mountains, or any natural features of the terrain; they were, instead, walls of words. Language divided us: Kerala was for speakers of Malayalam, the only palindromically-named tongue on earth; in Karantaka you were supposed to speak Kanarese.... Owing to some oversight, however, nothing was done with the state of Bombay; and in the city of Mumbadevi, the language marches grew longer and noisier and finally metamorphosed into political parties.[18]

One can see why in such circumstances many Indians have been drawn to English as a force for unifying their country culturally. The issue of language is of course highly controversial in postcolonial situations, with many arguing that to use the tongue of the old colonial master is to betray the cultural integrity of a newly independent nation.[19] But like many postcolonial authors, Rushdie has chosen to write in English, in part to reach an international audience but in part to be able to speak across the native language barriers in his homeland.[20]

Whatever one may ultimately think of Rushdie's writing in English, no one can accuse him of simply surrendering to the power of an alien tongue. Rushdie does not write the King's English. He states his linguistic goal firmly: "To conquer English may be to complete the process of making ourselves free" (*Imaginary Homelands*, p. 17). He has become the master of a hybrid linguistic form, an Anglo-Indian dialect that gives him one of the most distinctive voices in literature today. Rushdie's English is heavily influenced by the syntax, rhythms, and even the vocabulary of various Indian tongues.[21] When Rushdie writes of "kabobed saints" and "tandooried martyrs" (p. 26), we see vividly the hybrid texture of his prose. Whether he is dealing with a "tropicalised Victorian melodrama" (p. 100) or an "Indianised *Last Supper*" (p. 202), Rushdie's own art is the best example of the cultural hybridity he celebrates. Early in *The Moor's Last Sigh*, as if to demonstrate that cultural appropriation is a two-way street, and that the metropolitan heritage is now available for a former colonial to plunder, Rushdie quietly lifts a passage almost verbatim from Rudyard Kipling's short story, "On the City Wall" and makes it his own (pp. 39-40).[22] The way Rushdie in effect writes over Kipling's text as he incorporates it into his novel is an example of his central image for cultural hybridity in *The Moor's Last Sigh*: the palimpsest. For Rushdie, all culture, and especially Indian, is palimpsestic in nature. New cultural forces do not displace or erase prior ones, but simply write over them, giving culture the layered character Rushdie finds so interesting. Appropriately the final action of the novel centers around an attempt to uncover a portrait of Aurora that has been painted over with the alternate version of "The Moor's Last Sigh" by Vasco Miranda, perhaps a hint to us to be always on the alert for the layered quality of Rushdie's own art.

IV

And yet the course of Aurora's artistic career suggests a final twist in Rushdie's exploration of the problematics of multiculturalism: he comes to raise doubts about the value of cultural hybridity itself. That at least seems to be the burden of the transformation of the Moor figure toward the end of Aurora's life:

> He appeared to lose, in these last pictures, his previous metaphorical rôle as a unifier of opposites, a standard-bearer of pluralism, ceasing to stand as a symbol ... of the new nation, and being transformed, instead, into a semi-allegorical figure of decay. Aurora had apparently decided that the ideas of impurity, cultural admixture and mélange which had been, for most of her creative life, the closest things she had found to a notion of the Good, were in fact capable of distortion, and contained a potential for darkness as well as for light. This 'black Moor' was a new imagining of the idea of the hybrid.... Then slowly he grew phantom-like himself ... and sank into abstraction.... Reduced to mercenary status where once he had been a king, he rapidly became a composite being as pitiful and anonymous as those amongst whom he moved. (P. 303)

To understand this dark passage, and in particular what Rushdie means by the "mercenary status" of the Moor, we must return to his use of Spain in the novel, but this time to his vision not of the Spanish past but of the present. When Moraes comes to contemporary Spain in search of four of his mother's paintings that have been stolen, he encounters a strange simulacrum of the Moorish regime, a hollow echo of its genuine multiculturalism:

> I ...found myself in a most un-Spanish thoroughfare, a 'pedes-trianised' street full of non-Spaniards ... who plainly had no interest in the siesta or any other local customs. This thoroughfare ... was flanked by a large number of expensive boutiques—Gucci, Hermès, Aquascutum, Cardin, Paloma—Picasso–and also by eating-places ranging from Scandinavian meatball-vendors to a Stars-and-Stripes-liveried Chicago Rib Shack.... I heard people speaking English, American, French, German, Swedish, Danish, Norwegian, and what might have been either Dutch or Afrikaans.... This denatured part of Benengeli had become theirs. There was not a single Spaniard to be seen. 'Perhaps these expatriates are the new Moors,' I thought.... 'Perhaps, in another street, the locals are planning a reconquest, and it will all finish when, like our precursors, we are driven into ships at the port of Cádiz.' (P. 390)

Moraes finds the history of Moorish Spain repeating itself in Benengeli, but only according to Marx's famous formula: the second time as farce.[23]

Benengeli's multiculturalism is the product of what many regard as the latest form of imperialism, multinational capitalism. The town has been invaded by displaced persons from all around the world, who give it a cosmopolitan character, especially in terms of languages. But Rushdie finds this particular form of cultural hybridity empty. In his view, the commodity culture of capitalism abstracts from the local, from anything that roots a people in their soil, and substitutes instead a world of falsely universal brand names, epitomized by the fast-food chains that spring up everywhere and belong nowhere. This commercial cosmopolitanism *denatures* human beings; by ignoring all local customs, it dissolves their sense of cultural identity, which is always anchored in a larger sense of community. I believe that it is this process of dissolution that Rushdie has in mind when he speaks of Aurora's Moor figure as "reduced to mercenary status" and becoming "a pitiful and anonymous" "composite being." Cultural hybridity can take the form of a genuine and powerful synthesis of antithetical components, but it can also result in a mere pastiche, whose unity is superficial. When cultural artifacts are treated as pure commodities, they are unified only in the sense of being marketed together.[24] Already in *The Satanic Verses*, Rushdie was concerned that in the contemporary world "we have here a society capable only of pastiche: a 'flattened' world" (p. 261).

Indeed for all his celebration of cultural hybridity, Rushdie has always worried that it can degenerate into empty forms of amalgamation, in which the elements coalesce only because they have been stripped of all serious content and hence no longer come into conflict in any fundamental way. One of Rushdie's most eloquent evocations of multiculturalism occurs in *The Satanic Verses*, a vision so sweeping that it takes in all of India, encompassing in fact both East and West, eventually transcending all political boundaries, as a wife tries to match the universal knowledge of her schoolteacher husband in her own particular domain:

> In those days she had admired his pluralistic openness of mind, and struggled, in her kitchen, towards a parallel eclecticism, learning to cook the dosas and uttapams of South India as well as the soft meatballs of Kashmir. Gradually her espousal of the cause of gastronomic pluralism grew into a grand passion, and while secularist Sufyan swallowed the multiple cultures of the sub-continent—'and let us not pretend that Western culture is not present; after these centuries, how could it not also be part of our heritage?'—his wife cooked, and ate in increasing quantities, its food. As she devoured the highly spiced dishes of Hyderabad and the high-faluting yoghurt sauces of Lucknow her body began to alter ... and she began to resemble the wide rolling land mass itself, the subcontinent without frontiers, because food passes across any boundary you care to mention. (Pp. 245-46)

This passage reads like a parody of Rushdie's usual paeans to cultural hybridity. Here multiculturalism becomes a matter of a one-stop, full-service menu of Indian cuisine, and the inclusiveness of the vision is literalized in the form of the expanding girth of the cook involved. In this case ethnic differences in cuisine can easily be harmonized only because they have been in effect *aestheticized*, detached from any roots in a distinct way of life. Notice that this vision of multicultural cuisine works only because the woman's husband is a secularist. If he were a believing Muslim, she could not cook him pork, and if he were a practicing Hindu, she would not be serving him beef. In short, this example of cultural hybridity works only by ignoring the serious dietary commitments religions often demand from their followers, and thus trivializing the whole issue of food.

One of Rushdie's most famous images of cultural hybridity is the "eastern Western" in *Midnight's Children*, an Indian cowboy movie called *Gai-Wallah* with a distinctive Hindu twist:

> Its hero, Dev, who was not slim, rode the range alone.... Gai-Wallah means cow-fellow and Dev played a sort of one-man vigilante force for the protection of cows.... He stalked the many herds of cattle which were being driven across the range to the slaughterhouse, vanquished the cattlemen and liberated the sacred beasts. (P. 51)[25]

But this seemingly successful fusion of East and West turns out to have violent consequences:

> The film was made for Hindu audiences; in Delhi it had caused riots. Muslim Leaguers had driven cows past cinemas to the slaughter, and had been mobbed. (P. 51)

As Rushdie shows, cultural hybridity can go only so far; when it runs up against religious fundamentalism, the ability to bring about a larger synthesis comes to a screeching and sometimes violent halt.[26] In short, aesthetic traditions can be harmonized in a way that religious traditions strongly resist. We seem to have come full circle. I began by arguing that Rushdie offers multiculturalism as the antidote to religious conflict, but now I am saying that Rushdie views religious conflict as marking the inevitable limit to the success of cultural hybridity. I never claimed that Rushdie offers a simple solution to the profound problems he raises.[27] He would like to see people overcome their differences in larger cultural syntheses but he remains troubled that the price of doing so may be the aestheticizing of those differences, the effacing of precisely the fundamental beliefs that genuinely give meaning to life.[28] In particular, Rushdie worries that the very processes that produce multiculturalism may undermine a people's sense of community, dissolving the basic beliefs that traditionally provided a coherence and solidity to their culture.[29]

V

As Rushdie had shown in *Midnight's Children*, the history of India is complicated enough on its own, but in *The Moor's Last Sigh* he systematically juxtaposes it with the history of Spain, thus creating an imaginative hybrid world–a Mooristan or Palimpstine (p. 226)—that allows him to explore the full complexity of the problem of multiculturalism. Most surprisingly, he shows that multiculturalism and imperialism are not simply opposed, as is commonly thought, but may be intertwined. As Rushdie examines the variety of forms in which cultures may constitute themselves and interact with each other, he cautions against extreme positions and seeks to stake out a fruitful though precarious middle ground. He criticizes imperialism when it takes the form of simply trying to impose a monolithic, alien culture on a subject people. But at the same time he rejects postcolonial nationalism when, in its understandable reaction against colonial rule, it nevertheless repeats the error of its former masters and seeks to establish—or, as it claims, to re-establish—a pure native culture that in Rushdie's eyes can never be more than a convenient fiction. Rushdie celebrates the clash of cultures, even when produced by an imperialist encounter, as long as it involves a serious engagement of the cultures and results in a genuine fusion of antithetical traditions, styles, and ideologies—an outcome that he believes is in fact to be expected in such situations. Yet Rushdie cautions against a false hybridity of culture, in which the common currency is literally money and the cultural components are unified only by being reduced to a basket of commodities and thus emptied of all genuine content.

No one has done a better job than Rushdie of presenting the problems facing postcolonial regimes, torn between nationalism and internationalism, between trying to remain true to indigenous traditions and seeking to bring the benefits of an alien modernity to their people.[30] In works such as *The Moor's Last Sigh*, Rushdie has created a fictional world that mirrors the problematics of postcoloniality, a strange kaledioscopic universe in which figures out of Indian mythology like Shiva and Parvati rub elbows with characters out of American popular culture like the Lone Ranger and Tonto, a hybrid landscape in which a Spaniard and an Indian can communicate only because they have seen the same Hollywood Westerns ("Our common language was the broken argot of dreadful American films" [p. 385]). Given the difficulties of navigating through such uncanny terrain, it is no accident that Rushdie closes *The Moor's Last Sigh* with a fading vision of the dream of cultural synthesis, with a distant glimpse of what in the end may amount to no more than castles in Spain:

> The Alhambra, Europe's red fort, sister to Delhi's and Agra's—
> the palace of interlocking forms and secret wisdom, of pleasure-
> courts and water-gardens, that monument to a lost possibility

that nevertheless has gone on standing, long after its conquerors have fallen; like a testament...to that most profound of our needs, to our need for flowing together, for putting an end to frontiers, for the dropping of the boundaries of the self. Yes, I have seen it across an oceanic plane, though it has not been given to me to walk in its noble courts. I watch it vanish in the twilight, and in its fading it brings tears to my eyes. (P. 433)[31]

Notes

1. Quotations are taken from Salman Rushdie, *The Moor's Last Sigh* (New York: Pantheon Books, 1995). I reviewed the novel under the title: "Salman Rushdie: The Postcolonial Dickens" in *The Weekly Standard*, January 29, 1996 (pp. 41-43). A few passages in this essay are taken from that review; otherwise it discusses different aspects of the novel.

2. See, for example, pp. 393, 413, and 417.

3. Rushdie's interest in this period in Spanish history first surfaced in a short story called "Christopher Columbus and Queen Isabella of Spain Consummate Their Relationship," which originally appeared in the *New Yorker* and was republished in a volume of his stories called *East, West* (New York: Pantheon, 1995). As for Rushdie's sources for *The Moor's Last Sigh*, in an interesting review essay entitled "The Moor's Second Last Sigh," Martha Gould comes close to charging that Rushdie plagiarized the novel from a work called *The Last Sigh* by the Canadian author, Jacqueline Dumas, published in 1993. Dumas' novel evidently sets a story of contemporary Canada against the background of the story of Boabdil and his expulsion from Granada, and even features a character named Isabella who is compared to Spain's famous Queen. For more parallels between Rushdie's novel and Dumas', see Gould's essay in *Books in Canada* 25 (Feb. 1996): 16.

4. For a brief overview of the complicated history of the presence of the Moors in Spain, see Bernard Lewis, *The Arabs in History* (New York: Harper & Row, 1966), pp. 120-30, especially p. 123: "The non-Muslim protected communities were more numerous and better organised in Spain than anywhere else in Islam. The policy of the government towards them was generally liberal and tolerant, such repression as occurred being due largely to political considerations."

5. This is especially true of the writings of Averroës (Ibn Rushd). See, for example, Kalman P. Bland, ed. and trans., *The Epistle on the Possibility of Conjunction with the Active Intellect by Ibn Rushd with the Commentary of Moses*

Narboni (New York: Jewish Theological Seminary of America, 1982). For Rushdie's interest in philosophy in Moorish Spain, see the reference to Maimonides on p. 388 of *The Moor's Last Sigh*.

6. This view is advanced in an interesting postcolonial novel by the Pakistani author Tariq Ali called *Shadows of the Pomegranate Tree* (London: Verso, 1993), which is set in the Moorish community in Spain right after the Reconquest. See especially pp. 67-68 when a Muslim character tells a Christian: "Your [Catholic] Church put the axe to a tree that afforded free shade for all. You think it will benefit your side. Perhaps, but for how long? A hundred years? Two hundred? It is possible, but in the long run this stunted civilization is doomed. It will be overtaken by the rest of Europe. Surely you understand that it is the future of this peninsula which has been destroyed. The men who set fire to books, torture their opponents and burn heretics at the stake will not be able to build a house with stable foundations. The Church's curse will damn this peninsula." As odd as it may sound, I believe that, read carefully, *Don Quixote* presents the same view of Catholic policy in Spain.

7. On this general point, see John Tomlinson, *Cultural Imperialism* (Baltimore: The Johns Hopkins Univ. Press, 1991), pp. 73-74.

8. On this general point, see Tomlinson, pp. 91-92.

9. All quotations from *The Satanic Verses* are taken from the American edition (New York: Viking, 1988).

10. See also *The Moor's Last Sigh*, p. 201, for Rushdie's view of "endless talk about *the West as problematic* and *the myth of authenticity*" (italics in the original). Rushdie also speaks about "the bogy of Authenticity" in his essay "'Commonwealth Literature' Does Not Exist," *Imaginary Homelands: Essays and Criticism 1981-1991* (New York: Viking, 1991), pp. 61-70; see especially p. 67: "One of the most absurd aspects of this quest for national authenticity is that—as far as India is concerned, anyway—it is completely fallacious to suppose that there is such a thing as a pure, unalloyed tradition from which to draw. The only people who seriously believe this are religious extremists. The rest of us understand that the very essence of Indian culture is that we possess a mixed tradition, a *mélange* of elements as disparate as ancient Mughal and contemporary Coca-Cola American. To say nothing of Muslim, Buddhist, Jain, Christian, Jewish, British, French, Portuguese, Marxist, Maoist, Trotskyist, Vietnamese, capitalist, and of course Hindu elements. Eclecticism, the ability to take from the world what seems fitting and to leave the rest, has always been a hallmark of the Indian tradition." On the myth of authenticity and the inevitably syncretic character of postcolonial culture, see Bill Ashcroft, Gareth Griffiths, and Helen Tiffin, *The Empire Writes Back:*

Theory and Practice in Post-Colonial Literatures (London: Routledge, 1989), pp. 41-42, 110, 117-20, 195-96.

11. Rushdie has publicly admitted that the character of Raman Fielding is based on a prominent nationalist politician in India with the similarly Indian/British hybrid name of Balasebah Thackeray. The name "Fielding" may also be an allusion to the main British character in E. M. Forster's *A Passage to India*. Cyril Fielding.

12. See also Fielding's later comment: "If the new nation is to be born, there is much invader-history that may have to be erased" (p. 364).

13. Rushdie's model for this strategy, especially his focus on Jews, may be Joyce's *Ulysses*, which is increasingly being understood as a colonial/postcolonial novel, but one which deliberately avoids presenting Ireland as ethnically homogeneous and in fact emphasizes the multicultural aspects of the nation's heritage. On this subject, see Maria Tymoczko, *The Irish Ulysses* (Berkeley: Univ. of California Press, 1994).

14. See, for example, p. 50, where a number of Indians express their doubts about India's capacity to govern itself without British guidance.

15. Here Rushdie may be providing an answer to Kipling's famous poem, "Christmas in India."

16. For an example of such policies, see the quotations from Macauley on p. 376.

17. For the importance of the canon of English literature to British rule in India, see Gauri Viswanathan, *Masks of Conquest: Literary Study and British Rule in India* (New York: Columbia Univ. Press. 1989).

18. Salman Rushdie, *Midnight's Children* (New York: Avon Books, 1982), p. 225.

19. For the classic statement of this view, see Ngugi wa Thiong'o, *Decolonising the Mind: The Politics of Language in African Literature* (London: James Currey, 1986). Rushdie appears to voice his view of Ngugi's position when describing his appearance at a conference at which he "expressed his rejection of the English language by reading his own work in Swahili, with a Swedish version read by his translator, leaving the rest of us completely bemused" (*Imaginary Homelands*, pp. 62-63). For a brief discussion of Ngugi's view of language, see Ashcroft, *Empire Writes Back*, pp. 30, 131.

20. For the classic defense of this strategy, see Chinua Achebe, "The African Writer and the English Language," *Morning Yet on Creation Day* (Garden City, NY: Anchor Books, 1976), pp. 74-84. For a similar defense in Rushdie, see *Imaginary Homelands*, pp. 17, 64, and especially p. 65: "I've become convinced that English is an essential language in India, not only because of its technical vocabularies and the international communication

which it makes possible, but also simply to permit two Indians to talk to each other in a tongue which neither party hates."

21. For Rushdie's view of the Anglo-Indian dialect, see his essay "Hobson-Jobson" in *Imaginary Homelands*, pp. 81-83. See also Achebe's defense of the use of English in African literature: "But it will have to be a new English, still in full communion with its ancestral home but altered to suit its new African surroundings" (p. 84). Rushdie similarly argues in *Imaginary Homelands* (p. 64): "What seems to me to be happening is that those people who were once colonized by the language are now rapidly remaking it, domesticating it, becoming more and more relaxed about the way they use it." On this issue, see Ashcroft, *Empire Writes Back*, pp. 11, 38-40, 46, 61, and Benedict Anderson, *Imagined Communities* (London: Verso, 1991), pp. 133-34.

22. Rushdie acknowledges this debt on p. 435. For Rushdie's complex view of Kipling and of "On the City Wall" in particular, see the essay "Kipling" in *Imaginary Homelands*, pp. 74-80, especially p. 75: "No other Western writer has ever known India as Kipling knew it. ... nobody can teach you British India better than Rudyard Kipling."

23. For Marx's statement, see the opening of "The Eighteenth Brumaire of Louis Bonaparte" in Lewis Feuer, ed., *Marx and Engels: Basic Writings on Politics and Philosophy* (New York: Anchor Books, 1959), p. 320: "Hegel remarks somewhere that all facts and personages of great importance in world history occur, as it were, twice. He forgot to add: the first time as tragedy, the second as farce." For Rushdie's awareness of this formula, see *Midnight's Children*, p. 221: "Europe repeats itself, in India, as farce." A variant of the formula appears in *The Satanic Verses*, p. 424. In *The Moor's Last Sigh*, Marx's idea appears in this form (p. 352): "A tragedy was taking place all right, a national tragedy on a grand scale, but those of us who played our parts were ... clowns. Clowns! Burlesque buffoons, drafted into history's theatre on account of the lack of greater men." For a full understanding of tragedy and comedy in *The Moor's Last Sigh*, one would have to examine the many references to Shakespeare in the novel, especially to his two great plays about cultural hybridity, *Othello* and *The Merchant of Venice*. On Rushdie's relation to the theme of cultural hybridity in *Othello*, see my essay "*Othello*: The Erring Barbarian among the Supersubtle Venetians," *Southwest Review* 75 (1990): 296-319.

24. On this point, see Aijaz Ahmad, *In Theory: Classes, Nations, Literatures* (London: Verso, 1992), p. 128.

25. The parallel to the "eastern Western" in *The Moor's Last Sigh* is "'Country and Eastern' music, a set of twangy songs about ranches and trains

and love and cows with an idiosyncratic twist" (p. 209). The fact that this genre is invented by a character named Cashondeliveri, who performs under the stage name of "Jimmy Cash," is a good reminder that, for all Rushdie's criticism of capitalism, he presents it as one of the driving forces behind multiculturalism in the world today, as economic incentives work to dissolve tribal loyalties and bring about a globalization of culture.

26. Note that even in Rushdie's hopeful vision of cultural hybridity in the Indian Christmas in *The Moor's Last Sigh*, the religious dimension introduces an element of serious conflict: "But there are many Christianities here in Cochin, Catholic and Syriac Orthodox and Nestorian, there are midnight masses where incense chokes the lungs, ... there are wars between the denominations, R.C. v. Syriac, and *everyone* agrees the Nestorians are no sort of Christians, and all these warring Christmases, too, are being prepared" (pp. 62-63).

27. For this reason, Rushdie has drawn criticism from a variety of postcolonial critics who complain that he fails to come up with positive solutions to the problems of Third World communities. Ahmad (p. 151), for example, writes of Rushdie's novel *Shame*: "Rushdie's inability to include integral regenerative possibilities within the Grotesque world of his imaginative creation represents, I believe, a conceptual flaw of a fundamental kind." Or see Fawzia Afzal-Khan, *Cultural Imperialism and the Indo-European Novel* (University Park. PA: Pennsylvania State Univ. Press, 1993), who criticizes Rushdie's "failure to construct a viable alternative ideology for himself or for postcolonial society in general" (p. 142). One of the most critical discussions of Rushdie is to be found in Timothy Brennan, *Salman Rushdie and the Third World* (New York: St. Martin's Press, 1989), which basically argues that he is too cosmopolitan to be a true spokesman for postcolonial concerns and ends up contrasting him unfavorably with more genuine representatives of the Third World such as Roque Dalton and Obi Egbuna: "The fulness and complexity of their collective visions are often foreshortened in the personal filter of Rushdie's fiction" (p. 166). It seems that Rushdie's very success with Western critics has compromised him in the eyes of many champions of postcolonial literature.

28. In the story of Uma Sarasvati in *The Moor's Last Sigh*, Rushdie explicitly develops the tension between a "pluralist philosophy" and "fundamental verities" (p. 272).

29. The religious toleration and hence the multiculturalism in Moorish Spain resulted in part from precisely the weakness of the Islamic regime there-a consequence of the remoteness of Spain from the centers of Islamic

culture in the Middle East, as well as of all the internecine strife among the Islamic rulers in Spain.

30. For a broad discussion of this set of problems, see Michael Valdez Moses, *The Novel and the Globalization of Culture* (New York: Oxford Univ. Press, 1995).

31. To end on a personal note: I saw the Alhambra for the first time in October, 1995. It is one of the most extraordinarily beautiful architectural complexes in the world, especially if seen from a distance, when the grandeur of its conception becomes apparent. But the sublimity of seeing the Alhambra was undermined for me by three factors: 1) even in the offseason, it is swamped by hordes of international tourists; 2) much of it is reconstructed, and the aesthetic harmony is marred by later, incongruous additions, such as the palace of Charles V; 3) looking at its gardens and pavillions, I could not help thinking that here were the prototypes of every shopping mall I had ever seen in Southern California. Rushdie's dialectic between genuine cultural hybridity and its postmodern simulacrum is nowhere more evident than in the Alhambra as it stands today; with floodlit tours at night, the Alhambra is in danger of becoming a stagey imitation of itself.

J O S N A E . R E G E

Victim into Protagonist? Midnight's Children and the Post-Rushdie National Narratives of the Eighties

MIDNIGHT'S CHILDREN AS A BREAKTHROUGH

The 1981 publication of Salman Rushdie's *Midnight's Children* was a watershed in the post-independence development of the Indian English novel, so much so that the term "post-Rushdie" has come to refer to the decade or so afterwards in which a wave of novels appeared by established as well as by young writers that were clearly influenced by *Midnight's Children*.[1] Unashamedly self-centered, Rushdie's novel celebrates the creative tensions between personal and national identity, playing up and playing with both their polarity and their unity, recognizing, like its protagonist Saleem Sinai, that if the individual is "handcuffed to history" whether he likes it or not, he can make a virtue out of that necessity. Sparks fly between the private and public realms, making artistic fireworks where there had previously been deadening dichotomies. *Midnight's Children* neither denies nor seeks to transcend polarities, but embraces them as artistic method, rejecting nothing, celebrating the resulting chaotic multiplicity, even if it crushes the protagonist himself into a billion pieces. *MC* brings heresies into the open and transforms them into prophecies. What had been the Indian English novel's problems now suddenly became its trademarks.

The number of new Indian English novelists published throughout the 1980s testifies to *MC*'s tremendous influence, not merely on superficial

From *Studies in the Novel* 29, no. 3 (Fall 1997): 342-375. © 1997 by the University of North Texas.

145

would-be imitators (of which there were several), or on the metropolitan demand for Indian fiction (which was considerable), but also on the fundamental conception of the national narrative. My central claim in this essay is that *Midnight's Children* enacted a discursive reconfiguration of the relationship between Self and Nation. I seek to demonstrate how it did so, and also why and how it opened up new spaces for a new crop of writers in English. *Midnight's Children* declared that there were as many equally valid versions of Indian identity as there were Indians. This concept proved to be very liberating for many Indian English writers, allowing them to break the polarized stalemate between Self and Nation that had caught the Indian English novel in a kind of ideological and artistic holding pattern for two decades. The eighties and nineties have been distinguished by an Indian English literary explosion as writers have found themselves free to speak in a multiplicity of voices and write in a multiplicity of modes.

When *Midnight's Children* was published in 1981, winning that year's prestigious Booker Prize (and subsequently, the prize for the best of 25 years of Bookers), it was hailed both in and out of India as a literary masterpiece, and almost immediately became a kind of benchmark against which both writers and readers began to assess new novels. But it has become virtually impossible to look back at *MC* from the late nineties without seeing the novel through the filter of the events of the past 15 years. It is hard to remember, or even to acknowledge, the enthusiasm with which its publication was greeted in—India—not because of its politics (there were always quarrels with that), or because of the accuracy of its representation of Indian history (it did not even pretend to that), but because of its exuberance of language and style, its combination of hilarious comedy and scathing political satire, its triumphant over-confidence, and, not least, its very success. When Rushdie toured the country in 1983 in a "triumphal homecoming," hundreds of people flocked to see him.[2] At the British Council in Delhi, fully 700 people arrived at a reading where no more than 300 had been expected and the organizers had to set up loudspeakers on the lawns outside.[3] According to a 1988 article in the Indian weekly, *Sunday*, "copies of pirated editions [of *MC*] flooded the pavements before the paperback edition reached India."[4] In 1984, Shyamala Narayan wrote: "Publishers claim that the novel has sold 4,000 copies in hardcover, and 45,000 in paperback (in addition to the pirated editions); these sales figures are unprecedented for an Indian-English novelist."[5] *MC*'s commercial success certainly helped to pave the way for future Indian English writers as publishers in India became more attentive to the domestic market for fiction in English, and publishers in Britain and the United States became more receptive to new writers from India.[6]

In the late nineties, critics both inside and out of India are much more cautious, much less likely to embrace Rushdie or claim him for India; he tends to be discussed as a diasporic writer, and his influence on the Indian literary scene is often criticized as having negatively influenced a group of already elite, alienated, or expatriate Indian English writers, and intensified the neglect of Indian language writers.[7] Of course, chief among the events that have so radically changed our perceptions of *MC* and its author since 1981 has been the 1989 Irani *fatwa* on Rushdie's *The Satanic Verses*. Its intellectual and political fallout has been disastrous, both for the literary reputation and literal survival of Rushdie himself and for the dialogue between North and South, always strained, now more polarized than ever (ironic, this, for a writer whose stated aim was to open up space on the very horns of a dilemma). And at least as important as the *fatwa* to our changed view of *Midnight's Children* has been the deepening crisis of the Nation-state and the worldwide rise of myriad Indian and other sub-nationalisms throughout the eighties and nineties. To take a few landmark events in one rather prominent Indian family as an example: when *MC* was written, Indira Gandhi, demonized in the novel as the Widow, was still very much alive; she was assassinated by her Sikh body-guards in 1984. Her son Sanjay, whom she was grooming as her successor and who figured as the "labia-lipped" goon squad leader in *MC*, was still alive; but he was killed in a plane crash in 1980, after the novel had been completed. Her son the airline pilot, Rajiv, who was never meant for the limelight, and who received barely a mention in *MC*, succeeded her as Prime Minister and was himself assassinated by the Tamil Tigers in 1991. Historical events have indeed proven stranger than works of fiction, even one with Salman Rushdie's own fantastic mix of ingredients, and the megalomaniacal claim of protagonist Saleem Sinai, that the elimination of his family from the face of the earth was the hidden purpose of the entire Indo-Pakistani war of 1965, no longer seems so very far-fetched.

It may also be useful to remember that the publication of *MC* preceded the contemporary critique of nationalism and the social and political fragmentation of the large universalizing nation-state. It preceded the worldwide explosion of ethnic and religious nationalisms, from the Punjab to Bosnia. It also preceded the end of the Cold War, and the rise of the New World Order and the global economy of the nineties. And as for scholars of nationalism and postcoloniality, in 1981 Partha Chatterjee, Eric Hobsbawm, Benedict Anderson, and Ernest Gellner had not yet published their works on nationalism, colonialism, and the nation-state. Fredric Jameson and Aijaz Ahmed had not yet begun their now-famous debate about whether the Third World novel is necessarily a national allegory. Still years away from its now-

widespread "dissemiNation" was Homi Bhabha's *Nation and Narration*, and
scholars were not yet speaking of nations as acts of the collective imagination
and "India" in quotation marks. Rushdie's beloved Bombay was still a
tolerant, cosmopolitan city years away from the Muslim pogroms and
bombings of 1993, from the nativist Shiv Sena government of 1994, and
from changing its name to Mumbai in 1995. Rushdie as a Bombay Muslim,
albeit a thoroughly secular one, could in 1981 identify affectionately with the
elephant-headed God Ganesh, the scribe of the epic *Mahabharata*,[8] while less
than 15 years later in *The Moor's Last Sigh*, that chubby, endearing deity, the
epitome of auspiciousness, the one who brings all newly-begun enterprises to
a happy conclusion, becomes a "menacing grotesque" representing the
corrupt and cynically manipulative forces of the religious right. In 1981, the
world was certainly a fresher place in which to entertain notions of self and
nation, although perhaps also a more confined one. But, like the garrulous
protagonist of Rushdie's novel, I digress.

In the contemporary context, Rushdie's works have come to be seen as
the foundational texts for a new kind of postcolonial novel, one in which a
migrant, diasporic, cosmopolitan consciousness dominates, and also as the
foundational texts for a new kind of postcolonialism being established in the
metropolitan academy. Therefore few critics of whatever theoretical bent or
political stripe, especially those in the US-UK, have placed *MC* in its Indian
literary context, and investigated the nature of and reasons for its
considerable influence on the Indian novel in English and the legacy it has
passed on to a generation of new writers. This is what I want to begin to do
in this essay.

There has been a flood of critical writing, some of it very good indeed,
accounting for different aspects of *MC*'s success and literary influence.
Critics have written of Rushdie's multiple literary influences, his
postmodernism, his narrative art, and his deconstructive use of history.[9]
Critics in India have noted, first and foremost, that nothing succeeds like
success, and that the novel's commercial success outside India created a
metropolitan demand for Indian writing in English and a corresponding new
confidence and productivity on the part of writers in English within India.
For example, *Sunday* characterized *MC* as "a confident novel," one which
"offered no explanations, proffered no apologies sought no compromise."[10]
This confidence was seen as a "refreshing departure from the past," when
Indian writers were "far too apologetic about writing in English." Professor
Vrinda Nabar of Bombay University recalled the sixties, when "there was a
strong feeling against English and writers were criticized for using it." Indian
critics who might have tended to dismiss the expatriate Rushdie as a cocky,

elite, alienated outsider, found themselves prepared to be charmed by him (albeit sometimes grudgingly), at least until the controversy over *The Satanic Verses* erupted. But much of this criticism is descriptive or impressionistic, without closely examining the underlying conditions that contributed to the success. Many Indians were annoyed by the kind of reception with which *MC* was hailed, exemplified by the *New York Times* reviewer's phrase, "a continent finding its voice"—as if India's millions had been silent through the millennia until Rushdie came along to speak for them. And more relevant to my purpose, Indians have been critical of the weight, following *MC*, given to the narrative of nation—as if there were no other way for people to tell their story—thereby silencing or sidelining other voices using other terms.

In asserting the literary influence of *MC*, I do not assign it a uniquely privileged status or make an exaggerated claim for its centrality. Clearly I believe it had an important influence on Indian English fiction in the eighties. I employ it as a literary marker of the post-Emergency crisis in the Indian national idea, both expressing and embodying the crisis, both celebrating and mourning the idea. I discuss the formal and conceptual breakthroughs that Rushdie's novel achieved, how it set the tone for the eighties, how it broke out of a certain stagnation of both form and content that had characterized the Indian English novel of the previous two decades. I explore how both *Midnight's Children* and the increasing fragmentation of the times, primarily brought on by the crisis of the dominant model of nationalism, influenced other Indian English writers and enabled them to enter imaginatively into new relationships with the nation. I also suggest the limits and limitations of that influence.

One of the secondary relationships I want to chart in this essay is the relationship between the kind of discursive configuration Rushdie sets up in *MC* and the problematic relationship of Indian writing in English since Independence. Timothy Brennan has characterized Rushdie's novels as "metafictions ... novels about Third-World novels," and *MC* as a critique of the rise of the neocolonial élite that Rushdie links to "the production of Third-World fiction itself." Here Brennan is referring to what he sees as *MC*'s obsessive delineation, through the person and position of Saleem, of the degree to which the privileges of Third-World writers distance them from the realities of their subjects, and render them complicit with their subaltern compatriots' continued neocolonial suppression.[11] While I agree that a sense of distance and neocolonial complicity is certainly there, I also see a sense of rejection and hurt, accompanied by a concomitant desire to claim and be reclaimed by India. I would argue that *MC* is not so much about the neocolonial positioning of the Third-World novel(ist), but perhaps more accurately about the predicament of the neocolonial Indian nation-state and its inheritors, which is itself mirrored by the ambivalent position of the Indian English novel.

In a recent talk at Amherst College on post-Independence Indian writing, Rushdie referred to Indian English writing as "Empire's bastard child,"[12] which is exactly what Saleem Sinai was in *MC*; so at one level his protagonist can be seen *as* Indian writing in English, claiming centrality for itself. Rushdie himself is doing the same today when he asserts—characteristically over-aggressively—that the best prose writing in India since independence has been in English, which has by now become an Indian language. And furthermore, against all evidence and internal assertions to the contrary, he argues in his usual hyperbolic fashion that Indian English writing has not just a place for itself among other Indian literatures, but a pre-eminent place. I suspect that Rushdie's position here is something that needs to be understood in the light of his own feelings of rejection by and displacement from India. He needs to lay claim to India—and further, to centrality within it—in order to feel a sense of engagement, just as Saleem needed to feel an egotistical sense of mission in order to allow himself a new kind of engagement with India. Rushdie's act of claiming must also be seen in another light: he returned to India in the late seventies at thirty-something, in the aftermath of Indira Gandhi's Emergency, a time when large numbers of expatriate and emigrant Indians (many acting against their instinct not to wash dirty linen in public) had expressed their outrage at Gandhi and the Congress Party's betrayal of all the secular social-democratic ideals on which they, as the early post-independence generation, had been raised. In *MC*, Rushdie reaffirms and seeks to reclaim those ideals, even as he recognizes that their time may be past, and that he and his generation may be out of touch and out of time.[13]

MIDNIGHT'S CHILDREN'S CONCEPTUAL CONJURING

In *Midnight's Children*, Rushdie's reconfiguration of the relationship between the Self and the Nation opened up space that proved to be very enabling for new Indian English writers in the eighties. The novel's publication was a watershed for the Indian novel in English, coming at a time when the dominant Congress model of nationalism was cracking up—a time of fragmentation but therefore also a time of possibility. Many critics have commented upon *MC*'s influence on the Indian English novel, and several studies have analyzed the use of history and memory in the novel, its identification of Self and Nation, and its struggle to overcome duality. Few, however, have discussed how such elements of the novel combined to influence Indian writing in English.

In an early interview, Rushdie characterized *MC* as more a political novel than a historical novel, and most of all, as a novel about the nature of memory, "about one person's passage through history," in which the individual's version of the truth was presented as at once coherent and suspect. This personal view of history, Rushdie explained, allowed him to discuss and explore the nature of "the relationship between the individual and history, between private lives and public affairs."[14]

In his most recent novel, *The Moor's Last Sigh*, Rushdie's protagonist-narrator discusses his mother Aurora's artistic withdrawal in the decade after independence:

> It was easy for an artist to lose her identity at a time when so many thinkers believed that the poignancy and passion of the country's immense life could only be represented by a kind of selfless, dedicated—even patriotic—mimesis.
>
> Public opinion—not for the last time—swung against Aurora ... Scoundrelly patriots called her a traitress, the godly called her godless, self-styled spokesmen for the poor berated her for being rich ... "those artists truly in thrall to the West ... abused her for 'parochialism'", while "... other artists...reviled her just as loudly for 'losing touch with her roots.'" ...
>
> Aurora retreated somewhat from public life ... turned once and for all ... inwards, to the reality of dreams ... (and, in her bitterness and isolation), announced that neither Marathi nor Gujarati would be spoken within her wall; the language of her kingdom was English and nothing but.[15]

He could as accurately be speaking of the post-Independence Indian novel in English.

In the dynamic nationalist period of an independence struggle, individuals actively give themselves over to the struggle, willingly subordinating their personal desires to the urgency of the political moment, shaping themselves in the image of the nation. Quite naturally, the novels written during the period of the nationalist movement for independence, aptly called the Gandhian period of Indian literature, tended to identify themselves and their protagonists idealistically with the struggle. In order to unite the country in a shared vision, they portrayed the aspirations of the rural masses and the poor, and showed middle-class or educated characters either throwing in their lot with these masses or betraying them as enemies of the people. This period lasted into the first decade after Independence, and then, from the early sixties, tended to give way to a period in which writers expressed disillusionment with the corruption and failures of the government and its bureaucracy and often turned away from the public sphere altogether, in angry, bleak existentialist novels that charted alienation, interiority, and madness.

In the early post-independence period, the new-forged nation-state presses particularly heavily on the individual, molding the personal to the national, reproducing, maintaining and consolidating the national ideology at every level of society. In this ideological straitjacket, the Indian English novel which is, after all, the genre of the individual, stagnated and grew schizoid as the overriding story of nation increasingly gave the lie to individual realities. Nationalist speechmaking often gave way to deafening literary silences. Faced with a centrally imposed nationalism that purported to speak for the individual, many writers of the sixties and seventies turned away from the larger social realm, forced into alienation. Their protagonists were often destroyed by the tensions between their personal realities and the nationalist ideal, their novels deadened by the creative deadlock that ensued.

In this period of postcolonial consolidation of the nation-state, the Indian English novel, once caught up in the dynamism of the nationalist movement, settled into a rather tired social realism that no longer throbbed with urgency or captured the creative imagination. It seemed as if the drive toward freedom that had engaged the Gandhian novels now gave way either to mechanically formulaic, politically correct nation-building or, on the other hand, to rejections of the public sphere. The national idea, which had once been an inclusive vision of "unity in diversity," shrank into a more rigid, centralizing monolithic concept as the Congress Party sought to secure centralized state power.[16] In terms of the relationship between the individual and the state, it seemed that either one was a patriot, wholly identified with the nation and its symbols, or else a traitor; there was little middle ground. This was especially so for the Indian English novel, whose loyalties were already suspect in its use of the former colonizer's language. As a result, the Indian English novel—or Indo-Anglian novel, as it was more commonly called at that time—began to stagnate, robbed of "authenticity," unable to find an acceptable voice, form, or subject matter that was at once uniquely its own and indisputably Indian.

In the aftermath of political independence, as the new nation-state sought to consolidate its power, the expansive, multiple languages of the freedom movement shrank and hardened into a more limited, coercive discourse, in a kind of "collective failure of the imagination," as Rushdie might have characterized it. This meant that different worldviews no longer creatively interpenetrated, throwing up innumerable new possibilities, and that the arena of action narrowed into sharply opposed polarities in a postcolonial throwback to Orientalist categories of thought which privileged rationalism, action, and literalism, and invested them with state powers and legitimacy.[17] Thus the protagonists of the early post-independence novel were routinely faced with and forced to embody drastic, impossible choices: self or nation, loyalty or betrayal, modernity or tradition—choices which, because they did not reflect the richness of lived reality, often proved self-destructive to the characters. Such choices were conceptually limiting and artistically stultifying.

In general, then, the Indian English literary scene in the late seventies and early eighties was in the doldrums. In the official Sahitya Akademi publication, *Indian Literature*, the annual review of 1980 summed up the contemporary Indian English literary scene as "mediocre and ... meretricious."[18] The novel in English seemed to be stagnating, in terms of both content and form, neither engaged in social movements nor literary experimentation. By 1980, nation and novel had reached a state of impasse: both the unitary model of the modern nation-state and the narrative of the modern Indian English novel needed radical rethinking. The publication of *Midnight's Children* broke both deadlocks simultaneously: at once eulogy and elegy for the unitary model of nation-state that had failed to deliver the promises of the Indian freedom movement, and a new literary and conceptual model that opened new worlds of possibility for re-imagining and representing enabling relationships between individual and nation.

Without denying historical necessity, *MC* reconceptualized the dichotomy between personal and national identity in a way that made a new kind of social engagement possible. Rather than merely forcing the self into the image of the nation, Rushdie comically and mock-heroically insists on creating Nation in the imaginative image of Self. He takes on History, too, in the same way. The individual must either acquiesce to History's grand narratives or be destroyed—swept aside, or crushed underfoot. Rushdie's protagonist Saleem Sinai must also eventually succumb to the relentless march of History, but not before he tells his own story on his own terms.

Midnight's Children opened up space—conceptual and narrative—for play. Nevertheless, Rushdie's project is not merely post-modern free play, or flirting dangerously with a fashionable crisis of meaning, as Kumkum Sangari has argued in her influential essay, "The Politics of the Possible."[19]

Rushdie certainly does not seek to avert his—or our—eyes from the threatening loss-of-meaning implicit in the crisis of nation, but neither does he seek to trivialize it. Sangari suggests that through "double-coded" works like *MC*, "the crisis of meaning in the West" is imported into the "non-West." I recognize Sangari's concern that Rushdie's novel and others like it are all too easily appropriated into the academic discourse of poststructuralism as "texts of a near-canonical Euro-American postmodernism." However, the crisis that Sangari fears was already built into the epistemological categories of nation and history within which Rushdie was working, and these categories were already deconstructing themselves through their own inner conflicts. The crisis of the nation-state is inherent in the underlying formulations of the modern secular Nehruvian nation-state, and is one that *MC* prophesies, but surely cannot determine.

Identifying with Meaning itself, Saleem stands to lose everything by its loss, and thus making sense of the crisis takes on the proportions of a life-and-death struggle. "I must work fast," he pants as he introduces himself and underscores the urgency of his literary endeavor on the very first page of the novel, "if I am to end up meaning—yes, meaning—something. I admit it: above all things, I fear absurdity" (p. 9). While he is all too aware of his impotence and impending demise, his prophetic awareness does not lead him into fatalism or disillusionment. Instead, it spurs him on, not to struggle for his personal survival, but to reach toward, the meanings-within-the-loss-of-meaning of the national idea that he embodies.

INTERPENETRATION OF SELF AND NATION

Born on the stroke of midnight, August 14-15, 1947, baby Saleem Sinai receives a letter of congratulations from Prime Minister Nehru himself, worded with all the promises and truth-claims of the newly independent nation. Confidently identifying Saleem's life with the life of India itself, the letter links the unlimited potential of the newborn infant both with that of the nascent state, with all its future glory lying before it, and with the India of timeless antiquity, tales of whose past glories inspired and unified the nationalist movement: "You are the newest bearer of that ancient face of India which is also eternally young. We shall be watching over your life with the closest attention; it will be, in a sense, the mirror of our own" (p. 122).

"In what sense?" asks narrator-protagonist Saleem thirty-two years later as, battered by history, castrated by a Prime Minister, thoroughly disillusioned and "fullofcracks," he struggles desperately to preserve his version of India's history and his own before he completely falls to pieces. In what sense can it be said that his life and the lives of all the midnight's children—those 1001 babies born within an hour of the moment of independence—has mirrored that of the nation (which, it must be remembered, held out the promise of self-determination to the greatest and the least of its people)? And writer-storyteller Saleem answers his own rhetorical question, mock-heroically, pseudo-scientifically, in rhetorical terms, in "adverbs and hyphens":

> I was linked to history both literally and metaphorically, both actively and passively, in what our (admirably modern) scientists might term 'modes of connection' composed of 'dualistically combined configurations' of the two pairs of opposed adverbs given above. This is why hyphens are necessary: actively-literally, passively-metaphorically, actively-metaphorically and passively-literally, I was inextricably intertwined with my world. (P. 238)

The device of the "modes of connection" enables writer/narrator Saleem/Salman to grant his postcolonial protagonist multiple methods of engagement with the larger social realm and gives his characters room to move in ways which would be impossible within a unitary, social-realist structure, saving him, disillusioned as he becomes, from alienation and despair ("I was inextricably intertwined…"). Unlike a realistic novel form which privileges action and the actual, *MC* recognizes the passive and metaphorical modes as well, expanding the stage of action (at least) fourfold, and giving both formal and metaphysical realization to the fervent prayer quoted in Rushdie's essay, "Imaginary Homelands": "For God's sake, open the universe a little bit more."[20]

In *Midnight's Children*, women are seen to be the powerful practitioners of yet another mode of connection, the passive-aggressive. In spite of their seeming lack of control in the public sphere, they loom large in Saleem's family life, feeding all their repressed sorrow, guilt, jealousy, and bitterness into him like mother's milk, as did his Aunt Alia, who "fed us the birianis of dissension and the nargisi koftas of discord," and whose kormas, "spiced with forebodings as well as cardamoms," wrought a terrible vengeance upon his mother. Saleem's postcolonial status gives him an intimate connection with the passive modes of interaction with the world. Women's status within a patriarchal structure and the weapons of the weak that they wield mirror the weapons that the postcolonial subject can wield in the uneven struggle for self-determination. As the women do in the private sphere, so does Saleem in the universe of his narrative, namely, elevate the passive mode into equal significance with the active, and the metaphorical into equal prominence with the literal.[21] The Manichean dynamics of the neocolonial Indian nation-state maintain its sovereign subjects in a female/passive relationship to the Center even as the nationalist rhetoric exhorts them to work and action.

R. S. Pathak describes "the interplay of personal and national histories" as "the most significant feature of *Midnight's Children*," the inextricable intertwining of "the public and the private strands" as giving the novel its coherence, and "the interaction of historical and individual forces" as having "made the narrator what he is." Given that Indian history has been mutilated by the British, Pathak sees Rushdie's re-creation and reappropriation of Indian history and his charting of the "interlocking and interdependent relationships of history and the individual" as restoring a "much-needed sense of dignity" to the individual.[22] Pathak also points to Rushdie's savage satire and entertaining comedy as a winning combination, as does Thakur Guruprasad, who echoes similar sentiments in ascribing Rushdie's disarming charm to his having "conjured up a … new genre" that combines "fairy tale with savage political indictment" through "a fictional family story inter-twined with dismal political history in a comic strain."[23]

In an early review of *Midnight's Children*, Anita Desai hesitates to call the novel "historical" because of Rushdie's insistence upon the inter-penetration of the individual and the national, his belief that "while individual history does not make sense unless seen against its national background, neither does national history make sense unless seen in the form of individual lives and histories."[24] *MC* does not deny the nation's power over individual lives, neither does it subordinate individual to nation, but it acknowledges and makes creative capital of both their polarity and their unity. In the same review, Desai (in whose novels of the interior the protagonists are often helpless victims of History) speaks of the novel's purpose as "wholly serious" and its subject as tragic, "the tragedy of individual lives harried and wrecked by history, and of history harried and wrecked by individuals." However, part of the novel's appeal lies in its refusal to accept the relentless march of History as inevitably tragic. Rather than the individual being altogether obliterated by the Nation-state or matters of state being subordinated to the individual, it is the interesting space-in-between that is explored, and thereby what is patently the stuff of tragedy made comic. Rushdie doesn't deny the dichotomy between the private and the public; rather, he demonstrates how the two partake of each other in curious and often unexpected ways and how the possibilities of a situation may differ depending upon how it is perceived: baby Saleem was handcuffed to history, forcefed by events (passive-metaphorical), yet as the narrator, he can turn this around. History is *both* violent menace and nourishment for baby-to-be Saleem: "He, too, has to swallow all his past, all that made him— or, put another way, it feeds him" (pp. 107-08). Rushdie's triumphant technique in *MC* is simply yet supremely the discursive room-to-move gained by putting it another way.

Rushdie's playful handling of previously implacable categories opens up possibilities within language where there would seem to have been none, thus delivering a measure of discursive room-to-move. Says protagonist Saleem Sinai, "Setting my face against all indications to the contrary, I shall now amplify...my claim to a place at the centre of things." This is exactly what Rushdie's modes of connection enable him to achieve in *Midnight's Children*. Saléem and his age group have no agency in the active and the literal modes where he is perennially the victim, the one-to-whom-things-are-done; it is only in the metaphorical and, interestingly, in the passive realms of reality that he and his compatriots are controlling Subjects. "'Passive-metaphorical', 'passive-literal', 'active-metaphorical': the Midnight's Children's Conference was all three; but it never became what I most wanted it to be; we never operated in the first, most significant of the 'modes of connection'. The 'active-literal' passed us by" (pp. 238-39). Powerlessness and lack-of-choice continually characterize Saleem's predicament, yet he doggedly persists in positioning himself, the bestower of meaning and form, at the center of his story—as indeed he is, in the role of author-narrator. Even though Saleem is supremely the person to whom things have been done, it is Rushdie's magic that, "against all indications to the contrary," transforms victim to protagonist.

ACTION AND ENGAGEMENT

What does Rushdie achieve by the creation of his larger-than-life, tragi-comic hero and how might this fiat be said to have enabled a new kind of social engagement for a new generation of writers? Perhaps the success or failure of this engagement may be judged by the degree to which his protagonist Saleem is able to engage with the public sphere, if so, we may chart his progress through the novel. Or perhaps the success of failure of a character, who starts life with the optimistic faith that his country's achievements will be his own, tests the truth claims of a nation which has promised to deliver self-determination to the greatest and least of its citizens.

In a 1983 interview, Rushdie explained that his "comic inversion" of the relationship between the individual and history enabled him to discuss the problematics of that relationship in modern India. His protagonist Saleem begins his life with supreme confidence in his centrality and agency, but his unbounded optimism is besieged and eventually destroyed by disillusionment. Rushdie charts the disillusioning "series of retreats" that lead Saleem and the reader from his youthful omnipotence at the moment of Independence to his premature impotence and decrepitude at the age of thirty-two.

> Saleem believes that there is a relationship (between the individual and the nation), Saleem has a thesis, as it were, and the book tests the thesis. It turns out to be a destruction-test, because by the end of the book, it is clear that the thesis doesn't hold up: he's not in charge. And he can't stand it—at the moment at which he begins to be faced with the facts of life, he performs a series of retreats, whether into a kind of catatonic state, or into quiescence or acceptance, or finally, into the pickle factory.[25]

Midnight's Children is an ironic, quirky, but deadly serious critique of quiescence, of withdrawal, of forgetting. Being pulled forcibly from his roots by his parents' relocation to Pakistan begins the process of disconnection for Saleem. Across the political border he can neither receive nor broadcast signals to the midnight's children, and thereby becomes isolated within his own head. He succumbs first to a fatalism that allows him to accept all that is done to him. When he is struck by a flying spittoon in the Indo-Pakistan war of 1965, he loses his memory altogether, and with it, six years of his life. The narrative picks up in the midst of West Pakistan's foray into what was soon to become Bangladesh to quell the Eastern rebellion. Saleem is no longer the youthful. "I" but is presented at a third-person—remove as "the Buddha"—referring both to an old man, prematurely aged by history, and one who—like the prince who found enlightenment under the Bo tree— has withdrawn in spirit from the world of pain and sorrow.

Here Rushdie makes a stereotypical (mis)representation of Buddhism as escapism and quiescence. He depicts the Buddha's "not-living-in-the-world as well as living in it" as an act of weakness and submission; as indeed it is for his buddha, the former Saleem, who has become a man-dog, silently and obediently carrying out the function of a canine tracker for a Pakistani military intelligence unit, tracking down rebels—"undesirable elements"— and destroying them. Saleem's state of amnesia prevents him from taking responsibility for his betrayals of his own countrymen. "Emptied of history, the buddha learned the arts of submission, and did only what was required of him" (p. 350).

Withdrawal, however, is achieved at a price. The man-dog leads his unit into the Sundarbans, steamy jungles of the subconscious, where his own mind leads him tortuously and inexorably through fevered, shifting nightmare landscapes towards a recognition of his own true identity and the responsibility which he must take for his actions. As he runs from the conflicts of the physical battlegrounds, he is drawn into the depths of his insanity, an experience which may lead him towards a recognition of the truth of his situation, but is fraught with its own dangers—madness and the risk of never being able to return.

Even when the poison from a forest snake awakens him to himself and to the realities—and the dangers—of his predicament, he still cannot remember his name. It takes Parvati-the-witch to name him and recall him fully to himself. (Parvati, after Shiva, Saleem's arch-rival, his other half, who was also born on the stroke of midnight, is the child born next-closest to midnight, the Third who embodies a point of meeting for the polarized pair. Parvati is also the name of the Hindu goddess, consort of the god Shiva.)

It is Parvati's magic that conveys him safely back into India, but again, survival exacts a price. To survive, Saleem is made invisible, and carried into Delhi crouched inside a basket. But, ironically, the invisibility that saves him also carries the risk of robbing him of his very essence. What saves Saleem from the enervation that accompanies invisibility is anger, a righteous anger on behalf of India's oppressed people that brings with it an exalted sense of mission: a mission no less than that of saving the country. However, like the self-appointed leaders of the Indian nationalist movement, he is to betray the people he claims to represent, and he fails to overcome the isolation that followed his rejection of Shiva, his nemesis and polar opposite, and his loss-of-connection with the midnight's children. Far from saving the country, he is sucked down into the vortex of its crisis. In the attempt to restore his own fortunes by contacting his despicably toadying uncle Mustapha, who is a high official in the Indira Congress bureaucracy, he abandons Parvati and his adopted family in the communist magicians' ghetto. He returns, but what might have been is derailed by the squashy bellied, labia-lipped. Youth Congress leader and his goons as the slum is razed. He falls victim, like so many others, to "the Widow's" 1975 State of Emergency, in which he is tortured and made to reveal the names and addresses of all the surviving children of midnight, the hopes and possibilities contained within that moment of history. They are then given a fiendishly efficient operation—a "sperectomy"—which not only ensures their irreversible sterilization but also removes all hope.

For Saleem, it is a time of endings. For his son, however, and for the legion of bastard children whom Shiva has implanted in wealthy women across the nation, it is the beginning of a new chapter in India's history. Saleem's success in writing down his story—which is, in so many senses, the story of his generation—may or may not ensure that it is passed on and remembered. Against the evidence even of the narrative itself, the powers of Saleem's son and, by extension, of the new generation, project the hope that the times have bestowed upon them what it takes to survive and move forward—collectively—even to create new myths.[26]

Rushdie's narrative, which so fiercely advocates political engagement and social responsibility and so firmly condemns quiescence as betrayal, characteristically shows his naive protagonist's progressive withdrawal and eventual destruction to be both beyond his control and of his own making. Saleem's family, and his own sense of connection with the pulse of India, was destroyed by internal divisiveness as well as the will-to-power. In his bitter disillusionment and loss of his sense of centrality, he withdraws into himself, destroying himself and betraying his fellow-Indians. Rushdie explains social and political withdrawal of writers of his generation in terms of a profound disillusionment with the myths of the secular-socialist nation, myths which failed to deliver either material or spiritual results to a generation of believers. Yet at the same time, paradoxically, he reaffirms those very myths, even as he pronounces their obsolescence; both author and protagonist are bedevilled by duality and ambivalence.

DUALITY AND AMBIVALENCE

As Homi Bhabha points out in his introduction to *Nation and Narration*, nationalism is by definition ambivalent, and the ambivalence of the nation is mirrored in the very form of the national narrative. It is significant, too, that Bhabha uses Tom Nairn's term, "the modern Janus," for the nation, since the Indian English novel was, sometimes with dubious distinction, dubbed "Janus-faced" by Indian critics in the seventies. In this early post-independence context, the term was used in its sense of "two-faced," to cast aspersions on the pedigree of the Indian English—or "Indo-Anglian"—novel as insufficiently Indian, of dubious loyalty because of its dual parentage. This view, preceding the contemporary critique of nationalism, failed to consider the ambivalence inherent in nationalism and the nationalist discourse itself, which also has a dual parentage regardless of which modern Indian language it speaks through. Another sense of Janus-faced, however, is "sensitive to dualities and polarities," and this is the spirit in which Rushdie writes, sensitive to the dualities inherent in postcoloniality, accepting—even flaunting them rather than attempting to deny or conceal them, and elevating condition into method in his metanarrative.[27] Bhabha's use of the Janus metaphor aptly characterizes *MC*'s narrative approach, that of turning "the two-faced god into a figure of prodigious doubling," so that the condition of ambivalence is transformed into a dynamic process.[28]

Rushdie's successful inversion in *Midnight's Children*, his formula for overcoming post-independence alienation, whether in the postcolonial subject. Indian English, or the Indian English novel itself, might have been summed up in his latest novel, *The Moor's Last Sigh*, in the advice given to the freakish Moor by the boy-guru Lord Khusro: "Embrace your fate... Rejoice in what gives you grief. That which you would flee, turn and run towards it with all your heart. Only by becoming your misfortune will you transcend it." The Moor declares, "By embracing the inescapable, I lost my fear of it."[29] Rather than withdrawing in alienation if he is unable to identify fully with the nation, the individual may embrace his ambivalence, flaunting it publicly, rather than hiding in embarrassment, turning a liability into an asset, a birthmark into a trademark. Or in the words of the Anglo-Indian artist Vasco Miranda, himself doomed like Saleem: "A man's weakness is his strength, and versy visa" ... "Would Achilles have been a great warrior without his heel?"[30]

M. Keith Booker has rightly identified one of the central themes and strategies of Rushdie's fiction as "embracing contradiction," both constructing and deconstructing dual oppositions "by demonstrating that the apparent polar opposites are in fact interchangeable and mutually interdependent."[31] I think that Rushdie's approach to duality in *MC* functions as theme, as form, and as a method that enables a shift in postcolonial nationalist discourse by exposing and enacting the radical ambivalence of the Indian nation. However, as Booker also notes, Rushdie constructs and inhabits his opposing dualities only to expose their limitations; duality as method enables him to expose dualism as prison. I see Rushdie's reproduction, reconfiguration, and critique of nationalist dualities as creating new possibilities for postcolonial narrative discourse in the eighties, but also as raising doubts about the outcome of the swirling embrace of polar opposites: will it be perpetual motion, fusion, or fission?

Rushdie portrays Saleem as a victim of the paradoxes of Indian nationalism, among them the splits between pragmatism and idealism, the elite and the masses, centralization and federalism, rationalism and spirituality. As Krishna, in the *Bhagavad-Gita*, exhorted the doubt-torn Arjuna to rise above the pairs of opposites so that he might see clearly and act, so Rushdie's hero longs for a Third Principle that can overcome the dualities within and around him and break through to another level of truth. At meetings of the Midnight Children's Conference (or M.C.C.), through which the children meet telepathically, the idealistic young Saleem as convenor and central switchboard operator implores the squabbling midnight's children to overcome their differences. Their miraculous powers, so full of possibility, are powerless to prevent the apparently inevitable conflicts that break out among them:

> 'We,' I cried passionately, 'must be a third principle, we must be the force which drives between the horns of the dilemma; for only by being other, by being new, can we fulfil the promise of our birth.' (P. 255)

But Saleem himself—like the Indian nation and the Indian English novel—has internalized the very dualities that he seeks to unite. He is as yet unaware of his own mixed parentage, ironic evidence of the dual heritage of the Indian nation-state. And as he finds out, his own continued privilege is predicated upon the disinheritance of Shiva, his *alter-ego* and arch-rival. Even though Saleem desperately seeks to avoid Shiva, it would seem that the enmity between the two of them is inevitable: "Shiva and Saleem, victor and victim; understand our rivalry and you will gain an understanding of the age in which you live" (p. 432). And the enmity of Shiva and Saleem ("knees-and-nose, a nose and knees"), polar opposites, split selves, drives the novel to its tragic climax and its ambiguous conclusion.

When Saleem excludes Shiva from the *lok sabha* (lit. people's assembly or parliament) of his mind because he is afraid that Shiva will "insist on claiming his birthright" (p. 282), he closes off the option of regaining the harmony that the children had shared in the early days of the Midnight Children's Conference. It is this active rejection on his part, as much the passive-literal act of being taken across the border to Pakistan, that is responsible for his loss of connection with the midnight's children. Instead of accepting Shiva as an equal member of the group, even as equal to himself, Saleem perceives him as a threat (which, indeed, he is) and relegates him to the realm of an eternal Other. The possibility of a Third Principle is forever closed off for Saleem, as the polarization of knees-and-nose takes hold:

he became, for me, first a stabbing twinge of guilt, then an obsession; and finally, as the memory of his actuality grew dull, he became a sort of principle; he came to represent, in my mind, all the vengefulness and violence and simultaneous-love-and-hate-of-things in the world. (Pp. 298-99)

Still, Parvati-the-Witch, who always believed in Saleem, remains open to the possibility of reconciliation. Even as Saleem dreads the return of Shiva, the principle of destruction, Parvati is able to see him as a principle of Creation as well; after all, he is the father of her child—Saleem's son-who-is-not-his-son—and the father of thousands more throughout the land. Parvati the witch, perhaps the mediator/medium who can transform a vicious circle into a triangle, welcomes the return of the repressed: Maybe he will come when he has time; and then we will be three!" (p. 389).

Salman Rushdie is able to break the stranglehold of Manichean dualities in the realm of language, even though neither Saleem Sinai nor his creator is able to find a way to transcend duality in his own life. And he accomplishes this simply, just as he opened up more breathing space for the Self in his deadlock with the Nation. Can anything capture the essence of duality more simply and ineluctably than the children's game of Snakes and Ladders?

> ... implicit in the game is the unchanging twoness of things, the duality of up against down, good against evil; the solid rationality of ladders balances the occult sinuosities of the serpent; in the opposition of staircase and cobra we can see, metaphorically, all conceivable oppositions, Alpha against Omega, father against mother; here is the war of Mary and Musa, and the polarities of knees and nose ... but I found, very early in my life, that the game lacked one crucial dimension, that of ambiguity because, as events were to show, it is also possible to slither down a ladder and climb to triumph on the venom of a snake. (P. 141)

Beyond realizing the ability of each opposed half to turn into its opposite, Saleem begins to recognize that, rather than becoming paralyzed and alienated by seemingly irreconcilable dualities, an individual can aspire to partake of both (either/or becoming and ... and). He invokes the spiritual image of the *paramahamsa*, "symbol of the ability to live in two worlds, the physical and the spiritual" (p. 223). The *paramahamsa* symbolizes divinity and spiritual freedom, the creative ability to live in the world and rise above its dualities, at once engaged and detached.[32] Rushdie also employs as an antidote to Manichean dualism the traditional Indian conception of the multiple levels of correspondence between microcosm and macrocosm: "As a people, we are obsessed with correspondences ... It is a sort of national longing for form—or perhaps simply an expression of our deep belief that forms lie hidden within reality; that meaning reveals itself only in flashes" (p. 300). But the older Saleem, despite everything, remains earthbound like his grandfather before him, who was struck on the nose with a frozen clod of earth when, "foreign-returned," he attempted to pray. The cause? "Altered vision"—he "saw things differently" (p. 11). From the moment he returned to his native Kashmir from medical study in Germany and found himself unable to pray, Saleem's grandfather Aadam Aziz finds himself knocked into a place in which he is able neither to believe nor disbelieve in God. Throughout the novel, however, when real life continually breaks the bounds of reason, Saleem tells the reader, "believedon'tbelieve. But it happened anyway."

While Saleem is able to communicate with the midnight's children, he is able to inhabit two worlds; but when the powers and possibilities of the M.C.C. are cut off, his connections with both are severed. In his disillusionment, he bids farewell to his hopes: "If there is a third principle, its name is childhood. But it dies; or rather, it is murdered" (p. 256). Fear and cynicism murder it; it is blocked in the closing-off of possibilities, the hardening of the mind and heart, the loss of the ability or desire to put things another way.

Finally, *MC* accepts the dual legacy of midnight, a legacy split at the very root. Saleem does not come without Shiva, Shiva would not be Shiva if it had not been for Saleem. There is an acceptance of ambivalence, of the degree to which polarized opposites partake of each other, so much so that one cannot exist without the other, one feeds the other. Even as Saleem-the-narrator finally succumbs to the cracks and is trampled into dust, Rushdie-the-author triumphs. He has succeeded in creating a space between the horns of the dilemma, not by transcending them or denying them, but by reconfiguring them. For his generation are privileged *and* cursed "to be both masters *and* victims of their times."

Rushdie, as well as Saleem his creation, is a child of midnight, formed and raised by the secular ideals of the Nehru Congress in the days when Independent India itself was young. As a student of history and a left-leaning social democrat, he has recognized intellectually the limitations and ambivalence of the Indian inheritors of the colonial state, and *Midnight's*

Children subjects them to a serious critique. As an antidote to the paralyzing polarities of endlessly contending dualities, Rushdie poses the notion of multiplicity—many Indias, many versions of truth, and infinite capacities for regeneration. Nevertheless, ambivalence remains, because of his continued emotional investment in a unitary idea of India, the India of his lost innocence, and his own inability, despite everything, to conceive constructive possibilities in its demise.[33]

FRAGMENTATION AND THE WHOLE

Kathleen Flanagan, writing on the fragmented self in *MC*, recognizes divided selves in Rushdie's works as "the products of crises of faith in political and religious institutions" and stresses the importance for Rushdie of the individual's responsibility to society. She makes the important point that Saleem's act of writing down his story combines for him both "public good and private need" as it connects self to society by making the individual a "speaking subject" who recognizes his private acts as having public consequences. She further points out that Rushdie draws attention to the disjunction between the individual and the official views of history through what she calls the child Saleem's "ridiculous" and socially destructive self-centeredness. Taking from Lukacs a developmental view of Saleem's consciousness, she argues that he must progress from seeing "himself as the center of the state to seeing himself as a responsible part of the state." Although he desires to place himself at the controlling center of an "ordered reality," he is forced to recognize the power of "the fragmented forces of society" and the "preeminence of the social and the historical over the private." In Flanagan's Lukacsian argument, Rushdie's child-narrator starts with the problem of seeing history in isolated parts, and only as they relate to him as the center of his childish universe. His problem is that he should be seeing these parts "as aspects of the historical process and integrat[ing] them in a totality" if his knowledge is ever to be brought into line with reality, and that he must come to terms with the self as "decentered, yet responsible" *vis-a-vis* the state.[34]

It is here, in the insistence that Saleem's "absurd" self-centeredness must be decentered in order for him to mature into a truly responsible member of society, that I part company with both the teleology and the spirit of the argument. For while Saleem's childish megalomania is of course absurd, it is also quite clearly privileged in the novel. At the same time as Rushdie parodies and undermines the over-centralized nation-state that seeks to control and speak for all its "children," he also romanticizes the Congress Party ideal of "unity in diversity" in which the center provides a forum through which all the children can speak to one another. While the progression of the novel may certainly be seen as a movement from an immature megalomania to a more realistic, downsized sense of self, it is also a movement from idealism to disillusionment; from dynamic growth to castration and impotence, premature aging, and death; from a deep sense of connectedness with the pulse of India to alienation, betrayal, and insignificance. Saleem's irrepressible megalomania was precisely what post-Rushdie novelists found so attractive and inspiring. The lesson they drew was not that he needed to be cut down to size, so that he might learn to become a humble, socially responsible pickle-factory worker. They saw instead that, in spite of the fact that his story was just one story among millions, it was his own story, and therefore truer for him than any other. It was possible for an insignificant fragment to speak in his own voice from the center of his universe and tell that story. Ironically, however, even as Rushdie's novel may have inspired a myriad speaking subjects, his elite narrator Saleem recognized that it was only at the expense of his own sense of wholeness that the subaltern voices of the other midnight's children could begin to be heard. For Rushdie, as for Saleem, fragmentation presents both the terrifying prospects of chaos and the productive possibilities unleashed by the breakdown of the controlling center. But as a true child of his time he is unable, in spite of everything, to fully accept that breakdown.

An interviewer once reported that Salman Rushdie kept on his writing desk a little sculpture of an unpartitioned India. Even as he wrote of the realities of a divided subcontinent, he couldn't help but persist in holding on to India's geopolitical wholeness as both an idea and an ideal. His protagonist Saleem shares some of his creator's nostalgic idealism. Once a kind of radio who was able to tune in to voices from all over India, and more importantly, the instrument through which they were enabled to tune in to each other, Saleem has been drained of his powers, has aged prematurely, and is cracking apart. He hastens to record his memories before it is too late. And he seals his last chapter of pickled memories not a moment too soon, for now he is breaking into a myriad of fragments and his particles are being scattered and trampled into the Indian dust. And for Saleem, the vicissitudes of whose life are a mirror of his country's, whose battered, misshapen body is a grotesque caricature of the national map, fragmentation is something to be resisted to the end, even as he accepts its inevitability and indeed its desirability.

In 1957 Saleem was confidently in control—the prime minister, so to speak, of the "*lok sabha* of my brain," as he called the diverse, clamorous gathering of 581 ten-year-olds who convened inside his head. His idealistic quest for meaning and purpose drove him to declaim earnestly and endlessly to his agemates ("we must think...what we are for"), while his birth at the very stroke of midnight gave him greater powers than any other—excepting only one, his polar twin, his arch-rival, Shiva the cynical, Shiva the streetwise gang leader who mocked him and his ideals as a "pampered rich boy," Shiva whom he strove to shut out of his head, to his own cost. "... I was not immune to the lure of leadership," he acknowledges with rueful hindsight (p. 227). But then, while few of the children had his privilege, few had his larger sense of purpose or his powers. It was undeniable that the powers themselves had been granted hierarchically, and it was equally undeniable that, without Saleem, the children would have been unaware of the larger national arena, and unable to communicate with each other. Was the M.C.C. an institution of tremendous promise, or was it rather the vehicle of the children's eventual undoing?[35] Was Saleem, as its founder, their saviour or their betrayer? Was the break-up of the M.C.C., of Saleem, of India itself, the end of possibility, a tragedy to be averted at all costs, or was it, on the contrary, an opportunity to be welcomed? Like many others in *Midnight's Children*, the answer to all these questions is—well—both. And yet, from Saleem/Salman's personal perspective, it comes down quite clearly on one side.

As Saleem's bedeviled body begins to disintegrate, he naturally resists. Who in his position would not have striven to remain intact, healthy, whole?

> O eternal opposition of inside and outside! Because a human being, inside himself, is anything but a whole, anything but homogeneous; all kinds of everywhichthing are jumbled up inside him, and he is one person one minute and another the next. The body, on the other hand, is as homogeneous as anything. Indivisible, a one-piece suit, a sacred temple, if you will. It is important to preserve this wholeness ... Uncork the body, and God knows ... The consequences for the sphere of public action ... are ... no less profound. (Pp. 236-37)

The individual body, once intact and indivisible but now falling apart, allows a life to the myriad voices that it contained, controlled, suppressed, denied. It also allows the fragments to take on a life of their own.[36] It accepts the inevitability of the fragments breaking through but persists in holding on to an idea of the whole. Saleem's cracking up allows the voices to escape and be heard, and yet without Saleem they would not have been able to hear each other in the first place. "Midnight's other children ... are pressing extremely hard. Soon the cracks will be wide enough for them to escape" (p. 179). From the first page of the novel, the cracks signal the beginning of the end for Saleem as a unitary individual. He already more than half acknowledges the absurdity of his enterprise, yet persists stubbornly, ultimately succeeding in "pickling" all thirteen chapters of his story before the forces of disintegration prevail.

During the Quit India movement of 1942, Aadam Aziz, the patriarch, is infected with the optimism disease, the blind nationalism which prevents him from seeing the incipient divisions within nation and family, from failing to anticipate Partition and from responding to his wife's deep dissatisfaction. Later, the narrator/protagonist Saleem Sinai suggests that "the urge to encapsulate the whole of reality" is another Indian disease. Lifafa Das tries to put the whole world ("*Dunya Dekho*") in his peepshow. Nadir Khan's painter friend had drawn ever larger paintings, trying to "get the whole of life into his art." In the end he had committed suicide, saying, "I wanted to be a miniaturist and I've got elephantiasis instead." Saleem Sinai worries, "Am I infected too?"[37]

Richard Cronin's essay, "The Indian English Novel: *Kim* and *Midnight's Children*," asserts that Saleem's urge to encapsulate the whole of reality is "a disease to which only those like Rushdie who write about India in English are vulnerable," and that "it is only because he (the young Saleem) is an outsider that India seems one to him" and "he can aspire to encapsulate the whole of it."[38] Cronin calls Kipling and Rushdie, in the same breath, impudent "trespassers" in India. Further, he claims that, for Indians who write in a regional language, a regional identity "unavoidably" takes precedence over an Indian identity. Cronin's essay is full of categorical statements. First, if the young Saleem had a unitary conception of the nation, so did many of the educated Indians of his generation in the post-Independence Nehruvian era. Second, Rushdie's conception of the nation, while still holding emotional allegiance to the Nehruvian model, at the same time questions it deeply. Third, if Saleem is an "outsider" because he is from a wealthy family and does not speak Marathi or Gujarati in cosmopolitan Bombay, then legions of the Indian urban middle classes are outsiders as well. (In Maharashtra, the xenophobic Shiv Sena organization built its power base by organizing against South Indian "outsiders" in Bombay and it now seeks to expel the city's Muslims as well.) Fourth, the meaning of "reality" for Rushdie here is clearly not restricted to the unitary Indian nation—in fact, it is the very multiplicity of India, and beyond India, the multifaceted nature of reality itself, that he is attempting to convey.

Midnight's Children mocks its own melodrama but makes literary fireworks out of events which persistently refuse "to remain life-sized." Like India, Saleem Sinai finds himself cracking up into tiny pieces, like the pieces of his grandmother that his grandfather fell in love with and the pieces of his father that his mother tried to love; but, like Partition, it seems, his eventual fragmentation is inevitable, just as his grandfather never succeeds in seeing his wife whole and his mother is never able to love her husband wholly. The urge of the work is to resist (however vainly) fragmentation and compartmentalization, providing a strong contrary current of inclusiveness (like the epic *Mahabharata*, of which it is said that what is not in it, is not). Thus the text thrives on and is driven by a contrary dynamic, a dialectic that simultaneously undermines and valorizes its totalizing urges, recognizing their obsolescence while refusing to let go of their emotional power. In this dynamic polarization lies the explosive success of the novel—and perhaps; also, Saleem's ultimate fate. In the end, which is the madness and which the disease, the desire to embrace reality and to swallow the world whole, or the tendency to fragment, to compartmentalize oneself and the world into internally homogeneous, manageable, bite-sized pieces? Or is it both?

* * *

In this current crisis of the once-dominant Congress model of nationalism, polarized political forces intensify their struggle in a swirtling deathgrip, and it would seem that there is nothing beyond the dualities of endlessly contending extremes. And yet in the fragmentation of the national ideal of unity-in-diversity, of the Midnight Children's Conference, deep fissures in the once-impermeable national membrane allow new ideas entry; flames curl up through the cracks and set the nation able destroying but also illuminating, firing the national imagination. With final words, the disintegrating Saleem prophesies his fate and articulates the postcolonial condition of his generation:

> Yes, they will trample me underfoot, ... reducing me to specks of voiceless dust ... because it is the privilege and the curse of the midnight's children to be both masters and victims of their times, to forsake privacy and be sucked into the annihilating whirlpool of the multitudes, and to be unable to live or die in peace. (P. 463)

Even though Saleem is cracking into as many pieces as there are Indians, as there are stories to tell, he has successfully told his story—imperfect, unreliable, distorted, needing endless revising to be sure—but nonetheless triumphantly his own.

When Saleem Sinai tells his readers that they will have to swallow him and his story whole, "whole" does not imply unitary, seamless. Whole means multiple, fault-ridden, contradictory, "fullofcracks." Is he doomed? Yes, inevitably. But wholly defined by Nation and colonial History? Never! Stubbornly and against all the odds, Victim transforms himself into Protagonist, simply through the telling of his own story.

POST-*MIDNIGHT'S CHILDREN*: NATIONAL NARRATIVES OF THE EIGHTIES

When *Midnight's Children* was first published, Rushdie's refusal to censor or sanitize his story, his unembarrassed washing of dirty linen in public, was refreshing to the world of Indian English writing, which had trodden so carefully for so long, walking a tightrope between "Indian" authenticity and "English" correctness.[39] Unafraid either of public censure or government censors, Rushdie sought to embrace the sights, sounds, and smells of the India of his dreams and memories in all their multiplicity, and was determined to leave nothing out. Had he been living in middle-class Indian society, he might have been more circumspect. But then, surely, the novel would have lost much of its dynamism.

In an early review, written before *MC*'s success in India, Anita Desai expressed the belief that Rushdie's message would fall on deaf ears in the unself-critical intellectual climate of post-independence India. She wrote, somewhat bitterly, "… it is tragic to think how unlikely that it will be published, distributed or read in a land that prefers to avert its eyes from the intolerable reality and gaze upon *maya*, the shimmer of illusion." In fact, as noted earlier, the Indian sales of the novel were unprecedentedly high, heralding a new spirit of freedom and a willingness to experiment with subject, language, and narrative strategy. Desai, whose five novels of the sixties and seventies were pre-eminently novels of interiority, told me in a 1992 interview that *MC* gave her the courage and artistic room to move into the public sphere in her own fiction.[40] Rushdie's playfulness actually created discursive space for her where there was none before.

Indian English writers of the eighties found that Rushdie's paradigm allowed them a new freedom of both form and content. His narrative sleight-of-hand juggled multiple modes of engagement between the individual and the national narrative, teased apart the cracks within and between the master discourses, and conjured up space for (relatively) free play—or at least the illusion of it—in a terrain where there had previously been a polarized paralysis. New writers found his acknowledgement of multiplicity and his hybridity of language particularly liberating. It enabled them to tell their personal stories in their own voices as *national* epics. Just as the crisis of the unitary nation-state appeared to open up space for the clamor of a thousand contending claims, so it seemed that the crisis of the once-dominant nationalism opened up space for new discursive models.

Over the course of the eighties, a wave of Indian English novels followed *MC*, clearly influenced by it in language, style, and structure. Some prominent new novelists of the 1980s whose work is indebted to Rushdie include Namita Gokhale (*Paro, Dreams of Passion*), Amitav Ghosh (*The Circle of Reason* and *The Shadow Lines*), Upamanyu Chatterjee (*English, August* and *The Last Burden*), I. Allan Sealy (*The Trotter-Nama* and *Hero*), Boman Desai (*The Memory of Elephants*), Shashi Tharoor (*The Great Indian Novel* and *Show Business*), and Nina Sibal (*Yatra*).[41] Of course these novels did not represent the only tendency within Indian English writing during the period, but this was certainly the dominant one, and it brought a new vitality to what had become rather a stagnant tradition with little experimentation and few new names Rushdie-influenced works by new novelists have variously been seen to include one or more of the following features: 1) a multigenerational, mock-epic family saga, complete with family trees, maps, and a long list of *dramatis personae*, that tells the story of the protagonist's family as a national history; 2) a rejection of the traditional, social realist novel: larger-than-life allegorical characters and events in the tradition of magical realism; 3) both a fluency in standard English and a confidence with the language that allows the confident use of various kinds of Indian English; 4) a sprawling, rambling style, full of digressions and humor; 5) the use of myth, oral tradition, and different versions and ideas of history; 6) a playful irreverence for the sacred cows of nationalism and religion. Aside from these similarities, however, there is a broad range of tendencies among these post-Rushdie novels, even if one were to focus solely on their conception of the relationship of the individual to the nation and to History.

Less commonly noted is the opportunity these novels give to members of marginalized groups or national minorities to place themselves centerstage in the drama of national history, rather than feeling the pressure to subsume themselves in the mainstream, official version. For example, Parsis and Anglo-Indians are two groups whose "Indianness" is often called into question, but Parsis like Boman Desai (*The Memory of Elephants*, 1988) and Anglo-Indians like I. Allan Sealy (*The Trotter-Nama*, 1988), range back over the centuries in their novels to celebrate the long and colorful histories of their respective communities in India.[42] In his comic, digressive, mock-heroic mode, I. Allan Sealy's protagonist is able to present the checkered past of his "glorious" Anglo-Indian ancestors and to poignantly acknowledge their marginalization in post-independence India. Boman Desai draws on *MC*'s notion that there are competing histories that are equally valid—for the individual, at least—and that the individual has moral authority and willpower, if not political power. In *The Memory of Elephants*, Desai's protagonist gains access to the collective unconscious of his contentious family in particular and the Parsis in general, but although he is able to tune in to them, he has no control over the events he sees. However, just before he is forced to relinquish his dangerous powers, he is able, just for a moment and by a tremendous effort of will, to bring all his ancestors together and hold a united family tableau in his mind.

Besides giving new novelists the courage to tell their own stories *as* Indian stories, *Midnight's Children* also gave them permission to be ironic and ambivalent about their relationship to the nation-state. Upamanyu Chatterjee, in his first novel, *English, August: An Indian Story* (1988), is able to portray a disaffected protagonist within the Indian Civil Service who suffers deep and prolonged alienation and indecision in his provincial posting. And Shashi Tharoor, in *The Great Indian Novel* (1989), is able simultaneously to allegorize the story of modern India in terms of the epic *Mahabharata* and to question the very notion of using the authority of tradition to offer certitudes in the seeming chaos of the present.

Despite its conceptual freshness and vitality, *Midnight's Children* remains very much emotionally committed to the narrative of nation. In the end, it can only reconfigure the ideological categories, not step out of them altogether. If they were to remain within the self-as-nation framework, it might be that the new trajectories set in motion by Rushdie's reconceptualization of Self and Nation would eventually mire themselves in the same dualities as the novels of the earlier sixties and seventies, the possibility of alternative realities remaining just that, a possibility—a spectacular, but ultimately illusory, authorial conjuring trick. Is the discursive space in which they function merely in the realm of virtual reality, or do they posit alternate realities that in fact create new possibilities for public discourse?

In the eighties the new narratives of nation burst forth in a dazzling display of artistic pyrotechnics with a new confidence in self, language, and form. Their energy was based on a celebration of the simultaneous identity and duality of self and nation, a recognition of the creative potential of ambivalence. But ultimately life must be lived, and it cannot be lived for long on the fence—on the hyphen, as it were.[43] The energy that breaks forth from the crisis of the nation must eventually be redirected. As Rushdie/Saleem himself acknowledges, "new myths must be made." When allegiance to an idea is lost in disillusionment, new allegiances must be affirmed (or old ones reaffirmed) and new commitments made, in order for life to go on. In the meantime, of course, life goes on anyway, and the interregnum is characterized by "a great diversity of morbid symptoms."[44]

Just as the narrative of nation may marginalize other kinds of narratives, marginalized groups attempting to lay claim to the nation may themselves be written out of their own texts by the very terms in which the nationalist discourse is framed. Rajeswari Sunder Rajan observes in an essay on Nina Sibal's *Yatra* that women writers who have attempted to employ the narrative of nation find themselves condemned to rehearse a story that excludes them.[45] And recent feminist research on the colonial construction of Indian nationalism has demonstrated the extent to which 'traditional' conceptions of Indian womanhood have been bound up with the nationalist project. Women's experiences in the postcolonial period have shown, again and again, that their interests are incompatible with the interests of the nation-state. Protagonists of post-independence literary texts—particularly, but not exclusively, female protagonists—have become deadlocked when they have attempted to live out the conflicting demands of the nationalist synthesis. In general, minorities and women writers, who have found that the exclusive discourse of nation cannot be made to tell their story, have been less likely to employ the narrative of nation. Women writers, such as Shashi Deshpande and Jai Nimbkar, who have come to prominence recently in the late eighties and nineties, have been working relatively unnoticed for decades. Deshpande and Nimbkar, along with the younger Githa Hariharan and Anjana Appachana, are neither shoring up a disintegrating discourse of nation nor making dramatic departures from women's traditional conflicts and concerns, but are exploring the possibilities of coming to terms with the past in new ways.

Some of the new Indian English writers of the eighties used the nation as a framework to define themselves against, either as a peg on which to hang their identities or a boundary that demarcates their own liminal positioning. Thus they tended to gravitate towards two extremes, either a romantic clinging to the ideal of Nation, or its opposite, a fashionably disillusioned individuality answerable to no one: either an obsession with the need to belong to a Nation-state, or a defiant declaration of one's alienation. In a thoughtful review of Salman Rushdie's *East, West* in the *Indian Review of*

Books, Sanjay Iyer argues that the Rushdie-inspired narratives of nation have been privileged to the extent of obscuring other Indian novels that work out of different paradigms:

> In privileging the experiences of nation and post-colonialism, Rushdie, as a literary giant, has powerfully set the terms for inclusion in this countercanon [of Third World Literature]. The result is apparent to us every day, in the spate of novels that *do* take the personal as national ... The price of this has been the marginalization of countless works that are not obsessed with national experience.[46]

I would agree that the continued conflation of Self and Nation eventually ceases to be productive during a period when the Indian nation-state has quite clearly shown itself to be in a prolonged political and epistemological crisis. It is important to recognize that Rushdie's model in *MC* is not the only one operating in the contemporary Indian English novel, and perhaps no longer even the dominant one.

The first wave of exhilaration that produced a score of epic national/personal narratives directly inspired by *Midnight's Children* may well have run its course. For as long as post-Rushdie narratives remain ideologically bound to Nation, they will be forced to follow the contours of its crisis and recuperation in the eighties and nineties. If they are not to trickle out into what Saleem Sinai dreaded most, meaninglessness and flippant indeterminacy, they will have to move beyond ambivalence, and so perhaps beyond nation itself. However, from the vantage point of the late nineties, indications are that these fears are not being borne out. Rather than taking Indian English writing down a slippery slope into global capitalism, with its post-modern free play and radical indeterminacy, the post-Rushdie novel would seem to be moving beyond ambivalence to new commitments. For instance, in Mukul Kesavan's first novel, *Looking Through Glass* (1995), the protagonist starts out as a disengaged young photographer who looks at history and politics only through the lens of his camera, but moves progressively closer to his subjects until his point of view merges altogether with theirs. Sudden and involuntary time-travel magically plunges him into the politically turbulent period of the Quit India Movement of 1942 and forces him to live a Muslim Indian version of history from the inside. This was a period when Muslim points of view began to be erased first from Congress Party politics and later from official Indian histories, and Kesavan dramatizes this erasure by allegorizing it, Rushdie-style: overnight, hundreds of Muslims literally disappear. *Looking Through Glass* carries many of the hallmarks of the post-Rushdie novel: its portrayal of the vexed but intimate relationship of the personal and the political, the ambivalence of its protagonist, its challenging of official histories and parallel presentation of alternative versions, the magic realism of its time travel, the making concrete of its metaphors, and its valorization of political engagement.[47] In the tradition of *Midnight's Children*, it does not allow itself to be mired in disabling ambivalence. But we have seen that *MC* simultaneously challenges and reinforces the dominant model of Indian nationalism, and is ultimately unable and unwilling to step out of the framework of the nation. *Looking Through Glass* is equally caught up with national history, challenging the official nationalist version both by applying a corrective lens and by progressively removing the lens between history and life; it does not reject the national altogether, but replaces nationalist politics with a more local allegiance to people and to places.

Midnight's Children ends with the recognition that Saleem is at the end of a line. Nehru's promise has been drained of all possibility for him personally and perhaps even India itself has come to the end of that particular road in its history. Saleem recognizes that the country will have to fashion new ideals to inspire its people and move forward, but that will have to be the task of a new generation: "New myths are needed," he acknowledges, "but that's none of my business."[48] Another post-Rushdie first novel, Amitav Ghosh's 1986 *The Circle of Reason*, ends with its orphan protagonist's return to India. The discourse of secular rationalism that reared him has finally been discredited and consigned to the flames. He has been forced to live a life on the run from his own native land, and now he is free to return and make a new beginning. But it is clear that he will not be able to make it anew; he will have to work with the fragments he has. As one character says, "Nothing's whole any more. If we wait for everything to be right again, we'll wait for ever while the world falls apart. The only hope is to make do with what we've got."[49]

CODA, 1997

Ever since the advent of the novel in mid-nineteenth century colonial India, India writers have been reappropriating official versions of history to serve their own purposes. The Indian novel has had a role in the anti-colonial struggle as well as a role in forging an Indian national identity and an independent nation, its narrative vision shaping the ideal, and its language and discourse bodying forth the forms of the nation.[50] In the postcolonial period, with the crisis of the neo-colonial nation-state, the Indian novelist has both old tasks and new: first, in order to find, in Chinua Achebe's words, "where the rain began to beat us," to challenge official versions of history and nation and to recover the dignity and subjecthood of its people in their many and various voices; second, to envision and articulate new forms, new allegiances, that can carry them forward, giving meaning and coherence to fragmented, contending realities and forms of knowledge. In so doing, the novel necessarily becomes self-conscious, and the Indian English novel all the more so, because of its own complicity in the process of nation-building. I have argued that Salman Rushdie's *Midnight's Children* played a role in this process at a critical juncture in the postcolonial period, and that the novels that have succeeded it in the post-Rushdie period continue the tasks of vision and revision, telling their own stories in their multiple voices and imagining new languages and forms that can help give meaning and agency to individuals and communities during a time of crisis and change.

In April 1997, a new Prime Minister took office in Delhi for the third time in a year, heading a coalition of minority parties that is not unified or powerful enough to rule without the support of the formerly dominant Congress Party. Congress, the party that led India to independence and through more than forty post-independence years, was led by three successive generations of the Nehru family in an often-fantastic dynastic saga rivalled and mirrored by Saleem Sinai's own in *Midnight's Children*. Congress has lost the mandate of the Indian people and yet retains enough power to depose any coalition leader who threatens it too much. It is clear that a unitary, centralized model of nation no longer holds. But frightening as the seeming instability at the center may be, the present situation also may offer some hope for formerly disenfranchised fragments to realize a more decentralized vision, for the midnight's children—and their children—to continue talking to each other without any one privileged voice controlling them.

In these embattled, polarized times, it is perhaps all the more crucial to keep open the space for ambivalence, uncertainties, and multiple truths, rather than rushing to premature closure on questions of identity, whether personal or public. In spite of the resulting fear of instability and chaos, history has demonstrated the danger of imposing false unity upon either the nation or the novel form. Ultimately, *MC* is unable to reconcile the time-bound, linear model of history with the timeless, cyclical mode of myth. It is similarly unable to reconcile the unitary narratives of History and Nation with the multiple viewpoints of its individual and subaltern stories. And it fails to transcend the duality or reverse the fragmentation that defines its protagonist's life and eventually leads to his demise. But surely this failure is the novel's very point: its success lies in its willingness to point out the fatal flaws of the nation-state and to acknowledge its internal divisions and disjunctures, even at the risk of the protagonist's very life.

From the health and diversity of Indian writing in English in the eighties and nineties I would conclude that *MC* has had a salutary effect, but there are no easy conclusions to draw about the writers who have followed. Both nationalism and its critique continue to thrive in their work, which, like *MC* itself, simultaneously acknowledges and thematizes the limitations of the national narrative. And the latest crop of young writers—many of them women—have refreshingly begun to dispense with the language and forms of Nation altogether. Of course no single novel can be said to give a people agency, but the very multiplicity of modes and voices in the Indian novel of the nineties, even as the Indian nation-state flounders, is a testament to the hyperbolic claim of *Midnight's Children*, despite all evidence to the contrary, to have turned Victim into Protagonist.

* * *

Sitting down to write this essay, it seems an age since Saleem Sinai's opening lines sprang forth fresh on the page—almost when the world was still young. If *MC* were to be published today, sixteen years later, it might not receive the same positive welcome in the current social and political climate. If it had been published in India by an Indian publisher, it might not have won the Booker Prize. And without the acclaim outside India, it might not have been read with such eagerness inside India and been able to say things, and in a new way for the Indian English novel, that would otherwise not have been so well received. No doubt its post-Emergency timing was a factor in its success, and so was the novelist's gender, location, and positioning. But the novel's impact on Indian English writing of the eighties and nineties is undeniable. Re-reading *Midnight's Children*, I do not find it dated, neither do I read it merely as elegy/eulogy to a failed experiment; it remains a celebration of India, a paean to both unity and multiplicity, and both inspiration and challenge to a new generation to supercede it in style.

Notes

1. Salman Rushdie, *Midnight's Children* (London: Picador, 1982). Further references to this work will be abbreviated *MC* and all citations are from this edition.

2. Quoted from Shyamala Narayan, in the 1983 Bibliography, *Journal of Commonwealth Literature* 19.2 (1984): 79-82, Rushdie had lived in England since 1962, when his father sent him to Rugby at the age of fourteen. He went on to read history at King's College, Cambridge, during which time his family moved from Bombay to Karachi, Pakistan. Since his childhood, he had only been back to India once, in the late seventies, when *Midnight's Children* was conceived.

3. From Una Chaudhuri, "Imaginative Maps." (New York: Turnstile Press). A 1983 interview with Rushdie, conducted by Una Chaudhuri downloaded 3.8.97 from Subir Grewal's Rushdie pages: www.crl.com/ ~subir/rushdie/uc_maps.html).

4. Mukund Padmanabhan, et. al., "The Empire Writes Back," in *Sunday*, 4-10 December, 1988.

5. See Narayan's 1983 Bibliography, cited above.

6. See Debashish Mukerji's article, "An Area of Brightness," on the increased acceptance of Indian writers in English both in the west and in India itself (downloaded 11.28.96 from SAWNET: www.umiacs.umd.edu/ users/sawweb/sawnet/SAW.books.html).

7. Two examples of Indian critiques of Rushdie's literary influence are Aijaz Ahmed's *In Theory* (London: Verso, 1992) and Harish Trivedi's essay, "The St. Stephen's Factor," *Indian Literature* (Sept./Oct. 1991): 183-87. Trivedi also uses the term "post-Rushdie" critically in his *Colonial Transactions: English Literature and India* (Manchester: Manchester Univ. Press, 1995). Two recent studies of Rushdie as diasporic writer are Vijay Mishra's "Postcolonial Differend: Diasporic Narratives of Salman Rushdie," *Ariel* 26.3 (1995): 7-45, and Jean Kane's "The migrant intellectual and the body of history: Salman Rushdie's *Midnight's Children,*" *Contemporary Literature* 37 (Spring 1996): 94-118.

8. Rushdie accidentally (-on-purpose?) calls him the scribe of the *Ramayana*.

9. These are too numerous to list, but some of the scholars who have discussed the relationship of history, politics, and the individual in *MC* are Uma Parameswaran, R. S. Pathak, Dieter Reimenschneider, Aruna Srivastava, Neil ten Kortenaar, and Jonathan White. Thanks to Michael Reder for his useful review of the critical literature in "Narration and

Identity in Salman Rushdie's Midnight's Children," Unpublished Master's thesis, 1994.

10. "The Empire Writes Back."

11. Timothy Brennan, *Salman Rushdie and the Third World: Myths of the Nation* (New York: St. Martin's Press, 1989), p. 85.

12. Talk given at Amherst College (4/4/97) on the occasion of its award of an honorary degree to Rushdie.

13. Hence Saleem's desperate anxiety to set down his story before it is too late and his recognition that his son-who-is-not-his-son's generation will not live by his generation's ideals. Incidentally, "out of touch and out of time" also evokes a popular Rolling Stones' song of Rushdie's teen years, "Out of Time," whose lyrics express a lover's contemptuous rejection of a former love who has "been away for much too long."

14. Una Chaudhuri interview, 1983.

15. Salman Rushdie, *The Moor's Last Sigh* (London: Jonathan Cape, 1995), pp. 173; 178-79.

16. For an excellent discussion on the vexed relationship between literature and the post-independence Indian nation-state, see the Introduction to *Women Writing in India. Vol. II: The Twentieth Century*, S. Tharu and K. Lalita, eds. (New York: The Feminist Press, 1993).

17. For some of the ideas in the above paragraph, I am indebted to Shiv Visvanathan of the Center for the Study of Developing Societies in Delhi. He used Rushdie's phrase "collective failure of the imagination" in our 1993 conversation.

18. *Indian Literature* 25.1 (1982): 128.

19. Kumkum Sangari, "The Politics of the Possible," *Cultural Critique* (Fall 1987): 157-86.

20. Salman Rushdie, "Imaginary Homelands," in *Imaginary Homelands: Essays and Criticism 1981-1991* (New York: Viking, 1991), p. 21.

21. These passive-aggressive forms of resistance are reminiscent of suffragettes' tactics and—more relevant here—of Gandhi's use of mass non-violent civil disobedience. See Ashis Nandy's discussion of Gandhi's "feminine" modes of anti-colonial resistance in *The Intimate Enemy: Loss and Recovery of Self Under Colonialism* (Delhi: Oxford Univ. Press, 1983), pp. 47-57. For a feminist critique of these tactics, see Ketu Katrak's essay, "Indian Nationalism, Gandhian 'Satyagraha' and Representations of Female Sexuality," *Nationalisms and Sexualities*, Andrew Parker, et. al., eds. (New York: Routledge, 1992), pp. 395-406.

22. R. S. Pathak, "History and the Individual in the Novels of Salman Rushdie," in *The Novels of Salman Rushdie*, G. R. Taneja and R. K. Dhawan, eds. (New Delhi: Indian Society for Commonwealth Studies, 1992), p. 123.

23. Thakur Guruprasad, "The Secret of Rushdie's Charm," in *The Novels of Salman Rushdie*, G. R. Taneja and R. K. Dhawan, eds. (New Delhi: Indian Society for Commonwealth Studies, 1992), p. 169.

24. Anita Desai, "Where Cultures Clash By Night," *The Washington Post*, 3/15/81.

25. Una Chaudhuri interview, 1983.

26. The depth of Rushdie's current disillusionment with socio-political trends in India is reflected in *The Moor's Last Sigh* in which Saleem's son Adam, his last repository of hope in MC, has grown up to be a power-hungry, amoral, nineties-style yuppie capitalist.

27. William Safire, "On Language: Janus Lives," *New York Times Magazine*, 5.4.97: 22.

28. Homi K. Bhabha, *Nation and Narration* (London: Routledge, 1989), p. 3.

29. *The Moor's Last Sigh*, pp. 163-64.

30. Ibid., p. 155.

31. M. Keith Booker, "Beauty and the Beast: Dualism as Despotism in the Fiction of Salman Rushdie," *ELH* 57 (1990): 977-97.

32. "The gander is the animal mask of the creative principle, which is anthropomorphically embodied in Brahma ... a symbol of sovereign freedom through stainless spirituality ... The Hindu ascetic ... freed from the bondage of rebirth, is said to have attained to the rank of 'gander' (*hamsa*), or 'highest gander' (*paramahamsa*) ... The wild gander ... exhibits in its mode of life the twofold nature of all beings. It swims on the surface of the water, but is not bound to it. Withdrawing from the watery realm, it wings into the pure and stainless air, where it is as much at home as in the world below... Thus it is the homeless free wanderer, between the upper celestial and the lower earthly spheres, at ease in both, not bound to either ... it symbolizes the divine essence, which, though embodied in, and abiding with, the individual, yet remains forever free from, and unconcerned with, the events of individual life ... On the one hand earth-bound, limited in life strength in virtues and in consciousness, but on the other hand a manifestation of the divine essence ... we, like the wild goose, are citizens of the two spheres." See Heinrich Zimmer, *Myths and Symbols in Indian Art and Civilization* (New York: Harper Torchbooks, 1962), pp. 48-49.

33. In his essay, "The Riddle of Midnight: India, August 1987," Rushdie returns for the 40th anniversary of Independence and the 40th birthday of the "Class of 47." In view of the increasing exclusiveness of the nationalist idea in India, he muses over the "paradox: that, in a country created by the Congress's nationalist campaign, the well-being of the people

might now require that all nationalist rhetoric be abandoned." Given the continuing nationalist history India has been rehearsing, that does not look very likely anytime soon. See *Imaginary Homelands* (New York: Viking Penguin, 1991), pp. 32-33.

34. Kathleen Flanagan, "The Fragmented Self in Salman Rushdie's *Midnight's Children." Commonwealth Novel in English* 5.1 (Spring 1992): 38-45.

35. Whether it was either or both, M.C.C. is also the Marylebone Cricket Club. This is typical Rushdiesque deflationary humor, but with a serious point—the English democratic institutions inherited by independent India may have held promise at Independence, but it is increasingly being asked whether they hold the seeds of their own destruction.

36. To Rushdie, the fragment implies a whole, even if the whole is itself composite; it loses meaning in isolation. While he defends the fragment's right to a voice and an independent existence and condemns the coerciveness of the centralized State, he is clearly ambivalent about the loss of a controlling center. For a 1990s perspective, see Partha Chatterjee's *The Nation and Its Fragments* (Princeton NJ: Princeton Univ. Press, 1993).

37. Two of the protagonists in I. Allan Sealy's 1988 epic family-chronicle/national-narrative, *The Trotter-Nama*, are also ballooning miniaturists, literally and figuratively. As the Seventh Trotter's body balloons grotesquely, his paintings (ironically, copies of Mughal miniatures), get smaller and smaller. He claims that they do not simply imitate the original, but progressively improve upon it, eventually "dispensing with the world" altogether. His illustrious ancestor, also a portly figure, was killed while hot-air ballooning.

38. Richard Cronin, "The Indian English Novel: *Kim* and *Midnight's Children," Modern Fiction Studies* 33.2 (1987): 201-02.

39. "Washing dirty linen" inevitably calls to mind the episode of the washing-chest. If you hide in dirty laundry, you are bound to get exposed. You can only retreat "from the demands of parents and history" for so long before they catch up with you. And as with Saleem, both exposing and exposed, so also with Rushdie himself.

40. Anita Desai,. Personal Interview, S. Hadley, Massachusetts, November 1992. For a discussion of Anita Desai's novels in the sixties and seventies, see my essay, "Codes in Conflict: Post-independence alienation in Anita Desai's early novels," *Journal of Gender Studies* 5.3 (November 1996): 317-28.

41. Two recent India collections of essays on new Indian English writers of the 1980s are Viney Kirpal, ed., *The New Indian Novel in English: A*

Study of the 1980s (New Delhi: Allied Publishers, 1990) and Nilufer E. Bharucha and Vilas Sarang, eds., *Indian-English Fiction 1980-1990: An Assessment, New World Literature Series* 77 (Delhi: B. R. Publishing Corporation, 1994).

42. The Parsis came to India in the 7th Century A.D. and Anglo-Indians have been a presence since at least the late 18th Century.

43. Here I must acknowledge my colleague Pennie Ticen, who first used "on the hyphen" years ago in a conversation with me, long before it was in common use.

44. Antonio Gramsci *via* Nadine Gordimer, from the epigraph to her novel *July's People*: "The old is dying and the new cannot be born; in this interregnum there arises a great diversity of morbid symptoms." Gramsci's position here is that, while the precise direction is unknown, it is clear that the mass of the people have become "detached from their traditional ideologies...through the crisis of authority." There can be no easy resolution through a "restoration of the old," he asserts; it is necessary to create a new culture. "State and Civil Society," in *Selections from the Prison Notebooks*, Quintin Hoare and Geoffrey Nowell Smith, eds., p. 276.

45. Rajeswari Sunder Rajan, "The Feminist Plot and the Nationalist Allegory: Home and World in Two Indian Women's Novels in English," *Modern Fiction Studies* 39 (Spring 1993): 71-92.

46. Sanjay Iyer, "East, West: No Home is Best," *Indian Review of Books* 4.3 (Jan.-Feb., 1995): 2.

47. Mukul Kesavan, *Looking Through Glass* (New York: Farrar, Straus and Giroux, 1995). A young student in Delhi when Rushdie read on his 1983 tour of India. Kesavan has likened the event to a religious experience.

48. In her reading of *Midnight's Children*, Fawzia Afzal-Khan says that Saleem is trying to "debunk myth" when he declares that he will not see his son's miracles, that he will not see them "because, in fact, they will not happen." While it is true that Saleem does suggest that his son's generation will be more "pragmatic" than his own. I do not believe that he rules out "new myths" altogether. Saleem cannot partake of a new collective myth because he has been formed by the old one, and with its demise will come his own. See *Cultural Imperialism and the Indo-English Novel* (University Park, PA: Penn State Univ. Press, 1993), p. 159.

49. Amitav Ghosh, *The Circle of Reason* (New York: Viking, 1986), pp. 416-17. This is what Ghosh sets out to do in his next novel. *The Shadow Lines* (1988), in which he uses the structures of nation only to step out of them altogether.

50. For the history of the novel (including the historical novel) in colonial India, see Meenakshi Mukherjee's *Realism and Reality: The Novel and Society in India* (Delhi: Oxford Univ. Press, 1985) and Sisir Kumar Das's *A History of Indian Literature, 1800-1910, Western Impact: Indian Response*, and *1911-1956, Struggle for Freedom: Triumph and Tragedy* (New Delhi: Sahitya Akademi, 1991, 1995).

BRIAN FINNEY

Demonizing Discourse in Salman Rushdie's
The Satanic Verses

Salman Rushdie's *The Satanic Verses* (1988) is one of the relatively few works of fiction to have made a significant and permanent impact outside the enclosed world of literature. Despite W. H. Auden's assertion that "poetry [by which he meant imaginative literature in general] makes nothing happen" (242),[1] this novel has clearly made a number of things happen. It has led to the loss of over twenty lives. It made its author go into hiding from the Ayatollah Khomeini's *fatwa* of 1989, where he has remained under government protection ever since. Above all, coinciding with the ending of the Cold War, it has played a significant role in redefining the West's image of itself. The Other is no longer the threat of Communism, but that of Islamic fundamentalism—far more of a paper tiger than the very real nuclear menace offered by the USSR and its allies. The book was similarly used by Islamic clerics to reinforce their image of the US (and its Western allies) as the Great Satan—doubly ironical seeing what a fierce critic of American policy abroad Rushdie had shown himself to be in *The Jaguar Smile: A Nicaraguan Journey* (1987). The Iranian President Khamene'i told his followers, "*The Satanic Verses* ... is no doubt one of the verses of the Great Satan" (Appignanesi 87). In giving Rushdie's ironic title a literal reading (although itself figurative in another way) Khamene'i politicized the novel irrevocably. The Ayatollah Khomeini justified his *fatwa* against Rushdie by

From *ARIEL: A Review of International English Literature* 29, no. 3 (July 1998): 67-93. © 1998 by The Board of Governors, The University of Calgary.

similarly accusing him and "the world devourers" (the West) of publishing *The Satanic Verses* as "a calculated move aimed at rooting out religion and religiousness, and above all, Islam and its clergy" (Appignanesi 90). Considering that the clergy in Iran occupied the highest positions of political power, it can be seen how threatening Rushdie's novel must have appeared to the leaders of an Islamic theocratic state.

Whereas Western politicians have chosen to represent this conflict as a battle between democratic freedom of speech and autocratic censorship or even terrorism (the *fatwa*), Rushdie's ideological stance, both within the novel and in his numerous comments on its reception, is a great deal more complex and problematical. In an article written about responses to the book, "In Good Faith" (1990), Rushdie insists that he has "never seen this controversy as a struggle between Western freedoms and Eastern unfreedom." Instead, he asserts, his novel champions "doubts, uncertainties." "It dissents from the end of debate, of dispute, of dissent" (*Imaginary Homelands* 396). In defending his right to defend all issues endlessly, to postpone closure indefinitely, to oppose certainties of all kinds whether they originate in the East or the West, Rushdie is clearly positioning himself as a writer in a postmodern world where nothing can be asserted with assurance. "I am a modern, and modernist, urban man," he insists in the same essay, "accepting uncertainty as the only constant, change as the only sure thing" (404-05). This refusal to countenance any of the grand narratives that have governed Eastern or Western civilization is precisely the stance that Jean-François Lyotard identifies as central to the postmodern condition.[2] Rushdie has been simultaneously hailed by many critics as the preeminent practitioner of postcolonial writing which is normally characterized by its opposition to the values and ideology of the metropolitan centre. While postmodernism itself is said to embrace cultural relativity, it tends to prioritize relativity *per se*, whereas postcolonialism normally prioritizes non-Western cultural diversity. In other words there is an implicit conflict in the two positions: postcolonialism adopts specific political positions which postmodernism goes out of its way to relativize.

Rushdie's own life history further complicates this dichotomy. Brought up a Muslim in a Hindu country, he was sent to an English public school at the age of fourteen, and chose to stay on in England after obtaining a degree in History at King's College, London. Self-exiled from his native country, he was repeatedly rebuffed by the inherent racism he met with in his adopted country. Prior to the proclamation of the *fatwa* Rushdie was one of the acutest critics of the Thatcher regime's brand of racist politics. After he was placed in the care of the British security services, he found himself in the ambivalent position of an adopted citizen owing his life to a government that was simultaneously passing anti-immigrant legislation motivated by the fear of being swamped by alien races. Marginalized racially, Rushdie nevertheless belongs more to the centre of the dominant culture when considered in terms of class and wealth. He has turned the hybridity of his migrant (as opposed to immigrant) status into a desirable if uncomfortable mode of existence. It offers him freedom from "the shackles of nationalism," but it is "a burdensome freedom" (*Imaginary Homelands* 124). It means that writers in his position "are capable of writing from a kind of double perspective, because they, we, are at one and the same time insiders and outsiders in this society" (19). As an insider, Rushdie is postmodern in his validation of uncertainty. As an outsider, he is postcolonialist in his satirical subversion of the certainties of metropolitan (Thatcherite) politics and the center's exercise of power.

Rushdie attempts to reconcile these internal stresses by resorting to a trope—that of oxymoron—by means of which he seeks to celebrate the certainty of uncertainty, the singular affirmation of plurality. Inevitably he has been taken to task by each camp for supposedly embracing the opposing one. In particular, he has come under sustained attack for his quintessentially postmodern attitude by Marxists, especially by Aijaz Ahmad. Ahmad attacks Rushdie on the grounds that his fictional space is "occupied so entirely by Power that there is no space left for either resistance or its representation" (127). In Ahmad's eyes Rushdie lacks proper anti-imperialist political conviction. However, critics such as Ahmad embody a specific postcolonial interpretation of the political that is far too crude when applied to Rushdie's writings. Rushdie refuses to adopt any easy position in the postcolonial debate, because he stands on both sides of its divide. This enables him to discern in both dominant and emergent cultures the same desire to appropriate the truth for themselves and to use this truth to valorize their imposition of it on believers and dissenters alike.

Despite Rushdie's later protestations, there is no doubt that he set out in this novel to confront what he disparagingly calls "Actually Existing Islam" (by which he means "the political and priestly power structure that presently dominates and stifles Muslim societies") with the uncertainties governing the circumstances under which the Qu'ran came into existence (*Imaginary Homelands* 436). The original verbal battle between Muhammad and the poets who defended the polytheism he set out to replace, which is reenacted in Rushdie's fictional reconstruction of it, has since been replayed—verbally—between its author and the mullahs. Islamic fundamentalism squares off against Islamic secularism (Rushdie was brought up in a Muslim family where, however, "there was an absolute willingness to discuss anything." Appignanesi 30). As Aamir Mufti has put it, "in secularizing (and hence profaning) the sacred 'tropology' of Islam by insisting upon its appropriation for the purposes of fiction, the novel throws into doubt the discursive edifice within which Islam has been produced in recent years" (107). In effect Rushdie chooses to oppose the anti-imperialist discursive formation of Islam by pitting against it the alternative discursive formation of imaginative fiction. Rushdie seems to see in fictional discourse a neutral discursive space in which he can give free play to competing discourses that oppose both the discourse of Islam and that of Thatcherite nationalism. *The Satanic Verses*, then, can be seen as a bricolage of conflicting discourses framed by the controlling discourse of fiction. But just how neutral is a discourse that controls? In its postmodern form is not fictional discourse itself competing for dominance with the other discursive formations it seeks to incorporate within its all-embracing grasp?

The use of discursive formations, according to Michel Foucault, represents an attempt to control and contain the "barely imaginable powers and dangers," the "ponderous, awesome materiality" of language (*Archaeology/Discourse* 216).[3] Within *The Satanic Verses*, Rushdie pits secular against sacred, nationalist or racist against transnationalist or migrant, historical against ahistorical, and above all, authoritative against fictional forms of discourse. I want to concentrate on Rushdie's attempt to use fictional discourse to undermine the totalizing discourses of religion and nationalism. To undermine is not necessarily to destroy. Rushdie has said that the novel is an exploration of the "God-shaped hole" left in him after he had abandoned the "unarguable absolutes of religion" (Appignanesi 75). Apart from a brief moment of reverse apostasy during the period of the *fatwa*, he has remained a secular Muslim who has always aspired to achieve within an aesthetic context that transcendence experienced by the religious mystic. He maintains that art, like religion, can produce a "flight of the human spirit outside the confines of its material, physical existence" (*Imaginary Homelands* 421). Clearly the danger for someone holding this belief is that he will treat art or fiction as a transcendental signifier. Like many writers of the twentieth century, he is looking for an alternative religious experience outside the restrictive confines of an organized religion such as that of Islam (which literally means "Submission"). He would claim that, unlike Islamic funadamentalists, he does not seek to compel anyone to accept his aesthetic ideology. Nevertheless he clearly believes that this ideology is superior to that of either the fundamentalists or the imperialists. He has no wish to compel, but a strong wish to persuade.

This still leaves open to question why Rushdie should think that the discourse of art or fiction should have a truth-value unavailable to revealed religion. Can there be a hierarchy of discourses? According to Foucault all discourses are subject to their own particular confining sets of rules. If this is the case, why should the discourses of fundamentalist religion and nationalism find Rushdie's use of fictional discourse in *The Satanic Verses* so threatening? Is it because fiction claims to incorporate those other discursive formations within its own discourse and in doing so to reveal the will to power underlying their will to truth? (But doesn't the Qu'ran do the same thing in its treatment of contemporary poets?) Foucault identifies the will to truth as the most important of the three systems of exclusion that govern discourse. He claims that it has tended to assimilate the other two systems—prohibited words, and the division between reason and folly. Each discursive formation claims for itself the status of "true" discourse, concealing behind its will to constitute the truth of things its desire for power. This is obviously the case in the instance of a theocratic state such as Iran where Islamic faith (of the Shi'ite variety) is invoked to justify a war against even fellow (Sunni) Muslims of a neighboring state such as Iraq. By calling it a *jihad* or holy war, by definition a war waged against infidels, such a state draws on the discourse of "true" religion to sanction its naked nationalist and political ambitions. In a similar fashion Mrs. Thatcher appealed to the "truth" of the rights to self-determination by the Falkland Islanders to sanction her desire to retain political power back in the metropolitan center.

But Foucault insists that the same great systems of exclusion govern the discourse of literature. Literature too feels that it has to extend its power over its readers by claiming truth for itself. According to Foucault, "Western literature has, for centuries, sought to base itself in nature, in the plausible, upon sincerity and science—in short, upon true discourse" (*Archaeology/ Discourse* 219). One might argue that what is loosely referred to as postmodern literature does anything but base itself on nature. As Mimi insists in the novel: "I ... am conversant with postmodernist critiques of the West, for example, that we have here a society capable only of pastiche: a 'flattened' world" (261). Rushdie has obviously read his Jameson.[4] Yet when Rushdie comes to defend fiction in his own person he claims that postmodern writing offers the truest reflection of contemporary human experience: a "rejection of totalized explanations is the modern condition. And this is where the novel, the form created to discuss the fragmentation of truth, comes in.... The elevation of the quest for the Grail over the Grail itself, the acceptance that all that is solid *has* melted into air, that reality and morality are not givens but imperfect human constructs, is the point from which fiction begins" (*Imaginary Homelands* 422). This comes close to basing fiction in nature by redefining the natural. Rushdie is unashamedly pitting his naturalized fictional discourse against what he terms (with an acknowledgment to Lyotard) the unnatural, totalizing discourses of religion and national politics. As Foucault suggests, the will to truth "tends to exercise a sort of pressure, a power of constraint upon other forms of discourse" (*Archaeology/Discourse* 219).

In effect Rushdie claims for fictional discourse an imaginative form of truth where freedom reigns in place of institutional control. Fiction, he maintains, can flout the mundane facts and still appeal to the world of the imagination to claim that it represents the "true" or authentic transcription of human experience. In "Imaginary Homelands," he argues that "[w]riters and politicians are natural rivals. Both groups try to make the world in their own images; they fight for the same territory. And the novel is one way of denying the official, politicians' version of the truth" (14). Rushdie's figurative allusions here are revealing. While he is ostensibly arguing about claims to truthfulness, his vocabulary ("rivals," "fight," "territory") belongs to the the world of power.

In the opening chapter of the novel, Rushdie forces his readers to become conscious of the paradoxical nature of fiction's notion of "true" discourse: "Once upon a time—it was and it was not so, as the old stories used to say, *it happened and it never did*—maybe, then, or maybe not" (35). All fictional discourse is predicated by that "maybe." It is for the reader to decide on the probability of the imaginative construct. *The Satanic Verses* begins by flouting any sense of factual reality with an impossible rebirth—two actors (as the two main protagonists are tellingly characterized) falling to earth without parachutes or wings from a height of 29,000 feet. Other improbabilities follow. Gibreel acquires a halo and Chamcha goat hooves and horns. A dead lover visits Gibreel on a magic carpet. Gibreel tropicalizes London's climate. The British authorities turn immigrants into a water-buffalo, slippery snakes and a manticore, itself a beast of fictional invention. In effect Rushdie is exploiting the extended boundaries of fictional discourse to demonstrate that what is invented is not necessarily untrue if read figuratively. When Chamcha asks the manticore how "they" manage to turn the immigrants into such weird creatures, he promptly replies, "They have the power of description, and we succumb to the pictures they construct" (168). But the novelist, Rushdie goes on to imply, has a superior power of description, which should enable him to overpower the descriptive discourse of the racist immigration authorities. Like the novelist, these authorities make the "story" they concoct about how Chamcha came to be unconscious (mainly due to the beating they gave him) "more convincing" by incorporating into their fiction the fact that he was at any rate genuinely sick beforehand (169). Rushdie parodies their method of telling a story by starting off as they do with a fiction, such as the manticore, and then offering—not facts, but a figurative explanation for the seemingly unreal shapes they assume.

Interspersed with the "realist" chapters are chapters in which Gibreel is visited by unwanted dreams or nightmares. Paradoxically, within his surreal world of dreams Gibreel becomes the spectator or participant in a series of historically authenticated occurrences (suggesting that history itself is a collective dreaming about the past). His dream of Mahound (the Christian crusaders' demonic term of abuse for Muhammad) incorporates numerous incidents from accounts of the life of Muhammad. Similarly the story of Ayesha makes free use of a widely reported episode that happened in Karachi in 1983 when Naseem Fatima led thirty eight Shi'a followers into the sea which they expected to part for them. Another narrative strand in Gibreel's dream chapters—the account of the Imam's return from exile—resembles the Ayatollah Khomeini's return to Iran on the downfall of the Shah in 1979.

Gibreel is torn between a "real" world where the miraculous happens and a world of dreams where the miraculous is restored to an imagined but largely verifiable historical past. As Gibreel gradually drifts into a state of schizophrenia Rushdie further complicates the already confused distinction between material and imaginative reality by showing the barrier between waking and dreaming worlds slowly crumbling. Neither Gibreel nor the reader can be sure of where one world ends and the other begins. The resulting confusion can be either liberating or destructive. "The imagination," Rushdie admits, "can falsify, demean, ridicule, caricature and wound as effectively as it can clarify, intensify and unveil" (*Imaginary Homelands* 143). On the other hand, Rushdie reveals his own prejudice when he inconsistently insists that "the opposition of imagination to reality...reminds us that we are not helpless; that to dream is to have power." Here again we glimpse the will to power underlying fiction's will to (imaginative) truth. Rushdie continues: "Unreality is the only weapon with which reality can be smashed, so that it may subsequently be reconstituted" (*Imaginary Homelands* 122). But what does he mean by "reality"? Apparently "our conventional, habit-dulled certainties about what the world is and has to be," a world "in which things inevitably get worse" (122). The dream worlds of the artist have "the power ... to oppose this dark reality" (122). Their (postmodern) plurality, Rushdie asserts, brings the light of truth to a world benighted by the unitary truths of politics and religion. But the discourse of fiction is seen here to be as incapable as is all true discourse, according to Foucault, "of recognizing the will to truth which pervades it" (*Archaeology/Discourse* 219). It is as blind to its determination to establish its superior status as are the discursive formations of nationalism and Islam that it subordinates to its purposes. Discourse, like knowledge, is necessarily contaminated by its desire to dominate.

How does fictional discourse exercise its power of constraint on those totalizing discourses it opposes? Primarily by appropriation. It incorporates them into its own discourse, one which ostensibly throws all proclaimed truths into question. Whereas Muslims believe that the archangel Gabriel dictated God's verses to Muhammad, Mahound, in Rushdie's subversive version of the origins of the Qu'ran, exercises a form of telepathy by means of which he mesmerizes Gibreel into dictating what he (Mahound) needs from him. In other words Rushdie replaces the unauthored word of God by the psychologized interaction between the needful Prophet and his supposedly angelic mouthpiece—an internal projection. Since Gibreel is responsible for uttering under Mahound's spell both the Satanic verses and their angelic rebuttal, the fictional discourse places him in a position to throw doubt on Mahound's claim that the first set of verses came from Satan:

> Being God's postman is no fun, yar.
> Butbutout: God isn't in this picture.
> God knows whose postman I've been. (112)

Cast in fictional discursive form and undermined by Rushdie's use of a playful, punning tone, the absolutes of Islamic faith become humanized and relativized. The mere substitution of "postman" for "Messenger" reduces the sublime to the mundane. Rushdie repeatedly exploits the polysemantic nature of language to make us conscious of the possibility of alternative readings that were present at the moment that the discourse of Islam privileged one of them for its own use. For instance, *Bostan*, one of the two gardens of paradise, is also the name of the plane which is blown up by Sikh terrorists in the opening chapter of the book. Paradise, then, within a framework of fictional discourse, offers no haven from the uncertainties of this world. The sight of perfection that Allie Cone glimpsed on Mount Everest is seen by this representative figure of the postmodern world to be unattainable in the here and now. Perfection entails absolute silence, according to Allie: "why speak if you can't manage perfect thoughts, perfect sentences" (296)? Entry into the world of language, as the writer of fiction knows, entails the compromises and ambiguities that accompany imperfection, a fact that the believers in scripture deny. Within Rushdie's fictional universe most certainties (especially those consolatory absolutes held by religion) crumble. Uncertainty is the only unchanging certainty that Rushdie perversely posits in the novel.

Within his own discourse Rushdie performs what Foucault terms a genealogical analysis on the discourse of Islam. Such an analysis involves investigating how that discourse was formed, what were its norms, and what were the conditions for its appearance, growth and variation (*Archaeology/Discourse* 231-32). Indeed it is precisely this interest in what Foucault terms genealogy that predominates in this novel:

How does newness come into the world? How is it born?
Of what fusions, translations, conjoinings is it made? (8)

Mahound's discourse is founded on the insistence that there is only one God. He imposes this monotheistic idea on the people of Jahilia (meaning the period of ignorance prior to the advent of Islam), themselves polytheists who have constructed their city out of the shifting sands of the desert. Mahound's insistence on repetitive ritual washing is itself a threat to the survival of their multifold structures built of dry sand, as well as offering a paradigm of the difference in their ideological positions. The Jahilian polytheists (like contemporary postmodernists) can accept a greater degree of linguistic discontinuity in their belief in gods with overlapping powers and domains than can Mahound, who belongs to what Foucault terms the "'critical' group" which imposes "forms of exclusion, limitation, and appropriation" on the threatening linguistic universe (*Archaeology/Discourse* 231). Mahound's triumph represents the imposition of a unitary belief system on a society that resembled India where "the human population outnumbers the divine by less than three to one" (16). Here Rushdie combines a postcolonial admiration for Indian diversity with a Western postmodern endorsement of the polysemantic nature of language. But he seems to forget that diversity can be (and was in the case of the British Empire) used to divide and rule.

What also emerges from Rushdie's fictional historicization of the origins of Islam is that Mahound began life as a successful businessman (as Muhammad did) and subsequently used the new religion to consolidate in business-like fashion his secular hold on power. Mahound moves from the will to power to the will to truth which soon enough reveals the underlying will to power that resurfaces as the religious metamorphosizes into the political. Mahound is also likened to Ibrahim (Abraham), who at God's command abandoned his wife in the desert. The narrator comments, "From the beginning men used God to justify the unjustifiable" (95). Such an aside implicitly opposes a different discourse (humanism? feminism?) to that of religion. But simultaneously it gives narratorial approval to the opposing discourse, which defeats the ostensible postmodern stance of universal doubt. The context suggests that the primary discourse invoked is that of feminism. Much is made of Mahound's imposition of a maximum of four wives on his followers while permitting himself twelve. In a section of the novel that particularly inflamed Muslims Rushdie parodies Mahound's household by inventing the brothel in which Baal the poet (representative of the discourse of literature) parallels Mahound, and the twelve prostitutes he marries take on the names of the Prophet's twelve wives. Sacred (that is, divinely condoned) and secular sexuality, like sacred and secular verbal creativity, are made to appear virtually identical in a fictional context. The distinctions that define Islamic discourse (Foucault's external rules of exclusion) are subtly elided until that discourse merges into the discourse of fiction where it becomes just another imaginative textual construct. In this instance Rushdie is more successful in undermining a unitary discourse by placing it in a discursive context that deliberately equates sacred and secular through the use of literary parallelism.

Rushdie has a more difficult task attempting a genealogical analysis of the discourse of nationalism, if only because the formation of nations predates recorded history. In the case of Britain he chooses instead to invoke the Norman conquest of 1066 (an event used by English historians to mark the beginning of the Middle Ages) by having Gibreel and Chamcha fall to earth at Hastings, the site of the battle in which William the Conqueror defeated Harold and replaced Anglo-Saxon civilization with a new regime. Just as William swallowed a mouthful of sand on landing at Hastings, Gibreel swallows a mouthful of snow, while Chamcha had already been forced to swallow a kipper, bones and all, "the first step in his conquest of England" (44). The narrative reminds us from the start that Britain is the product of countless invasions each of which has put new blood into its system. Gibreel invokes another royal foreigner, William of Orange, whose bloodless revolution in 1688 brought with it an influx of new ideas from the Continent. Gibreel reflects, "Not all migrants are powerless.... They impose their needs on their new earth, bringing their own coherence to the new-found land, imagining it afresh" (458). The newest conquerors are immigrants from the West Indies and the Indian subcontinent. Conquest, however, is not without its dangers. Both Williams died of unnatural causes—Rushdie refers in the novel to the later William's death from falling off his horse onto the hard earth he'd civilized. Similarly one of the two migrant protagonists and other immigrant characters in the novel meet unnatural deaths, some at the hands of the xenophobic British authorities who remain blind to their own mixed racial origins.

Margaret Thatcher, who had been in power for over nine years by the time the novel was published, comes in for harsher treatment than does Mahound, being referred to as "Torture. Maggie the Bitch" (269). Rushdie had been particularly enraged by a speech she had made after Britain's victory against Argentina in the Falkland Islands (Las Malvinas) in which she "most plainly nailed her colours to the old colonial mast, claiming that the success in the South Atlantic proved that the British were still the people 'who had ruled a quarter of the world'" (*Imaginary Homelands* 92). Unconsciously she was betraying the fact that she did not consider immigrants like Rushdie who had come from the ruled quarter to be a true part of the national identity. Rushdie goes further, arguing that "the British authorities, no longer capable of exporting governments, have chosen instead to import a new Empire, a new community of subject peoples," referring to the post war immigration from the Caribbean (*Imaginary Homelands* 130). It is this attempt to reverse the course of history that enables Rushdie to establish a link between Mrs. Thatcher and the Imam, the contemporary representative of Islamic fundamentalism. When Mrs. Thatcher called for a return to Victorian values, Rushdie wrote, "she had embarked on a heroic battle against the linear passage of Time" (*Imaginary Homelands* 92). In the novel, Valance makes the same point more colorfully to a disconcerted Chamcha. The connection to the Imam becomes clear when the Imam tells an equally disconcerted Gibreel that he will smash all the clocks when he comes to power in the name of God's "boundless time, that encompasses past, present and future; the timeless time, that has no need to move." "I am eternity," he asserts (214). Whereas Lyotard and Fredric Jameson both claim in their way that the postmodern entails a denial of the forces of history, Rushdie's satire at the expense of these two modern leaders who have set out to reverse the chronological progression of time emanates more from his postcolonial belief in the need to acknowledge the historical effects of imperialism if these are to be overturned and left behind by the newly liberated peoples of the old empires. The truly postmodern response to Mrs. Thatcher's and the Imam's reversal of historical time would be to allow temporal and atemporal forces equal play.

Instead Rushdie attempts to subvert the uncreated word of God by rehistoricizing the origins of Islam (just as he undermines the Thatcher regime's desire to return to the Victorian days of Empire by staging a race

riot that is representative of contemporary immigrants' militant rejection of
the ideology of imperialism). He does this by turning to a distinctive
characteristic of literary discourse—literary form—in order to subvert the
claims to truth of Islamic discourse. He employs a form that begins by
attempting to distinguish through alternating chapters between the waking
present-day "reality" of London (and Bombay) and Gibreel's dreams of his
participation in phantasmagoric historical events, and that deliberately
engineers the collapse of that distinction as the fictionality of the controlling
literary discourse asserts itself. In framing history within a fictional context
this novel is not behaving like a typical postmodern work of art in which, as
Jameson puts it, "the past as 'referent' finds itself gradually bracketed, and
then effaced altogether" (18). Rather, the mythologized past of the origins of
Islam is given a sense of lived historical actuality by being dramatized within
the novel; in the process it is demystified and returned to the fallible world
of human need and error. Simultaneously the fictionalized episodes involving
Gibreel's and Chamcha's escapades in Ellowen Deeowen (itself a product of
fiction, a child's nursery rhyme name for London) incorporate recognizable
elements from contemporary history references to Enoch Powell's famous
prediction in a speech to the House of Commons in 1969 that rivers of blood
would flow if immigration to Britain were not severely restricted;
recognition that Mrs. Thatcher was attempting "literally to invent a whole
goddam new middle class in this country" (270); the easily identifiable
London ghetto of Brickhall where the harassment of immigrants from the
Indian subcontinent by police and white youths boils over into a full scale
race riot. In these and other similar sections of the book contemporary
reality constantly erupts into and disrupts the impression that we are
occupying a world of pure imagination. This bricolage of historical and
fictional components is not available to the discourse of religion for which a
condition of the discourse is that the truth be accepted as of divine origin.
Whereas religion asserts the truth of its discourse (itself a will to power),
postmodern fiction ostensibly questions all forms of truth—those of both
historical fact and fictional invention.

Or does it? Behind the postmodern pastiche artist cannot one discern
the traditional writer as seer? However, instead of finding truth in long
established shared verities, Rushdie privileges a non-totalized, pluralistic,
open-ended form of discourse that coincides with postmodern writing
practices. Truth-value in his view is multiple and conflicting; it comes closer
in definition to the satisfactoriness of belief favored by pragmatic
philosophers. But the will to truth persists. A radical postmodern stance, on
the other hand, would proclaim the inaccessibility of truth and confine itself

to undermining all claims to absolute truth by and in discourse. Rushdie's position entails an assumption of superiority over those claiming to represent the truth by demonstrating the impossibility of doing so. Yet Rushdie implicitly elevates the multiple and conflictual nature of fictional discourse to a position of higher "truth." The very fact that it can incorporate the truth of religion into its manifold discourse—and *The Satanic Verses* certainly accomplishes this—is intended to show the superiority of plural fictional discourse to the unitary discourse of Islam. But, as Sara Suleri has acutely pointed out, "the desacrilizing [sic] of religion" in *The Satanic Verses* "can simultaneously constitute a resacrilizing of history" (190). Even history, however, is subordinated in the novel to the playful and irresistible powers of the artistic imagination. And, despite Rushdie's assertions to the contrary, the imagination goes well beyond the raising of questions in Rushdie's fiction. He tends to say one thing while accomplishing another. "Answers are cheap. Questions are hard to find," he asserted on the occasion of his emergence from hiding in September 1995 to talk about his latest novel, *The Moor's Last Sigh* (Montalbano E7). Yet the new novel shows him once again implicitly going beyond mere questions when deploring "the tragedy of multiplicity destroyed by singularity, the defeat of Many by One" (Wood 3). Why the insistence on binary polarity? What is wrong, for instance, with the One *and* the Many? Is this not the more genuine postmodern alternative to the exclusivity of the One?

Another characteristic of fictional discourse which Rushdie uses to subvert the truth claims of other unitary discourses is its ability to exploit a disparity between tone and substance. Having already written one comic epic (*Midnight's Children*), Rushdie considered *The Satanic Verses* the most comic of his first four novels (Jain 99). By "comedy" he understands "black comedy" "that doesn't always make you laugh" (Haffenden 240). Black comedy, which applies a comic tone to serious, even tragic subject matter, is a mode that in its written form is largely appropriated by literature. It is much used by postmodern writers confronted with a world on the brink of self-annihilation. Rushdie makes skillful use of this mode to undercut the serious tone which religious and political discourse employs most of the time. As the narrator says at one point, all he can offer in place of tragedy is the echo of it, a "burlesque for our degraded, imitative times, in which clowns re-enact what was first done by heroes and kings" (424). So heroes of the past (like Muhammad) are transformed into burlesque images (like Mahound) of their heroic models in this contemporary retelling of their stories.

Rushdie's use of black comedy is particularly evident in the passages concerning politics, capitalist greed and racism, all of which tend to mutually support one another's rhetoric. The epitome of this ethos is a minor character in the book, Hal Valance, an advertising executive who used to employ Chamcha for the voice-overs in his commercials. His hero is Deep Throat, who advised Bob Woodward: follow the money. Hal takes this advice to heart. Over lunch he confides to Chamcha:

> "I ... love this fucking country. That's why I'm going to sell it to
> the whole goddamn world, Japan, America, fucking Argentina.
> I'm going to sell the arse off it. That's what I've been selling all
> my fucking life: the fucking nation. The flag." (268)

Hal uses market research to justify removing all signs of black immigrants from his commercials, ending up by sacking Chamcha for being "a person of the tinted persuasion" (267). His justification: "ethnics don't watch ethnic shows" (265). Chamcha's media image is "just too damn racial" (265). (It is interesting that most of Hal's racial prejudices echo actual instances of racism that Rushdie records encountering while working for the advertising industry; see *Imaginary Homelands* 136-37.) Hal has no compunction about projecting his racism onto the immigrant community by accusing Chamcha of being too alien even for his fellow immigrants (for the "ethnic universe" as Hal puts it in his execrable commercialized jargon).

Political opposition to Hal's television show in which Chamcha starred comes from a black activist, Dr. Uhuru Simba. The police claim that, while under arrest, he fell off the lower of two bunks in his cell on waking up from a nightmare and broke his neck falling to the floor. The absurd improbability of this explanation is typical of the way Rushdie employs black humor to expose the repeated instances of racial bias offered during the eighties by the British police, who habitually employed a quasi-legal terminology (such as is used by the Community Relations Officer in the book) to lie their way out of their illegal actions. It is interesting to reflect that the reality of the lies told in court by the police during the prosecution of the Birmingham Five (or by Mark Fuhrman during the O. J. Simpson trial) was actually more subversive of social justice than the hilarious and absurd explanations offered in Rushdie's novel for the death in jail of Dr. Simba. The exposure effected by the supposedly superior discourse of fiction is less credible, if more enjoyable, than the simultaneous press exposure of police perjury by the supposedly inferior discourse of the media. Comedy, in this case black comedy, may expose the hypocrisies of those in authority, but cannot and does not attempt to affect the course of social history in the way that more utilitarian discourses can and do. In his role as a postmodern writer, Rushdie, in "bracketing off the real social world," (as Terry Eagleton writes of all postmodernists) "must simultaneously bracket off the political forces which seek to transform that order" (67-68).

The feature of fictional discourse that, it is claimed, distinguishes it from all other discourses is its unique and special use of language. Ever since the Russian Formalists argued that literary language defamiliarizes "everyday" language (but which? and whose?), there seems to have been general agreement that the discourse of fiction has at its disposal uses of language that other discourses may borrow but do not deploy systematically. If one accepts Foucault's assertion that discursive formations are governed by internal and external thresholds and limits "to master and control the great proliferation of discourse, in such a way as to relieve its richness of its most dangerous elements" and "to organize its disorder so as to skate round its most uncontrollable aspects" (*Archaeology/Discourse* 228), then the question arises whether literature is privileged above other forms of discourse because it allows within its borders more of the dangers and disorder of uncontrolled discourse, ostensible chains of signifiers refusing all semblance of closure. Foucault at times suggests as much, as when he writes, for instance, that literature's task is to say the most unsayable—the worst, the most secret, the most intolerable, the shameless" (*Power, Truth, Strategy* 91). Surely this is just what *The Satanic Verses* is doing? In a key essay, "Is Nothing Sacred?" Rushdie claims that one way in which his use of literary language acts in just this fashion is by undermining the monologic discourse of religion: "whereas religion seeks to privilege one language above all others, one text above all others, one set of values above all others, the novel has always been *about* the way in which different languages, values and narratives quarrel, and about the shifting relations between them, which are relations of power" (*Imaginary Homelands* 420). If Rushdie begins to sound like Foucault here this may be because he has read him and goes on in the essay to quote extensively from his "What Is an Author?"[5] It is significant, however, that neither Foucault nor Rushdie are entirely consistent in their claim to see in literary discourse a (negative) superiority over rival discursive formations.

By placing the monologic discourses of Islam and of nationalism within the polyglossic and heteroglossic discourse of fiction, Rushdie is able to decentre them and reveal the self interest that lies behind all special uses of language—except that of fiction to which he remains largely blind. Rushdie is extremely adept at using literary language to expose the polysemantic nature of terminology given a unitary (or, as Bakhtin would say, a centripetal) interpretation by the forces of authority. His sheer linguistic inventiveness

produces neologisms whose uncomfortable conjunctions expose the
contradictions inherent in the original word—"Bungledish" and
"BabyLondon" come to mind. With one inventive word combination,
London, the imperial center, the epitome of wealth and power, that held its
colonial peoples in captivity as Nebuchadnezzar did the Jews, is by verbal
association made to share the downfall of Babylon and become "the
habitation of devils" (Rev. 18.2). Similarly he strings words together the
effect of which is to undermine the conventional distinction between them:
"angelicdevilish," or "information/inspiration." Another linguistic feature
that enables Rushdie to make seemingly impossible connections in this
particular novel is his multiple use of the same proper names. He takes from
Islamic history Ayesha, the name of the Prophet's favorite wife, and uses the
same name for the most popular of the prostitutes in the Jahilia brothel, for
the Muslim visionary who led her fellow villagers to drown in the sea, and
for one of the girl prostitutes in London. Sacred and profane versions of
womanhood become fused and indistinguishable by this linguistic sleight of
hand. Whereas all the Ayeshas exist in Gibreel's dreams, the name of
Gibreel's lover, Alleluia Cone, who belongs to the waking world, becomes
metamorphosed via her nickname, Allie, to Al-Lat, the goddess denounced
by Mahound, and to Mount Cone (the equivalent to Mount Hira in Islamic
tradition) which Mahound ascends to receive the words of Allah, both of
which feature in Gibreel's dream world. In this instance Rushdie is using
language to reinforce the lack of distinction between material and
imaginative worlds. Many other characters share their name with characters
who belong to a different narrative sequence, such as Mishal, Hind, and
Salman, Mahound's scribe, who bears the same name as the author. Salman,
when he starts deliberately mistranscribing Mahound's dictation, discovers
that his "poor words could not be distinguished from the Revelation by
God's own Messenger" (367). Rushdie's mischievous use of his own name for
this character cannot help privileging Salman's subversive discourse in which
the natural slippage of language undermines the divine status of the Q'uran.
Is this deliberate on Rushdie's part?—an attempt to escape from his own
logocentrism by acknowledging it? Or is he once again giving narrative
sanction to the superior status of literary discourse?

Rushdie repeatedly dramatizes the heteroglossic quarrel between
languages that he, like Bakhtin, considers the special province of fictional
discourse. Heteroglossia, according to Bakhtin, is *"another's speech in another's
language ... a special type of double-voiced discourse"* (324). On two occasions
Rushdie pits a poet's linguistic dexterity against the thunderings of,
respectively, a politician and a prophet. Enoch Powell's racist speech

threatening rivers of blood is appropriated by the immigrant Jumpy Joshi as the title and subject for a poem in which the river of blood of the slain is transformed into the river of blood of humanity in all its variety: "Reclaim the metaphor, Jumpy Joshi had told himself. Turn it; make it a thing we can use" (186). The second instance involves the linguistic battle between Baal, the satirical poet, and Mahound who stands opposed to all poets and poetry. Baal pits his poetic satires against Mahound's Recitation. The role of the poet, Baal declares, echoing Foucault, is to "name the unnamable, to point at frauds, to take sides, start arguments, shape the world and stop it going to sleep" (97). Words, it turns out, can be mortal (as Rushdie knows to his cost). When Mahound finally has Baal in his power he orders him and the twelve prostitutes he married to be executed. "Whores and writers, Mahound," Baal shouts as he is dragged away. "We are the people you can't forgive." To which Mahound replies, "Writers and whores. I see no difference" (392). The grand narrative of religion can only see the plural and contradictory discourse of literature, what Rushdie has called "the schismatic Other of the sacred (and authorless) text," as a prostitution of the one truth (*Imaginary Homelands* 424). But doesn't the decentered discourse of postmodern literature equally see the grand narrative of religion as a prostitution of the truth? Why does its plurality and fragmentation make it preferable to a unitary master narrative? Different, yes. More comprehensive, because less insistent on the unitary nature of truth, maybe. But superior? It still betrays the same will to power as those grand narratives that it despises.

Although Foucault at times appears to suggest that fictional discourse enjoys some exemption from the limitations governing other discursive formations, in "The Discourse of Language," he treats literary discourse as an exemplary case when outlining the program for a critical (as opposed to a genealogical) analysis of discourse. Critical analysis involves identifying the forms of exclusion, limitation and appropriation that enable us "to conceive discourse as a violence that we do things, or, at all events, as a practice we impose upon them" (*Archaeology/Discourse* 229). Rushdie sees fictional discourse as an opportunity to counter "false" narratives, such as that of national politics, with the supposedly superior truth-value of imaginative literature. "I think it is a curious phenomenon of the twentieth century," Rushdie has said, "that politicians have got very good at inventing fictions which they tell us as the truth. It then becomes the job of the makers of fiction to start telling the (real) truth" (Interview, BBC). Whether the "(real)" is Rushdie's or Malise Ruthven's explanatory addition when she transcribed this excerpt, the claim to have access to the truth (and what is an unreal truth?) reveals the contradiction that lies at the heart of Rushdie's fictional polemic. The "real truth" is exactly what every discourse aspires to embody, according to Foucault. In Foucaultian terms *The Satanic Verses* has the same truth-value as those discourses it sets out to undermine. Its author unabashedly asserts that its own set of truths consist of "hybridity, impurity, intermingling, the transformation that comes of new and unexpected combinations of human beings, cultures, ideas, politics, movies, songs" (*Imaginary Homelands* 394). Rushdie additionally claims that his use of non-naturalistic material in his books constitutes "a method of producing intensified images of reality" (Haffenden 246). In privileging the non-naturalistic, is not Rushdie displaying his own discursive rules of exclusion, limitation and appropriation that do as much violence to things as do discourses privileging the naturalistic? Certainly others have interpreted his use of magic realism in less positive ways. Sara Suleri, for instance, felt that in *Shame* it represented a "startlingly conservative need to take refuge in formalism" (175). What appears to be a form of freedom in one discourse, that of literature, appears to be a sterile retreat within the context of another, that of liberal politics.

Rushdie's stream of comments about the nature of his work falls under one of Foucault's internal, as opposed to external, set of rules whereby "discourse exercises its own control" (*Archaeology/Discourse* 220). Foucault's diagnosis of the function of commentary is amusing, paradoxical and disturbing (for those of us engaged in the act of commentary). "Commentary," he writes, "averts the chance element of discourse by giving it its due: it gives us the opportunity to say something other than the text itself, but on condition that it is the text itself which is uttered and, in some ways, finalized" (221). Commentary, in other words, is charged with restricting the potentiality of discourse to proliferate uncontrollably by the use of repetition. Very few other novels have generated the volume of commentary that *The Satanic Verses* has in the short period since it was published. Most of these commentaries have attempted to appropriate the book to a particular ideology—anti-Islamic, pro-Islamic, secular, postcolonial, postmodern. By ignoring the totality of voices and discourses within the novel, they seek to fix its meaning within their particular discursive field. Rushdie's own voluminous commentary focuses on the plurality of meanings that postmodern fiction nurtures and exploits. But he remains blind to the fact that the indeterminacy and universal doubt which his commentary champions is frequently abandoned in the novel, not just when he assumes his post-colonial mantle, but also when satirizing the abuses of Islamic religion. Incidents such as the burning of the wax effigy of Mrs. Thatcher and the Imam's swallowing whole the armies of his supporters demonize the two leaders of racist nationalism and extreme Islamic militancy respectively in such a way as to leave little or no room for alternative readings. Rushdie might argue in his defence that he has also demonized his narrator, although his treatment of him is more ambivalent—and therefore truer to the spirit of the postmodern—than is his representation of the two leaders. Often posing as the Devil, the narrator is careful to leave open the possibility that he may as readily represent "Ooparvala," the "Fellow Upstairs" as "Neechayvala," the "Guy from Underneath" (318). Under cover of this ambivalence the narrator in his own commentary on the action betrays a fundamental vacillation between a postmodern open-endedness and an older humanist defense of liberal values.

But what of my own and similar instances of literary commentary that focus on (and thereby implicitly endorse) the novel's plurality of discourses, its multiplicity of voices, its postmodern resistance to totalizing explanations, positivist ideologies and narrative closure? Do not I have Rushdie's own commentaries as a guarantee of authenticity? Could not I argue that Rushdie and I in our commentaries are both opening up his fictional discourse, rather than circumscribing its fortuitousness, its propensity to semantically proliferate? After all the novel undermines not just Islamic fundamentalism but Christian fundamentalism (Eugene Dumsday, the American evangelist), not just British racism, but Indian racism (Hindu nationalism). It even makes fun of Baal, the representative of literary discourse within this literary discourse, Baal whose poems as he grows old degenerate into celebrations of loss. And yet does it really put down Baal's poetry? What form does his loss take? "It led him to create chimeras of form, lionheaded goatbodied serpenttailed impossibilities whose shapes felt obliged to change the moment they were set, so that the demotic forced its way into lines of classical purity and images of love were constantly degraded by the intrusion of elements of farce" (370). Is not this a description of Rushdie's own style of writing? Is not one of the features of postmodernism its conjunction of the demotic with the classical—what Jameson terms "aesthetic populism" (2)? Compared to the (modernist) clarity and finished quality of Mahound's verses, are not Baal's an anachronistic anticipation of postmodern literature? Does not Baal conveniently conform to Rushdie's definition of his own position within the contemporary literary universe? And do not Baal and Rushdie claim a privileged status for that position? And by writing this commentary am I not employing what Foucault calls "the infinite rippling of commentary" in order "to say *finally*, what has silently been articulated *deep down*" (*Archaeology/Discourse* 221)? Am I not privileging those qualities of semantic plurality and endless signification that characterize his and other postmodern literary discourses at the expense of the monologic utterances of religious, political and other authorities? Bakhtin, on the other hand, insists that "[l]anguage...is never unitary" (288). He claims that "[e]very concrete utterance of a speaking subject serves as a point where centrifugal as well as centripetal forces are brought to bear" (272). If *The Satanic Verses* is intent on exposing the centrifugal forces concealed within the discourses of politics and religion, then it would be appropriate for a commentator on the novel to concentrate on centripetal forces lurking behind its postmodern carnivalesque facade.

Instead, even the best commentators attempt to impose their own circumscription on the novel's polysemantic potential. Homi Bhabha views Rushdie's contextualization of the Qu'ran within the discourse of postmodern fiction that has brought on the charge of blasphemy:

> It is not that the "content" of the Koran is directly disputed; rather, by revealing other enunciatory positions and possibilities within the framework of Koranic reading, Rushdie performs the subversion of its authenticity by the act of cultural translation— he relocates the Koran's "intentionality" by repeating and rein- scribing it in the locale of the novel of postwar cultural migrations and diasporas. (226)

Bhabha is intent on revealing the impersonal operations of cultural translation. Blasphemy, he contends, constitutes "a moment when the subject-matter or the content of a cultural tradition is being overwhelmed or alienated, in the act of translation" (225). "Secular translation of the origins of Islam is itself the product of 'the disjunctive rewriting of the transcultural, migrant experience'" (226). Bhabha is clearly employing a postcolonial critical perspective. So he is endorsing, by reinterpreting, Rushdie's implicit ideological stance, on the grounds that it is representative of the way postcolonial newness makes its contribution to the postmodern world. As Foucault ironically observes, "the novelty lies no longer in what is said, but in its reappearance" (221). The apparent openness of postmodernism to both or all sides of an argument seems calculated to invite readers and commentators (even Rushdie) alike to try to tie down and circumscribe the plurality of meanings playfully offered by the text.

Foucault has not finished with me/us yet. Literary discourse, he argues, is also a prime example of a "fellowship of discourse" whose function is "to preserve or reproduce discourse, but in order that it should circulate within a closed community" (*Archaeology/Discourse* 225). Ridiculous, the reader will say; anyone who wants to can read *The Satanic Verses*. But then we look at what happens to those who attempt to read it outside the literary fellowship. Enraged Muslims are reminded by those within the fellowship of literature that this is mere fiction. To read into a novel an act of blasphemy is to misunderstand the nature of fictional discourse. As Billy Batusta, the producer of a "theological" movie about the life of Muhammad says in the novel, when asked if it would not be seen as blasphemous, "Certainly not. Fiction is fiction; facts are facts" (272). Rushdie has echoed this argument privileging the literary reading over all others in his many commentaries defending the novel. So have most of the book's commentators. When Margaret Thatcher and her foreign secretary dared to apologize on behalf of the British nation for any offense the book might have caused and expressed a dislike of its contents, the *Financial Times* published a rebuke from within the literary community proclaiming that "they are wholly unqualified, in their capacity as elected politicians, to have a useful opinion" on matters of literary taste (Appignanesi 148)—a perfect instance of the operation of a fellowship of discourse claiming exclusive right to comment on one of its own productions.

So where do I stand as a critic of this novel within the fellowship of discourse? Should I, in typical poststructuralist fashion, explore the semantic multiplicity of this text, its inclusion of competing discursive formations, its selfconscious deconstruction of its apparent thematic position(s)? Yet is there not something hypocritical about this impersonal stance? Like Rushdie, I lost my religious faith long ago, and share with him his dislike of religious dogmatism as well as his admiration for the state of transcendence that religion can produce. Like him, I was politically opposed to the Thatcher government's implicitly racist attitudes while living in London during her period in office. I have no patience with the concept of blasphemy (which incidentally illustrates another of Foucault's rules determining conditions under which discourse may be employed—ritual, which restricts who may even talk about the discursive content). Am I to pretend that I have no opinions of my own? Would not my readers and students simply lose patience with my liberal refusal to take sides? The appeal to plurality, with which much of the time I find myself in sympathy, seems to me totally inappropriate when faced with the need to take a unitary stand on subjects like the Thatcher government's immigration policy.

Is not, then, what is missing in Rushdie's fiction any critique of the pluralist position he espouses in his fiction? In his commentaries on the novel, he is prepared to adopt, as we have seen, a unitary (and superior) attitude to the dogma of Islamic fundamentalism and Thatcherite racism.

What is missing is any recognition on his part of this contradiction between his defence of his unitary stance as commentator of his own work and the creative plurality lying at the centre of his imaginative fiction. So there appears to be no escape from the blindnesses and limitations of discursive formations within which we operate. All I can do, and have done, is to make explicit the limitations of the literary discourses that on the one hand Rushdie and on the other hand I are working within. They are not superior to others. I choose to read and comment on fictional discourse finally because I personally feel more comfortable within it, because I like to enter that impossible world where writers name the unnamable, where language is a tool of power, where dreams hold their own with material reality, and where as Blake wrote (whom Rushdie quotes in the novel) "a firm perswasion that a thing is so" will "make it so" (338).[6]

NOTES

1. Cf. "Art is a product of history, not a cause ... so that the question of whether art should or should not be propaganda is unreal.... If not a poem had been written, not a picture painted, not a bar of music composed, the history of man would be materially unchanged" (Auden 393).

2. "I define *postmodern* as incredulity toward metanarratives." "Postmodern knowledge ... refines our sensitivity to differences and reinforces our ability to tolerate the incommensurable" (Jean-François Lyotard 38).

3. Foucault makes a point of distinguishing discourse analysis from the history of ideas. Discursive formations consist of statements which, like equations and unlike sentences, are functional, and, like events, are material but incorporeal. A discursive formation, Foucault asserts, "is made possible by a group of relations established between authorities of emergence, delimitation, and specification." It is "defined (as far as its objects are concerned, at least) if one can establish such a group; if one can show how any particular object of discourse finds in it its place and law of emergence; if one can show that it may give birth simultaneously or successively to mutually exclusive objects, without having to modify itself" (*The Archaeology of Knowledge* 44).

4. Rushdie is echoing Fredric Jameson's remarks in "The Cultural Logic of Late Capitalism." There he refers to "the pastiche of the stereotypical past" which "endows present reality ... with the spell and distance of a glossy mirage." He also identifies "the emergence of a new kind

of flatness or depthlessness" as a distinguishing feature of postmodernism (*Postmodernism* 9).

5. In "The Discourse on Language," Foucault groups the use of the author (by which he means the unifying principle in any group of writings that guarantees their coherence) within what he calls "principles of constraint," because, like commentary and disciplines, the author principle limits the hazards of discourse. He had already offered a more elaborate explanation of the author as a function of discourse in his essay "What Is an Author?" (*Language, Counter-Memory, Practice* 113-38).

6. I am indebted to Michael North for his helpful comments on an earlier version of this essay, which resulted in substantial alterations to it.

WORKS CITED

Ahmad, Aijaz. *In Theory: Classes, Nations, Literatures*. London: Verso, 1992.

Appignanesi, Lisa, and Sara Maitland, eds. *The Rushdie File*. London: Fourth Estate, 1989.

Auden, W. H. "The Public v. the Late Mr. William Butler Yeats." *The English Auden*. Ed. Edward Mendelson. London: Faber, 1977. 389-93.

Bakhtin, M. M. *The Dialogic Imagination: Four Essays*. Trans. Caryl Emerson and Michael Holquist. Ed. Michael Holquist. Austin: U of Texas P. 1981.

Bhabha, Homi K. *The Location of Culture*. New York: Routledge, 1994.

Eagleton, Terry. "Capitalism, Modernism and Postmodernism." *New Left Review* 152 (1985): 60-73.

Foucault, Michel. *The Archaeology of Knowledge and the Discourse on Language*. Trans. A. M. Sheridan Smith. New York: Pantheon/Random, 1972.

———. *Language, Counter-Memory, Practice. Selected Essays and Interviews by Michel Foucault*. Ed. Donald F. Bouchard. Ithaca, NY: Cornell UP, 1977.

———. *Michel Foucault: Power, Truth, Strategy*. Trans. Paul Foss and Meagan Morris. Ed. Meaghan Morris and Paul Patton. Sydney: Feral Publications, 1979.

Haffenden, John. *Novelists in Interview*. London: Methuen, 1985.

Jain, Madhu. Interview. *India Today* 15 Sept. 1988: 98-99.

Jameson. Fredric. *Postmodernism, Or, The Cultural Logic of Late Capitalism*. Durham: Duke UP. 1991.

Lyotard, Jean-François. *The Postmodern Condition: A Report on Knowledge.* Trans. Geoff Bennington and Brian Massumi. Minneapolis: U of Minnesota P, 1984.

Montalbano, William D. "Salman Rushdie Moves Out From the Shadows." *Los Angeles Times* 14 Sept. 1995: E1, 7.

Mufti, Aamir. "Reading the Rushdie Affair: An Essay on Islam and Politics." *Social Text* 29 (1991): 95-116.

Rushdie, Salman. *Imaginary Homelands: Essays and Criticism 1981-1991.* New York: Granta Books/Viking Penguin, 1991.

———. Interview. Desert Island Discs. BBC Radio 4, London. 8 Sept. 1988.

———. *The Satanic Verses.* New York: Viking Penguin, 1989.

Ruthven, Malise. *A Satanic Affair: Salman Rushdie and the Rage of Islam.* London: Chatto & Windus, 1990.

Suleri, Sara. *The Rhetoric of English India.* Chicago: U of Chicago P, 1992.

Wood, Michael. "Shenanigans." *London Review of Books* 7 Sept. 1995: 3, 5.

JOHN CLEMENT BALL

Pessoptimism: Satire and the Menippean Grotesque in Rushdie's Midnight's Children

In October 1988, Salman Rushdie cracked a joke during a panel discussion at Toronto's International Festival of Authors. With Indira Gandhi's assassination and Zia ul-Haq's recent airplane crash presumably on his mind, Rushdie remarked that his novels had featured a select group of politicians and that most of them had subsequently died. "Many met violent ends, he said: "I've come to believe maybe this is a service I could perform" (Remarks). This quip by a popular and influential author—whose construction by himself and his admirers as a secular, postmodern, post-colonial, Third World, cosmopolitan migrant makes him the very model of a valorized contemporary subject—ironically has the writer in opposition sounding like a very ancient figure: the fearsome curser-satirist of Robert C. Elliott's influential study *The Power of Satire*, a person whose words were seen by "primitive" peoples to have the power to kill (47).[1] Versions of such a figure populate Rushdie's novels. In *Shame*, Old Mr. Shakil and Iskander Harappa, spewing multi-directional oaths, call death upon enemies local and foreign. Gibreel as angel of destruction does the same to London in *The Satanic Verses*, and Baal, the satirist of Jahilia in that novel, composes "assassination songs" against murdered men's killers (98). But however noisy and fearsome they may be and however morally correct their objections to the status quo, such characters are inevitably compromised in Rushdie's

From *English Studies in Canada* 24, no. 1 (March 1998): 61-81. © 1998 by John Clement Ball.

narratives. They are variously shown to be delirious or desperate and out of synch with their times. The most concrete achievement of their ravings and curses is usually to hasten their own deaths.

Perhaps the jesting tone in which Rushdie allied himself with Elliott's primitive satirist was an expression of uneasy ambivalence about the role. In awe (or mock-awe) at the success of his previous satiric representations, Rushdie might nonetheless have had reason to wonder about the consequences of his latest satiric attack: would he hit another target or bring on his own death? *The Satanic Verses* had just been published, a novel whose biggest target was not a politician, or even a national political culture, but an international faith. It was already controversial for being deemed officially unwelcome in India. (Rushdie had a joke for this too, that day. When asked why Rajiv Gandhi had banned the book, he said that perhaps it was due to the fact that in a previous novel, "I was rude to his mother" (Remarks).) While *The Satanic Verses* was seen by many Muslims as a violent assault on sacred tradition, the real death-blow came not from Rushdie's text but from the words of the Ayatollah Khomeini. As Srinivas Aravamudan describes the logic of what became "the Rushdie affair,"

> The satirist's arrow, once it is defined as *literal*, as well as performative—through the workings of defamation or blasphemy—is often matched with a countershaft designed to accordingly damage the originator of the verbal attack. But the respondent in this war game can choose to raise the stakes, adopting more violently persuasive means. (17)

It was not Rushdie's text but the words pronouncing the *fatwa* against him that held the real power; as Aravamudan notes, "[the question] 'what can Khomeini do?' is entirely inseparable from 'what does Khomeini say?'" (18). Through this rebound effect, the satiric words of Rushdie's novel provoked the most notorious literary event of our time, and the author was left hoping that the Ayatollah's murderous words would be of the ineffectual sort and not cause his own violent end.

Rushdie has always been ambivalent about satire; before and after the *fatwa* he has alternately embraced and resisted association with it. But, while this paper does not attempt to steer its discussion of satire through the treacherous waters of the *Satanic Verses* debate, it does hope to show a very particular kind of ambivalence in Rushdie's earlier novel, *Midnight's Children*. It reads thematic and political cross-currents in the novel as functions of genre—specifically manifest in tensions between two countervailing types of satiric energy and the contrasting images of the body that most vividly show the differences between them. Rushdie's novels all exhibit this dynamic to some degree, and many of the interpretive questions swirling around the work of an author so often labelled a "satirist" can be usefully addressed by probing beyond the illusion of transparent meaning implied by casual uses of this signifier and asking what kinds of satire Rushdie's first major book actually contains.

In two famous essays Rushdie associates the writing of which he approves—and his own directly or by implication—with satire. "Outside the Whale" argues for recognition of the socio-political, referential contexts of all "works of art" and challenges George Orwell's "quietist option" for the writer (*Imaginary* 92, 97). Rushdie insists that writers take sides in debates and make "as big a fuss" as possible about injustices and oppressions; using "comedy, satire, deflation," the artist must not be "the servant of some beetle-browed ideology," but rather "its critic, its antagonist, its scourge" (98, 99). In *The Satanic Verses*, the satirist Baal describes his work, "[a] poet's work," in similar terms: "To name the unnamable, to point at frauds, to take sides, start arguments, shape the world and stop it from going to sleep" (97). Satire, in such statements, becomes the very essence of responsible art. "In Good Faith," Rushdie's post-*fatwa* response to attacks on his novel, defends the artist's "freedom to challenge, even to satirize all orthodoxies, including religious orthodoxies" (*Imaginary* 396). He denies that satire is an alien, unfamiliar mode to Islamic culture that can therefore be read only literally as blasphemy, yet feels he must contextualize the "forceful, satirical" language of the character Salman the Persian as the product of Gibreel's destabilized dreaming mind (399). His own purpose in writing the book was not to offend against Islam, he says; rather, "dispute was intended, and dissent, and even, at times, satire, and criticism of intolerance, and the like" (414). Here Rushdie appears comfortable with the idea of his writing as intentional satire (if not with its reception as such).

But if oppositional referentiality makes him a satirist, elsewhere Rushdie asserts that his work's social and political grounding makes him a realist, even a naturalist. While *Shame* may be "as black a comedy as it's possible to write," it is so "not for easy satirical reasons, but for naturalistic reasons. Because that seemed to be the only way that one could come somewhere close to describing the world that was there" ("*Midnight's*" 15). Here Rushdie asserts the fidelity of his representations against a literary snobbism that might discredit "easy satirical" techniques of caricature, fanciful exaggeration, and symbolic violence. He says that only in the West are his novels seen as fantasies, and only Westerners are likely to forget that

Shame is about a real place and real dictators. In India, he proudly observes, nobody talks about *Midnight's Children* "as a fantasy novel; they talk about it as a novel of history and politics" (*"Midnight's"* 15).

From a theoretical standpoint, none of this is very rigorous (nor should we necessarily expect it to be). Rushdie uses "realistic" and "naturalistic" loosely as synonyms for "referential." And referentiality has always been a component of satire, easy or otherwise. It is also a popular option for fantasy, if only as the recognizable context against which the fantastic appears *as* fantastic (Todorov, *Fantastic* 25). Rushdie's ambivalence about satire transcends the kill-or-be-killed fate that faces the ancient curser-satirist. It can be read as an expression of a time-honoured ambiguity inherent in the protean manifestations and shadowy generic status of satire. If satire is principled dissent against specific instances of terror, injustice, authoritarian coercion, and shameful behaviour, then yes, Rushdie writes it. If satire is cheap-shot caricatures and a will to power over easily conjured phantasms, then no, it is not a term that he would have us use.

Rushdie's critics often link his novels with satire and the satiric.[2] Typically, they presume a conventional definition of satire as a playfully didactic mode of referential attack using various deforming techniques of representation and rhetoric. Target-specific satiric jabs are certainly prevalent in all of Rushdie's work, yet it is hard not to agree with James Harrison when he argues that overemphasizing Rushdie's activity as a satirist may limit other interpretive possibilities. Although Harrison favours a reading of *Shame* as "a satire" with "close to a single satiric purpose—almost a single target" (5), he argues that its predecessor cannot be adequately accounted for under that rubric. *Midnight's Children*, despite its very "angrily written" Book Three, and despite many incidental "rapier thrusts...en passant" towards specific Indian phenomena in Books One and Two, is not, as Harrison says, predominantly satiric in tone: "The targets for such satire are too scattered, and there is too much else going on" (46, 48).

This view is preferable to Tariq Ali's early reading of *Midnight's Children* as "centrally an attack on clearly identifiable targets: the indigenous ruling classes in South Asia"—"a devastating political indictment" characterized by "pessimism and nihilism" (87, 93). To Ali one is compelled to respond, "Is that all? Is the novel *only* pessimistic, *only* an attack, and *only* on the ruling classes?" Ali dismisses Rushdie's own view that the book's apparent despair and pessimism are countered by its "optimistic" inscription of "the Indian talent for non-stop self-regeneration" through its teeming density of stories (*Imaginary* 16). Versions of this positive reading are put forward by many other critics, however, and a recurring debate over

Midnight's Children concerns whether it is best seen as celebration or critique, as ultimately optimistic or pessimistic about the overarching referent behind its fictions: post-independence India.

The temptation here, as with all polarities, is to seek a middle ground. In a recent article Neil ten Kortenaar, acknowledging the novel's "paradoxical" reception "as both a celebration of India and a withering satire on the very possibility of the nation-state" (41, 57), performs a subtle and compelling reading of its historical allegory that challenges Timothy Brennan's view of Rushdie as one of the Third World's "satirists of nationalism and dependency" (Brennan 81). Showing in detail how Rushdie's allegory literalizes conventional metaphors of national history, ten Kortenaar argues that such metaphors, once exposed as the fictions they are, can nevertheless offer a form of "truth." In his view, "Rushdie's novel explodes the notion of the nation having a stable identity and a single history, then invites a sceptical, provisional faith in the nation that it has exploded" (41–42). It is a critique that ultimately affirms.

While ten Kortenaar's may be the most nuanced reading yet of the novel's allegorical gestures, the same critical paradox may be approached through a different generic category. Allegory is undoubtedly central to the novel's meanings, but there are many other genres, sub-genres, and modes at work, including autobiography, epic, bildungsroman, picaresque, magic realism, fantasy, and satire. As a generic medley, Rushdie's novel can be reconfigured through the lens of a subsuming and controlling genre: the Menippean satire. Not only does *Midnight's Children* fit the chief characteristics of this genre (most notably theorized by Mikhail Bakhtin), but the question of whether it optimistically celebrates or satirically negates the nation can be seen as a function of a generic tension between Menippean satire and a more conventional negative satire involving referential attack. That tension, revealed in large part through contrasting images of the grotesque body, results in an ambivalent and at times conflicted vision of national history best captured in the term "pessoptimist," a neologism that Rushdie once borrowed from Edward Said (who in turn borrowed it from the Palestinian novelist Emile Habiby) (*Imaginary* 168; Said 26).

Midnight's Children exemplifies many features of Menippean satire (or "menippea") as discussed by Bakhtin.[3] When Saleem narrates his familial and personal histories, he aspires "to encapsulate the whole of reality" (75)— the multiplicitous reality of the Indian subcontinent that he claims to contain within him and to reflect metaphorically through his life. He fears absurdity and seeks the meaning and purpose of his life history as well as, by extension, his nation's. Likewise, Bakhtin's Menippean satire, also called "encyclopedic satire" (Payne 5), is characterized by "an extraordinary philosophical universalism and a capacity to contemplate the world on the broadest possible scale. The menippea is the genre of 'ultimate questions'" (*Problems* 115). It deals with topical issues, addresses the ideologies of the day, and arises in periods of social change "when national legend was already in decay, … in an epoch of intense struggle among numerous and heterogeneous religious and philosophical schools and movements" (*Problems* 119). Rushdie's 63-year narrative begins in 1915, the year of Mohandas Gandhi's return from South Africa to join nationalist agitation, and ends in 1978, shortly after the end of Indira Gandhi's Emergency. Its chronological centrepoint and thematic focus is the moment of independence in 1947, when an imposed and hierarchical imperial order gave way to a post-colonial democratic self-rule. Menippean satire is a "utopian" genre (*Problems* 118), and Rushdie captures the utopian spirit of freedom, optimism, and newness of the transitional period both through images of celebratory crowds and of Saleem's birth, growth, and adoration by his family. It is also evident in an exuberant and transgressive narrative style reflective of the multiplicitous energies of carnival.

Menippean satire in Bakhtin's account is based on his theory of carnival as a liberating and subversive challenge to the political status quo. Carnival (as social event and transcendent principle) represents a utopian transgression of ossified hierarchies; its literary manifestation, the Menippean satire, is thus a positive, future-oriented genre in which pluralism and festive laughter represent signs of renewal, hope, and incipient democracy. Rushdie establishes such principles as working norms in portraying newly independent India's proliferating possibilities. Bakhtin's privileging of discovery over certitude, participation over detachment, unstable becoming and transformation over official authority's stasis and negation is echoed by Rushdie's own preferences. The colourful "carnivalization of speech" (*Rabelais* 426) that Saleem's polyphonic medley of discourses and languages achieves makes his monologue a "microdialogue," which Bakhtin sees as possible when a voice incorporates a multiplicity of mutually conflicting and interrupting voices (*Problems* 75). Indeed, embedded genres and a mixed style are key features of Menippean satire. Saleem's physical, spiritual, and mental mutability establishes identity and character as process. Like the heroes of the Dostoevsky novels that are Bakhtin's privileged specimens of post-Rabelaisian Menippean satire, Saleem's richness as a character is a direct function of the fact that he "never coincides with himself" (*Problems* 59). For if, as Saleem constructs his identity, "I am the sum total of everything that went before me, of all I have been seen done, of everything done-to-me ... everyone everything whose being-in-the-world affected was affected by mine" (370), then that identity will be not only multiple but also changing constantly. In the essays collected in *Imaginary Homelands*, Rushdie regularly voices his approval of such Bakhtin-friendly concepts as hybridity, pluralism, impurity, transformation, and newness. He prefers questions to answers, and opposes absolutism in favour of provisional, indeterminate truths. He insists on a social grounding and social mandate for art and believes, like Bakhtin, that "the novel is one way of denying the official, politicians' version of truth" (*Imaginary* 14).

Menippean satire for Bakhtin involves "*an extraordinary freedom of plot and philosophical invention*"; it boldly uses the fantastic and extraordinary for "the provoking and testing of a philosophical idea, a discourse, a *truth*" (*Problems* 114). Saleem proposes that events such as the telepathic Midnight Children's Conference have allegorical or symbolic value intimately bound to the truths that he wants to confirm. In comments that seem custom-made for *Midnight's Children*, Bakhtin notes the genre's combination of

> the free fantastic, the symbolic, at times even a mystical-religious element with an extreme and (from our point of view) crude *slum naturalism*.... The idea here fears no slum, is not afraid of any of life's filth.... The menippea loves to play with abrupt transitions and shifts, ups and downs, rises and falls, unexpected comings together of distant and disunited things, mésalliances of all sorts. (*Problems* 115, 118)

Bakhtin also identifies abnormal psychological states—including split personality, unusual dreams, and strange passions—as characteristic of Menippean satire (116). Saleem's dream of the Widow, his telepathy, his amnesiac "man-dog" phase, and his obsession with Jamila Singer are just a few of Rushdie's many uses of "abnormal states." The novel also features the "scandal scenes," "eccentric behavior," and violations of norms and customs noted by Bakhtin (117), and displays the "passion for spatial and temporal expanses" characteristic of the genre (Stam 134).[4]

But if Menippean principles attain a normative value by their congruence with central features of *Midnight's Children's* style, plot, characterization, and thematic concerns, as well as with statements of authorial philosophy, Rushdie also shows those valorized principles under siege by tyrannic forces of monologic authority. The darkening of tone that so many readers experience in Book Three marks a defeat—in India's political realm as well as Saleem's personal realm—of optimism and joy by the very retrograde powers that the carnival-minded Menippean satirist would wish to subvert or relegate to the past. Overcome by a reality that no longer coheres with its principles, Menippean satire gives way to a more negative, attack-oriented satire. The Menippean vision remains implicit, however, as the normative basis from which the negative satiric attack is launched.

Book Three's general shift in tone from optimism to pessimism, from hope to its absence, is actually not as great or as sudden as some critics suggest. There is plenty of incidental satire in Books One and Two. Targets include India's class- and caste-based prejudices (through the snobbery of the participants in the Midnight Children's Conference), war propaganda, election-day thuggery, political corruption and inefficiency, Eurocentric history-writing (in which Europeans "'discovered'" India [13]), and Indian mimicry (displayed by the inhabitants of Methwold's Estate and metaphorically conveyed in the description of businessmen turning white). These satiric jabs are certainly subordinate to the predominant themes of Saleem's and India's early years, which cluster around Menippean concepts of hope, newness, becoming, and possibility. But they do help to show that such optimism is a construct made from a deliberately selective vision. Indeed, this optimism comes at a great cost: in order to stress the positive excitement of "the infant state's attempts at rushing towards full-sized adulthood" (232), Rushdie must occlude the horrors of violence and displacement experienced by millions during the Partition riots. Books One and Two do contain many episodic portrayals of anti-Menippean energies—denial, oppression, and monologism. But from the standoffs between Reverend Mother and Aadam Aziz to the careerist misrepresentations of Jamila Singer, these episodes do not inspire Saleem's anger because, like the Partition riots, they do not directly harm him. They can be sent up with playful detachment and thus domesticated to the exuberant manipulations of Menippean satire. Until the loss of his hair tonsure and fingertip, the most significant act of direct and unasked-for imposition upon Saleem is Mary Pereira's baby-switch; this, of course, has the positive effect of giving him a family and moving him out of the slum. Those later bodily mutilations, however, mark the formal introduction, long before Book Three, of the darker, more negative satiric energies that will increasingly dominate the narrative. In fact, the body is a primary locus on which the novel's generic tensions are enacted.

Saleem's body functions as an extreme example of what Peter Brooks calls the discursive, textualized body. In *Body Work*, Brooks defines the body in modern literature as "a site of signification—the place for the inscription of stories—and itself a signifier, a prime agent in narrative plot and meaning"

(5–6). Saleem engages in what Brooks calls the semiotic retrieval of the body in order to make it signify, or represent, or mean (8, 22). But for Saleem as actor-protagonist *in* narrative, that body has already been written upon in the sense that it has been marked and scarred. To inscribe the body is to recognize the artistic dilemma inherent in the contradiction between generating meaning and discovering meaning—between writing (or speaking) the body oneself and reading (or listening to) a body already written-upon by others. Subsumed in that structural tension of writing/reading and speaking/listening are the dualities of subject/object, self/other, controller/controlled, creation/destruction, active/passive, and affirming-Menippean-satire/negative-debunking-satire. The novel encourages us to evaluate all such pairings hierarchically: the first element is valorized, the second the endangering threat to it. Thus the objectifying inscription of negative historical events on Saleem's body (border disputes, wars, the Emergency) determines and largely limits his freedom to inscribe his body positively as a subject in history. His "buffetted" (38) body affects the stories that can be told, as well as the manner of their telling, which is "faster than Scheherazade" (11). Saleem, after all, is much more convincing as "the sort of person to *whom things have been done*" (232) than as the central, determining influence on Indian history that he sometimes claims to be, no matter how scandalously appealing the Menippean empowerments of the latter may be. Saleem's body in its grotesque aspect—an irregular body whose open apertures exist in a dynamic give-and-take with the world that increasingly favours take over give—becomes the primary site on which a normative Menippean ethos is overwhelmed by a bitter, angry satire of negation and despair.

The first step in tracing this process in detail—in explicating the complex and varying connections of grotesque body images and satiric ethos—requires the recognition of a central device in Rushdie's novel: the literalized metaphor. When the freezing of Muslim assets causes Ahmed Sinai's testicles to freeze and Sinai babies to cease issuing forth, or when Saleem as mirror of India literally comes to contain its multiplicity in his head, connections that in a realistic novel would remain metaphorical—enacted in language only—are turned into literal events by the freedom of magic realism, or what we might call the Menippean fantastic. Many critics have remarked on Rushdie's use of this device in the novel.[5] Most useful for our purposes, however, is a general theory advanced by Geoffrey Galt Harpham in *On the Grotesque*. Harpham views the merging of metaphoric and literal as a property of mythic narrative, which traverses normally separate categories such as animal and human, or animate and inanimate. "At the margin of figurative metaphor and literal myth," he writes, "lies the grotesque, both and neither, a mingling and a unity" (53). This blending of realms has a levelling effect on modern Western hierarchies of meaning and Aristotelian logic (54). It offers instead an infinitely inclusive field of significance that embraces contradiction—one in which "no realm of being, visible or invisible, past or present, is absolutely discontinuous with any other, but all equally accessible and mutually interdependent" (51).

Under Harpham's rubric, the trope of the literalized metaphor can be contextualized within Rushdie's project in several ways. First, it expresses Rushdie's preference for contradiction and multiplicity instead of a totalizing, unitary truth. Second, it captures the mythic sensibility of a novel steeped in Hindu mythology, a novel that can be read as a creation myth of independent India. Third, it evokes a traditional Hindu cast of mind that makes no distinction between the divine and the human or man and nature; all are interconnected, and all are equally real (Younger 15). As Wendy Doniger O'Flaherty notes, Hindus accept contradiction and pluralism and reject attempts to eliminate alternative views (5–7). Fourth, if the literalized metaphor is compatible with Rushdie's worldview and with Hindu thought, it also agrees with the carnival spirit of Menippean satire which favours contradictory conjoinings, juxtapositions, and the revolutionary inter-penetration of "officially" bounded and stratified realms of human life and of literary representation. Fifth and finally, this trope translates abstract ideas into physiological conditions. Virtually all of Rushdie's literalized metaphors manifest themselves as bodily abnormalities and thus participate in the multiplicitous indeterminacy of the grotesque. In the literalized metaphor, then, the valorized transgressive openness of Menippean satire joins forces with the valorized transgressive openness of Bakhtin's related notion of the grotesque body.

The two concepts of Menippean satire and grotesque body are never linked in Bakhtin's work.[6] But he clearly finds both Menippean satire and grotesque realism preferable to what he sees as the deriding, oppositional type of satire. "The satirist whose laughter is negative," Bakhtin says, "places himself above the object of his mockery, he is opposed to it" (*Rabelais* 12). Menippean satire and the grotesque are associated with a participatory, ambivalent laughter that enables both affirmation and critique (*Rabelais* 11; *Dialogic* 26). Both ideas are theorized in conjunction with the concepts of carnival, dialogism, and ambivalence, and both involve top-to-bottom reversals of hierarchy, crude naturalism, and bodily imagery suggestive of incompleteness and becoming and a spirit of renewal and liberation from the status quo. Bakhtin's Menippean satire and his grotesque body have enough in common to warrant yoking them together in what we might call "the Menippean grotesque."

As noted above, Bakhtin locates the origins of the modern Menippean spirit in "a carnival sense of the world" (*Problems* 134) associated with medieval folk culture. Carnivalesque energy represents liberation from official orders, hierarchical fixities, and prevailing truths through a celebration of change, incompleteness, and renewal. In the work of Rabelais, through which Bakhtin's theory of carnival is largely developed, the primary symbol that makes concrete the transformative potential of the carnival spirit is the grotesque body: the ingesting, defecating, urinating, and fornicating body of open apertures, where the physiological self flows into and out of the world. This conception of the unfinished body "blended with the world, with animals, with objects" turns it into a version of the "cosmic" realm, "the entire material bodily world in all its elements" (*Rabelais* 27).

Bakhtin's ethical view of the grotesque body as a valorized semiotic medium challenges traditional alignments of grotesque images with satiric attack. Wolfgang Kayser, for instance, sees the grotesque as having origins in "a satiric world view" (186–87) although he takes pains to distinguish the two concepts (37). Theorizing the grotesque as "experienced only in the act of reception" (181), Kayser identifies the feelings it evokes variously as estrangement, alienation, confusion, disparagement, and helplessness in the face of a disintegrating order. For him, the grotesque is a glimpse of "a chaos that is both horrible and ridiculous" (53), and it reinforces "the discrepancy between world and Self" (146–47). Bakhtin, for whom a disintegrating order is cause for joy, explicitly challenges Kayser for stressing the negative, the alien, and the terrifying at the expense of what Bakhtin sees as a positive counterpart:

> The existing world suddenly becomes alien (to use Kayser's terminology) precisely because there is the potentiality of a friendly world, of the golden age, of carnival truth. Man returns unto himself. The world is destroyed so that it may be regenerated and renewed. While dying it gives birth. (*Rabelais* 48)

This rhapsodic view of the grotesque's liberating, revolutionary, and democratizing potential is at the heart of Bakhtin's theory. That power and potential are a function of the carnivalesque and of the grotesque body's unfinished nature and unbounded interaction with the world. Images of what Bakhtin calls "the material bodily stratum"—with its open orifices producing urine, excrement, and reproductive fluids—may in one sense be associated with debasement: for Bakhtin, "debasement is the fundamental artistic principle of grotesque realism; all that is sacred and exalted is rethought on the level of the material bodily stratum or else combined and mixed with its images" (*Rabelais* 370–71). But these images are also ambivalent as they are associated in various ways with fertility, renewal, and regeneration. The grotesque can therefore serve traditional satiric purposes of attacking established pieties or stratifications of power. Bakhtin emphasizes, however, the constructive changes and "progress" (406) that such an attack can inaugurate, rather than the deconstructive, leveling effect of the attack itself. This orientation towards the optimistic over the pessimistic, the transformative over the critical, marks Bakhtin's greatest departure from other theorists.

Inscriptions of idea on the body in *Midnight's Children*—whether literalized or simply metaphoric—are normatively offered as positive, enabling events. Saleem's first self-description is as "a swallower of lives" who has "consumed multitudes" (11); he says, "To understand just one life, you have to swallow the world" (108). The individual gives way to the crowd, and for Rushdie this can be a good thing with enormous potential, just as Bakhtin's grotesque, unfinished body fulfills itself when it "swallows the world and is itself swallowed by the world" (*Rabelais* 317). For Bakhtin, the important parts of the grotesque body are the open cavities, orifices, and apertures where "the confines between bodies and between the body and the world are overcome; there is an interchange and an interorientation" (317). In *Midnight's Children*, the most important apertures are the nose and the genitals. Aadam Aziz's nose, described in the novel as "the place where the outside world meets the world inside you" (19), is said to have "dynasties waiting inside it" (15), thus affiliating itself with the motifs of intermingling, fertility, and regeneration that Bakhtin associates with bodily orifices and protruberances. Saleem's "mighty cucumber of a nose" (152) leaks into the world in the early years when he seems to have the greatest power and stature in his world; these are also the years when India as a new nation inspires the greatest optimism. But after the accident in the washing-chest Saleem's nose becomes a conduit for a greater form of access to and interaction with the world through his telepathic mind. It becomes a channel of communication (Stam 163). In this mode, the nose offers great hope and potential, but for the idealistic Saleem the results of his telepathic activities are as disappointing as the political events with which they overlap. When the nose is later surgically drained, the effect is a disconnection from the multiple voices of community. The drainage is described through images of absence, isolation, and infertility: "A connection broken (for ever). Can't hear anything (nothing there to hear). Silence, like a desert" (295). The most important subsequent use to which his nose's interactive capacities are put is the aiding and abetting of death in the 1971 war. Increasingly over the length of the novel, the interaction between body and world through the nose is associated less with possibility and achievement and more with futility and ignoble deeds.

The nose is only one location for the novel's important imagery of leaking or dripping. In other instances, the images are also normatively positive. When Saleem says that "'things—even people—have a way of leaking into each other ... like flavours when you cook'" (39), he sees this as not merely inevitable but good. Leaking leads to transformation, creation, and newness—to a productive impurity. And the fact that "the past has dripped into me" (39) allows Saleem to perform the creative act of narration. But there are many negative, or at best ambivalent, uses of this imagery. The young Saleem's enormous dripping nose may be a metaphor of growth, potency, and potential, but "Toxy Catrack, of the outsize head and dribbling mouth," is an image of isolated imbecility (129). And any positive associations attendant on baby Saleem's "heroic programme of self-enlargement" by draining successive women's breasts is qualified by corollary associations with greed, excess, unnaturalness, and the sterility of life-giving bodily organs rendered "dried-out as a desert after only a fortnight" (124).

Examples abound. When the Rani of Cooch Naheen turns white, her disease leaks into history and infects businessmen after independence. Saleem's later speculation that his lust for meaning and centrality leaked into Indira Gandhi has clearly negative connotations: the leakage has produced the demagogic, multiplicity-denying slogan "*India is Indira and Indira is India*" for the post-Emergency election campaign (406). In a particularly negative use of the leak image, Saleem tells us that "children are the vessels into which adults pour their poison, and it was the poison of grown-ups which did for us" (249). The Midnight Children's Conference fails because the children begin replicating the poison of their parents' prejudices and can no longer collaborate. Saleem's cousin Zafar receives a heavy dose of adult poison after leaking urine into his bedclothes: his father hurls abuses ("Pimp! Woman! ... Coward! Homosexual! Hindu!" [281]). Later, Zafar's fiancée discovers his leakage and responds by willfully obstructing her own—the menstrual flow—so that she can put off becoming an adult and avoid marrying him. When Aunt Alia impregnates her cooking with negative emotions as a means of bitter revenge, the emotions leak into the members of Saleem's family who consume "the birianis of dissension and the nargisi koftas of discord" (320). The effect is to drain the family of strength, sense, competence, coherence, love, and hope.

Saleem himself goes through a series of drainings, beginning with the loss of his finger. As noted above, this event marks the first step in the darkening, more pessimistic tone that finds its most intense expression in Book Three. The finger-mutilation is described by Saleem in apocalyptic terms that clearly challenge the Bakhtinian vision of the unbounded body as an emblem of the positive and regenerating flow between realms. In fact, Saleem takes pains to separate the non-material intermingling of *identities* from any material affront to the body's boundaries:

> O eternal opposition of inside and outside! Because a human being, inside himself, is anything but a whole, anything but homogeneous; all kinds of everywhichthing are jumbled up inside him, and he is one person one minute and another the next. The body, on the other hand, is homogeneous as anything. Indivisible, a one-piece suit, a sacred temple, if you will. It is important to preserve this wholeness. But the loss of my finger … has undone all that. Thus we enter into a state of affairs which is nothing short of revolutionary; and its effect on history is bound to be pretty damn startling. Uncork the body, and God knows what you permit to come tumbling out. Suddenly you are forever other than you were; and the world becomes such that parents can cease to be parents, and love can turn to hate. (230–31)

A finger, of course, is not one of Bakhtin's orifices of interaction between the body's internal and external spheres. The unnatural, externally imposed flowing of blood from a finger is a different order of event from a dripping nose or feeding breast—hence Saleem's dire tone. And the novel's instances of leaking and draining are in general increasingly imposed, increasingly the outcome of external assault on the body, distinct from the normal flow of orifices. At the end of his life Saleem's body, "buffeted by too much history," begins unnaturally to crack and crumble as a result of being "subjected to drainage above and drainage below" (38). The drainages above (of Saleem's nose) and below (of his testicles) are both violent, inflicted processes that prevent further natural drainings (of snot and sperm). In some instances, then, drainage means the natural transgressions of the body's limits through the emissions of apertures associated in Bakhtin's system with abundant excess, new life, hope, and Menippean satire. In others, drainage means imposed transgressions of the bounded body and is associated with monologic tyranny and negative satire; the sterilization of the midnight children as "the draining-out of hope" during Emergency rule (421) is the novel's central satiric moment.

Depending on contexts, then, images of the grotesque body draining into the world may have either positive or negative thematic value. In the first case they serve a Menippean vision of renewal and progress referentially directed towards the qualities of Indian society that Rushdie valorizes: pluralism, democracy, hybridity, and change. In the second case they serve as an angry satiric attack on forces in modern India and Pakistan that deny those principles: fundamentalism, despotism, purity, and stasis. In both cases the satiric method and philosophy match the perceived primary qualities of the referents. The imagery is ambivalent, but not in Bakhtin's sense, which posits the positive associations (birth, community, and renewal) as accompanying and ultimately triumphing over the negative associations (death, degeneration, and alienation) embedded in the grotesque.

Some of these negative, target-oriented satiric images of death by draining do, in fact, come with corollary suggestions of fertility, but they take on an attenuated, parodic form. Saleem's surreal vision of a field of "crops" on a field near Dacca after the 1971 war turns out to be a pyramid of dead and dying soldiers—including three childhood friends—"leaking nourishing bone-marrow into the soil" (360). This image of wasted youth supports Rushdie's satiric indictment of the agents behind a gruesome and unnecessary war far more powerfully and relevantly than it offers mitigating optimism through images of human crops and fertilizer; if anything, these images mock the very notion of fertility. Similarly, Saleem's alter ego Shiva is said to fulfill both aspects of his divine namesake (425): he represents destruction by helping sterilize his fellow midnight children and procreation by "strewing bastards across the map of India" (395). But if Saleem is unequivocal in aligning the removal of the midnight children's reproductive powers with a satiric denunciation of Emergency as "the draining-out of hope" for India's future, he seems hesitant to celebrate the next generation, Shiva's offspring, as a countervailing cause for optimism. Young Aadam Sinai and his peers will be a "tougher" generation, "not looking for their fate in prophecy or the stars, but forging it in the implacable furnaces of their wills" (431). If this description suggests an agency and effectiveness never achieved by Saleem and *his* peers, it sounds closer to the selfish, bloody-minded, and totalitarian agency of Shiva than the democratic idealism of Saleem. If these children of a darker era can challenge the current tyrannical powers of negation, it will be to replace them with something equally monologic and just as scary. A sense of apprehensive awe inheres in Saleem's description of this group as "fearsomely potent kiddies, growing waiting listening, rehearsing the moment when the world would become their plaything" (431). This image of regeneration proves no more encouraging than the Emergency's other horrific contribution to reproduction imagery, the multiply cloned versions of Sanjay Gandhi that parody and discredit the very idea of regeneration.

A number of Western literary and sociological traditions are evoked by Rushdie's satiric imagery of tyrannic bodily abuse. English satirists from Swift to Huxley have championed the rights of the individual body against state interference. In Michel Foucault's pessimistic vision, the body is always institutionally coerced and ideologically conditioned to meet the utilitarian demands of "discipline" and "power," which see a docile and subjected body as socially, politically, and economically productive ("Body"; "Docile"). For Foucault, moreover, the body "manifests the stigmata of past experience"; as "the inscribed surface of events," it is necessarily "a volume in perpetual disintegration" because a body imprinted by history is a body destroyed by history ("Nietzsche" 148). The chief targets of Rushdie's negative satiric anger in *Midnight's Children* are institutionalized policies and procedures of a post-independence Indian state whose short history, written upon Saleem's body, ultimately destroys it.

But for Rushdie the body is not always necessarily the controlled, acted-upon body of Foucault. His novel is equally interpretable through a more traditional view espoused by the Enlightenment thinkers Adam Smith and David Hume, who in Catherine Gallagher's words "maintained a two-millenia-old tradition of seeing the individual body as sign—both as metaphor and as source—of the health or infirmity of the larger social body" (83). The healthy baby Saleem reflects a generally healthy young Indian state, while the bodily deterioration of the older Saleem is both a metaphor and a literal effect of ill health in the realms of the state and the body politic. Again, as a process these changing connections accommodate both Menippean-optimistic and critical-pessimistic forms of satiric energy. Interestingly, Rushdie's novel is also compatible with the major eighteenth-century challenger to Smith's and Hume's traditional alignments of bodily and social health. Thomas Malthus argued that healthy individual bodies may reflect a healthy social body in the present, but could cause its enfeeblement in the future by proliferating themselves and causing overpopulation. The healthy "body is a profoundly ambivalent pheno-menon" for Malthus because of its capacity to "destroy the very prosperity that made it fecund, replacing health and innocence with misery and vice" (Gallagher 84). Malthus's pessimism resonates strongly in the context of

India's burgeoning population and the various state campaigns of suasion aimed at curbing the social body's growth through birth control. It resonates too with the uncertain promise attributed to the second generation of midnight children sired by Shiva.

Indian concepts of the body are equally ambivalent, equally multiple and contradictory, and resonate in equally complex ways with Rushdie's satiric intents. As Gavin Flood shows in a survey of views among different Indian philosophical-religious groups, the body is thought of variously as the only criterion of personal identity, as an inseparable part of unitary reality, as a place of bondage and suffering, or as a locus of liberation (47). Saleem's body is all of these at different points. And if both Saleem and Rushdie value certain kinds of impurity and intermingling, the novel also invokes and gains satiric power from a significant strain in Indian thought that privileges bodily perfection and purity. In orthodox Brahminism the body is seen as "polluted through its effluents"; passion and spontaneity must be suppressed to keep it safe from possession by malevolent forces (Flood 49). Indian art typically takes the perfect yogic body as a standard of perfection; discipline and penance make the body "etherealized so that it may become a fit vehicle for the realization of moksa [release from earthly bondage]" (Mukerjee 129).

A fascinating example of bodily discipline and perfection is documented in Joseph S. Alter's study of Indian wrestling, *The Wrestler's Body: Identity and Ideology in North India*. Alter describes the wrestler as embodying an ideology of social duty and nationalist reform through somatic disciplines of diet, exercise, and abstinence. Wrestling bouts disregard caste strictures of touchability; by positing the body as the sole criterion of identity, such bouts critique the hierarchical construction of "the Hindu body [as] the docile subject of a pervasive political anatomy" (24, 167–97). Because Hindu philosophy sees mind and body as "intrinsically linked," not separable into a "simple duality," the wrestler's physical exercise and mental meditation are seen as one indivisible activity (92). Wrestlers take from the world a customized diet with special emphasis on milk, almonds, and ghee, and they voluntarily block what their bodies might leak into the world by abstaining from sex and masturbation. Semen is seen to contain the essence of the body and of life. It is the quintessential fluid that distills all other fluids, including blood and marrow, and becomes for wrestlers "the locus of a person's moral character and physical prowess" (129, 137). Wrestlers extend their somatic enterprise into a self-congratulatory nationalist ideology in which the wrestler represents "the perfect citizen" standing against the hedonistic bodily indulgences of the modern body politic. Reforming the body is valorized by wrestlers as civic duty and patriotic act through which individuals, one by one, can counteract social degeneration. Alter undercuts the utopian idealism of the wrestlers' ideology with gentle irony: "Eventually, it is thought, the whole country will exercise and eat its way toward a civic utopia of propriety and public service" (247); celibacy will curb population growth, and "poverty will fall before an inspired work ethic fueled by the natural energy of the wrestler's good health" (248).

Saleem's individualization of national destiny is no less preposterous, and if his experience is ultimately of the mutual failure of the body and of history, then a primary sign of the bodily and societal collapse that he narrates—for him as for the wrestlers—is the draining out of semen. Enormous symbolic and satiric value is attributed to this event, "the draining-out of hope" is also the beginning of Saleem's death. In her discussion of ancient (Vedic and Post-Vedic) beliefs about bodily fluids, O'Flaherty notes that while women's loss of blood (menstruation) and milk (nursing) were symbols of creation and fertility, the male's loss of blood and semen (his equivalent of female milk) were associated with death (40–44). The flow of male fluids was to be strictly controlled; a belief that semen was stored in the head made castration a form of symbolic beheading that resulted in a loss of more general powers, including the powers of the imagination (81–87). As they are for Alter's modern-day wrestlers, women were seen as potential threats to men's precious fluids (O'Flaherty 57); a particularly dominant woman could drain a man of his life (77). When Saleem is drained of semen by a dominant Widow, he begins to die, and India irrevocably enters a period of darkness. Saleem musters his remaining powers to narrate his story, although even the powers of imagination that serve him so well throughout begin to fail him as his disintegration becomes acute. The draining of fluids from his body is the final literalization of the intermingling of realms and transgression of boundaries that as metaphor— as idea—proves enabling, but that as material bodily fact manifests itself increasingly as failure or destruction.

Rushdie's novel thus navigates a complicated course between the metaphoric and the literal, between inclusive Menippean optimism and exclusive negative satiric pessimism, and between an orthodox Indian valorizing of purity and a secular migrant preference for impurity. Any simple conclusion about his vision of the nation is therefore hard to come by. If we let genre be our guide, however—and for Bakhtin, genre always has sociopolitical implications—we can see Rushdie's vision of India residing in the pessoptimistic divide between these countervailing forces. As his controlling image of the leak proves life-enhancingly dialogic in principle but damagingly hostile to dialogue in practice, and as Menippean energies are overwhelmed by satiric, so Rushdie celebrates the Nehruvian vision of the newly independent India as a secular and pluralistic democracy, but scourges the historical assaults on that vision that culminate in virtual "death" during Indira Gandhi's Emergency.

But if the novel seems to end with the gloom and despair of the satirist in his conventional role as defeated victim, there is a sense in which the defeat is not total. Graham Pechey writes of Bakhtin that

> his theory of social hegemony is written almost exclusively from the stand-point of a perennial counter-hegemony always in the making—always having the last laugh as it were on the monoglot powers-that-be but never *winning* in any properly political sense. In other words, the true priority of heteroglossia is never realised as decisive victory: the forms of its militant self-assertion constantly imply that priority which the monoglot and centralising forces have constantly to posit themselves against. (52)

At the end of *Midnight's Children*, if we are to locate such a counter-hegemonic challenge anywhere, it must be in the novel itself. Rushdie's most Bakhtinian essay "Is Nothing Sacred?" is a paean to the novel as a "'privileged arena' of conflicting discourses" where "we can hear *voices talking about everything in every possible way*" (*Imaginary* 426, 429). The novel is a privileged genre for Rushdie for the same reasons it is for Bakhtin: insofar as literary genres have the power to "transform our awareness and conceptualization of external reality" (Gardiner 22), the dialogic world of the novel involves a "decentering of the ideological world" (*Dialogic* 367). Rushdie's novel, so often seen as teeming with India's diversity and bursting forth "the *fecundity* of the repressed" (Sangari 166), exemplifies not only these aspects of Bakhtinian novelness but also those of its hyper-inclusive sub-species, the Menippean satire. The cracking-up of Saleem's body, which in one sense figures the destructive assaults of ignoble history, in another sense, as Mujeebuddin Syed has shown (103), draws on a Vedic tradition to figure creation—the pouring-out in narrative of the multitudes that Saleem has swallowed over his life. Saleem's pouring-out is Rushdie's pouring-in: together they create a polyphonic novel that can claim to include a wide spectrum of the nation's diversity. By contrast with the narrower scope of the nation's rulers, and as the normative ideal on which satire is based, the Menippean novel provides a subversive alternative to official state ideology. It asks its readers to return from the final moment of imminent death to the initial moment of exuberant birth, of first principles. It is in this India, the visionary secular democracy that has always fallen short in practice, that Rushdie wants to put his faith.

NOTES

Much of the research for this article was conducted at the University of Toronto in connection with my doctoral thesis on post-colonial satire. I am grateful for the generous support of a SSHRC doctoral fellowship, and for the helpful comments of W.J. Howard, J. Edward Chamberlin, Chelva Kanaganayakam, Randall Martin, and the *ESC* readers.

1. Elliott's account of satire's origins in death-dealing magical curses traced through various ancient cultures does not draw on specifically Indian examples, although he asserts the universality of the belief "among people of every stage of civilization" (285). The prevalence of magic and superstition in ancient India is well documented, and belief in the power of the words contained in curses and black-magic spells is discussed in books by Banerji and Chakraborty (163) and Gupta (177–202).

2. Rao, for example, proposes that "irony and bitter satire become the mainstay of Rushdie's worldview" (163), and most of the Indian critics collected in *The Novels of Salman Rushdie* (Taneja and Dhawan) invoke satire in discussing matters of tone, vision, or literary style. The trajectories and targets of Rushdie's satire are discussed incidentally or at length by numerous critics, including Harrison (36–48), Brennan (109, 164), Booker (990), Kanaganayakam (95), Nair (1000), and Fletcher (99–111).

3. Bakhtin is not, of course, the only twentieth-century critic to theorize Menippean satire. Frye devotes several pages of *Anatomy of Criticism* to the genre (308–12), and while his ideas have been influential, it is hard not to agree with Griffin when he describes Frye's theory as "sketchy," "cryptic," and of limited use. Moreover, Griffin says, when Frye's theory is set beside the more elaborate and very different formulation of Bakhtin, "it almost seems as if Frye and Bakhtin are describing different forms" (32–33).

4. Payne, in a book on Chaucer's debt to classical Menippean satire, uses Bakhtin's definition and adds several of her own, all of which apply to *Midnight's Children*. These include paired and opposed characters in dialogue (Saleem and Shiva, up to a point); a virtually endless quest assisted by a "helping" and commenting character (Saleem's search for meaning aided by Padma); non-pornographic obscenity; a sense of "unquenchable hope and a

titanic energy"; and the absence of unquestioned theological authority or abstract certainty (9–11). Indeed, when Payne says Menippean satire "requires that we accept as necessary the presentation of simultaneous unresolved points of view," and that it questions "the possibility of ideal standards" by showing that "the world is largely what we make it" (4–6), the genre can be seen not only to be compatible with Rushdie's views (in his essay "Is Nothing Sacred?" for instance) but also to predate certain "contemporary" theories commonly used to explain his work; Hutcheon describes the postmodern world view in virtually identical terms (x, 43).

5. These include ten Kortenaar, Durix (61), and Sangari (164).

6. Bakhtin's theories of the grotesque body are outlined in *Rabelais and His World* (especially 303–436), whereas his views on Menippean satire are contained in *Problems of Dostoevsky's Poetics* (especially 112–22), and in the essay "Epic and Novel" (especially 21–28) in *The Dialogic Imagination*. Todorov remarks on the difficulty of making links among Bakhtin's theoretical texts, including *Rabelais* and *Problems*; it is hard to reconstruct a coherent "general system," since the texts are not cross-referenced (*Mikhail* xii).

WORKS CITED

Ali, Tariq. Rev. of *Midnight's Children*, by Salman Rushdie. *New Left Review* 136 (1982): 87–95.

Alter, Joseph S. *The Wrestler's Body: Identity and Ideology in North India.* Berkeley: U of California P, 1992.

Aravamudan, Srinivas. "'Being God's Postman is No Fun, Yaar': Salman Rushdie's *The Satanic Verses,*" *diacritics* 19.2 (1989): 3–20.

Bakhtin, M. M. *The Dialogic Imagination: Four Essays.* Trans. Caryl Emerson and Michael Holquist. Ed. Michael Holquist. Austin: U of Texas P, 1981.

——. *Problems of Dostoevsky's Poetics.* Ed. and trans. Caryl Emerson. Minneapolis: U of Minnesota P, 1984.

——. *Rabelais and His World.* Trans. Helene Iswolsky. Bloomington: Indiana UP, 1984.

Banerji, Sures Chandra, and Chhanda Chakraborty. *Folklore in Ancient and Medieval India.* Calcutta: Punthi Pustak, 1991.

Booker, M. Keith. "Beauty and the Beast: Dualism as Despotism in the Fiction of Salman Rushdie." *ELH* 57 (1990): 977–97.

Brennan, Timothy. *Salman Rushdie and the Third World: Myths of the Nation.* New York: Macmillan, 1989.

Brooks, Peter. *Body Work: Objects of Desire in Modern Narrative.* Cambridge: Harvard UP, 1993.

Durix, Jean-Pierre. "Magic Realism in *Midnight's Children.*" *Commonwealth: Essays and Studies* 8.1 (1985): 57–63.

Elliott, Robert C. *The Power of Satire: Magic, Ritual, Art.* Princeton: Princeton UP, 1960.

Fletcher, M. D. *Contemporary Political Satire: Narrative Strategies in the Post-Modern Context.* Lanham: UP of America, 1987.

Flood, Gavin D. "Techniques of Body and Desire in Kashmir Saivism." *Religion* 22 (1992): 47–62.

Foucault, Michel. "The Body of the Condemned"; "Docile Bodies." *The Foucault Reader.* Ed. Paul Rabinow. New York: Pantheon, 1984. 170–87.

———. "Nietzsche, Genealogy, History." *Language, Counter-Memory, Practice: Selected Essays and Interviews.* Trans. Donald F. Bouchard and Sherry Simon. Ed. Donald F. Bouchard. Ithaca: Cornell UP, 1977.

Frye, Northrop. *Anatomy of Criticism: Four Essays.* Princeton: Princeton UP, 1957.

Gallagher, Catherine. "The Body Versus the Social Body in the Works of Thomas Malthus and Henry Mayhew." *Representations* 14 (1986): 83–106.

Gardiner, Michael. *The dialogics of critique: M. M. Bakhtin and the theory of ideology.* London: Routledge, 1992.

Griffin, Dustin. *Satire: A Critical Reintroduction.* Lexington: UP of Kentucky, 1994.

Gupta, Beni. *Magical Beliefs and Superstitions.* Delhi: Sundeep Prakashan, 1979.

Harpham, Geoffrey Galt. *On the Grotesque: Strategies of Contradiction in Art and Literature.* Princeton: Princeton UP, 1982.

Harrison, James. *Salman Rushdie.* New York: Twayne, 1992.

Hutcheon, Linda. *A Poetics of Postmodernism: History, Theory, Fiction.* New York: Routledge, 1988.

Kanaganayakam, C. "Myth and Fabulosity in *Midnight's Children.*" *Dalhousie Review* 67 (1987): 86–98.

Kayser, Wolfgang. *The Grotesque in Art and Literature*. Trans. Ulrich Weisstein. 1963. Gloucester MA: Peter Smith, 1968.

Mukerjee, Radhakamal. *The Cosmic Art of India: Symbol (Murti), Sentiment (Rasa) and Silence (Yoga)*. Bombay: Allied, 1965.

Nair, Rukmini Bhaya. "Text and Pre-Text: History as Gossip in Rushdie's Novels." *Economic and Political Weekly* 6 May 1989: 994–1000.

O'Flaherty, Wendy Doniger. *Women, Androgynes, and Other Mythical Beasts*. Chicago: U of Chicago P, 1980.

Payne, F. Anne. *Chaucer and Menippean Satire*. Madison: U of Wisconsin P, 1981.

Pechey, Graham. "On the Borders of Bakhtin: Dialogisation, Decolonisation." *Bakhtin and Cultural Theory*. Ed. Ken Hirschkop and David Shepherd. Manchester: Manchester UP, 1989, 39–67.

Rao, M. Madhusudhana. *Salman Rushdie's Fiction: A Study ("Satanic Verses" Excluded)*. New Delhi: Sterling, 1992.

Rushdie, Salman. *Imaginary Homelands: Essays and Criticism 1981–1991*. London: Granta, 1991.

———. *Midnight's Children*. 1980. New York: Knopf, 1984.

———. "*Midnight's Children* and *Shame*." *Kunapipi* 7 (1985): 1–19.

———. Remarks as participant in "Conservative Fictions: A Panel Discussion." Mod. Alberto Manguel. Wang International Festival of Authors, Toronto. 17 Oct. 1988.

———. *The Satanic Verses*. London: Viking, 1988.

———. *Shame*. London: Cape, 1983.

Said, Edward W. *After the Last Sky: Palestinian Lives*. New York: Pantheon, 1986.

Sangari, Kumkum. "The Politics of the Possible." *Cultural Critique* 7 (1987): 157–86.

Stam, Robert. *Subversive Pleasures: Bakhtin, Cultural Criticism, and Film*. 1989. Baltimore: Johns Hopkins UP, 1992.

Syed, Mujeebuddin. "*Midnight's Children* and Its Indian Con-Texts." *Journal of Commonwealth Literature* 29.2 (1994): 95–108.

Taneja, G. R., and R. K. Dhawan, eds. *The Novels of Salman Rushdie*. New Delhi: Indian Society for Commonwealth Studies/Prestige, 1992.

ten Kortenaar, Neil. "*Midnight's Children* and the Allegory of History." *ARIEL* 26.2 (1995): 41–62.

Todorov, Tzvetan. *The Fantastic: A Structural Approach to a Literary Genre.* Trans. Richard Howard. Cleveland: Case Western Reserve UP, 1973.

——. *Mikhail Bakhtin: The Dialogical Principle.* Trans. Wlad Godzich. Minneapolis: U of Minnesota P, 1984.

Younger, Paul. *Introduction to Indian Religious Thought.* Philadelphia: Westminster, 1972.

STEPHEN BAKER

"You Must Remember This": *Salman Rushdie's* The Moor's Last Sigh

Salman Rushdie's fiction is the writing of capitalist neo-colonialism. We see this in the fiction's celebration of cultural eclecticism and hybridity, the reification of local cultures and traditions into so many consumerist choices and lifestyle options. Rushdie's fiction has come to stand, almost emblematically, for the writing of postcolonial literature, a literature that somehow reconciles the untroubled textual playfulness of a consumer culture with the historical and political legacy of anti-colonial struggle. The writing allows us to evade the necessity of concrete political and ethical choices. It provides us, as in the case of Rushdie's *The Moor's Last Sigh*, with a text self-consciously constructed from a multitude of other texts, each chosen to further the eclectic range of the hybrid, postcolonial work. Every dilemma faced by a character, each troubled judgement reached by a reader, all are absorbed into the *mis-en-abyme* of the novel's textuality. The narrator of *The Moor's Last Sigh*, Moraes Zogoiby, tells us in the novel's opening pages of his frantic escape from death and of the pain he still feels at the loss of his treacherous beloved. It is difficult, though, to engage with the gravity of Moor's situation and confusion when we have seen his tale's reliance on references (some explicit, some implicit) to *The Tempest*, Vasco da Gama, Luther, *Don Quixote* and *Tristram Shandy*. The novel starts to seem less an

From *The Journal of Commonwealth Literature* 35, no. 1 (2000): 43-54. © 2000 by *The Journal of Commonwealth Literature*.

attempt to address the complexity of Indian national identity and statehood than an exercise in self-reflexive literary game-playing.

Or so at least it might seem to a Lukacsian-inspired, Marxist critic. Aijaz Ahmad, both in his book *In Theory: Classes, Nations, Literatures* and in his article "The Politics of Literary Postcoloniality", has undertaken a major and thorough critique of many of the features commonly associated with postcolonial literature and its criticism (such as "migrancy", "hybridity", "contingency"). The following premise informs much of Ahmad's analysis:

> I am reminded of something that the Cuban–American critic, Roman de la Campa, said to me in conversation, to the effect that "postcoloniality" is postmodernism's wedge to colonise literatures outside Europe and its North American offshoots— which I take the liberty to understand as saying that what used to be known as "Third World literature" gets rechristened as "postcolonial literature" when the governing theoretical framework shifts from Third World nationalism to post-modernism.[1]

Ahmad rehearses much of the Marxist critique of postmodern writing and culture in his critical analysis of postcolonial literature. With specific reference to the work of Salman Rushdie, he writes:

> How very enchanting, I have often thought, Rushdie's kind of imagination must be for that whole range of readers who have been brought up on the peculiar "universalism" of *The Waste Land* (the "Hindu" tradition appropriated by an Anglo-American consciousness on its way to Anglican conversion, through the agency of Orientalist scholarship) and the "world culture" of Pound's *Cantos* (the sages of Ancient China jostling with the princely notables of Renaissance Italy, with Homer and Cavalcanti in between, all in the service of a political vision framed by Mussolini's fascism). One did not have to belong, one could simply float, effortlessly, through a supermarket of packaged and commodified cultures, ready to be consumed.[2]

Ahmad's argument is based on extending the Marxist ideology critique of postmodernism as "the cultural logic of Late Capitalism" (in what Ahmad calls "Jameson's superb phrase") to postcolonial literary and theoretical writings, such as those of Rushdie, Said, Spivak and Bhabha.

Ahmad's critique of Rushdie often seems to be based on similar grounds to Georg Lukacs's critique of modernist writing. Following Lukacs's prescription of a Realist aesthetic based on the representation of a social totality, he laments Rushdie's unwillingness or inability to represent in *Shame*, for example, the full complexities and conflicts of Pakistani politics and society. Insisting on an economic model with which to unmask the hidden ideology of major features of postcolonial writing, he compares the theme of migrancy, to which Rushdie is so irredeemably attached, to the financial practices of multinational corporations.

There is, no doubt, much justification for such a critique. But it is perhaps worth asking whether the strategies of traditional, Marxist ideology critique do not in fact themselves reify the literary text, defining it as a finished, passive object, ready for the critic's analytical dissection. This is itself a questionable practice, ignoring the creative "event" (to borrow Jean-François Lyotard's term) of reading itself. It may be seen as a form of critique that has already posited the literary text as some retified object to be subjected to the critique of equally reified and transhistorical criteria of judgement. Critical thought itself need have little part to play, while the text is processed through an already defined set of analytical criteria, to be catalogued according to the inherited set of critical categories. Salman Rushdie's fiction is the writing of capitalist neo-colonialism.

It may be possible, though, to insist on a more creative analysis of Rushdie's writing, an analysis that is open to the demands that Rushdie's texts make of us each time we read them, and open to the dependence of the texts on the correspondences we draw and the links we establish. Above all, it is worth retaining a sense of the unique experience of the event of each reading of the texts. The creation and recreation of new texts, new narratives, in the reading of Rushdie is not merely an adjunct to the novels' political and historical content; it reintroduces a sense of political and historical content to the act of reading the novels themselves. Following Aijaz Ahmad's association of the postcolonial and the postmodern, I want to argue that a postmarxist approach to the contingency and fragmentation of postmodern narrative is useful in rediscovering a political, historical and ethical dimension to those same textually playful and self-reflexive features of postcolonial writing of which the Marxist tradition remains so suspicious.

Thomas Docherty's identification of the "elusiveness of character" in postmodern fiction would produce little dissent from critics writing from within the Marxist tradition. Docherty, in *Alterities*, draws upon Italo Calvino's *If On A Winter's Night A Traveller* to explain what he sees as the consequences of reading postmodern characterization. The reader of

Calvino's novel constantly has to readjust to different perspectives, situations, indeed different texts as the novel continually changes from one narrative to another. The act of reading *If On A Winter's Night A Traveller* becomes itself the principal subject matter of the novel, and the focus of its most sustained narrative, as it charts the developing love affair of the Reader and the Other Reader. "This multiplication of 'the Reader'," writes Dochert, "(and the confusion of the *character* of the Reader with 'real' readers of the text) is an analogue of what happens to characterization in postmodern narrative generally."[3]

At least part of what Docherty seems to be suggesting is that postmodern narrative both generates and reflects on questions of ontology. David Harvey, in *The Condition of Postmodernity* argues that the ontological plurality of postmodern texts is mimetic of an age of consumer capitalism.[4] This interpretation would seem to identify the ontological instability that Docherty sees in postmodern characterization with the reproduction of what Marxists such as Jameson, Harvey and Ahmad see as the ideological effects of late capitalism. In other words, Docherty's initial description of postmodern characterization is generally consistent with the analysis and ideology critique of Marxist critics. His interpretation of that initial description, though, is completely different.

Docherty reads this playful disruption of characters' and readers' identities as profoundly radical and enabling strategies. "Postmodern narrative," he writes,

> seeks to circumvent the phenomenological elaboration of a definable spatial relation obtaining between a transcendent ontological reading subject and an equally fixed and non-historical object of that reader's perception, the "character".[5]

Docherty reads the implicit assumptions of a static, definable (and defining) relationship between a Self and Other as being contested by postmodern characterization. This mode of characterization, he argues, opens the narrative to the possibility of change—thereby opening it to historicity itself. The postmodern historical novel, to the postmarxist critic, is not principally the reproduction of a historical narrative (something which, for Jameson and Ahmad, it does inadequately) but is more concerned with the creation of history, the rediscovery of a creative, historical dimension in the reading process itself.

Docherty claims that "[t]o read postmodern characterization is to reintroduce the possibility of politics, and importantly of a genuinely historical political change, into the act of reading."[6] The justification for this claim is important. He argues that in a narrative of this sort the reader is forced to understand herself or himself as Other. Denied the stable perspective of the more "traditional" reader and the fixed identities of equally "traditional" characters, the reader of postmodern fiction develops an endlessly differing series of subject positions, grasping a sense of "dissident" subjectivity, a subjectivity marginalized from "a centralized or totalized narrative of selfhood."[7] This, for Docherty, is a profoundly ethical and political manoeuvre. It involves the reader in the event of her or his own positioning and repositioning as a reading subject. It confronts the reader with the necessity of continual revision and reconstruction, the acknowledgement of the inescapable contingency of all narratives. Each subject position, always already acknowledged as a fiction, and each narrative proposition is held to imply immediately an innumerable number of alternatives.

In "The Harmony of the Spheres", one of the short stories collected in Salman Rushdie's *East, West*, the narrator Khan describes his memories of Eliot Crane, a friend who has recently killed himself. Eliot, he explains, had been mentally unbalanced for some time, suffering from paranoid delusions provoked by his interest in the occult: "What human mind could have defended itself against such a Babel, in which Theosophists argued with Confucians, Christian Scientists with Rosicrucians?"[8] Rushdie uses Eliot's paranoia to aim an easy jibe at those "concerned" about immigration:

> Eliot had elaborated a conspiracy theory in which most of his friends were revealed to be agents of hostile powers, both Earthly and extra-terrestrial. I was an invader from Mars, one of many such dangerous beings who had sneaked into Britain when certain essential forms of vigilance had been relaxed.[9]

On hearing of Eliot's death, Khan goes to see his widow Lucy; she asks him to read through his dead friend's papers. "There were," he comments, "only ravings." For the most part, these seem ridiculous occultist tracts or self-pitying, autobiographical speculation. "Harder still to read," adds Khan,

> were his fantasies about us, his friends. These were of two kinds: hate-filled and pornographic. There were many virulent attacks on me, and pages of steamy sex involving my wife Mala, "dated", no doubt to maximise their auto-erotic effect, in the days

immediately after our marriage. And, of course, at other times.
The pages about Lucy were both nasty and lubricious.[10]

At the end of the story Khan tells his wife about Eliot's hurtful sexual
fantasies. "'Those weren't fantasies,' she said".[11]

"The Harmony of the Spheres" is a rewriting of a passage from "The
Angel Azraeel" section of *The Satanic Verses*. Saladin Chamcha tortures the
fanatically jealous Gibreel, in a multitude of different voices, claiming sexual
knowledge of his girlfriend Allie Cone:

> superb Byronic aristocrats boasting of having "conquered
> Everest", sneering guttersnipes, unctuous best-friend voices
> mingling warning and mock-commiseration, *a word to the wise,
> how stupid can you, don't you know yet what she's, anything in trousers,
> you poor moron, take it from a pal.*[12]

Here the claims are, of course, false; they are part of Saladin's revenge for
Gibreel's earlier abandonment of him. Rushdie, though, integrates quite
specific echoes of this episode into his short story. Before he begins his hoax
calls, Saladin visits Gibreel and Allie in their Scottish retreat. Allie tells him
something of Gibreel's neurosis:

> "He can't get very far without transport, but you never know,"
> she explained grimly. "Three days ago he stole the car keys and
> they found him heading the wrong way up an exit road on the
> M6, shouting about damnation."[13]

Khan visits Eliot and Lucy (this time travelling to Wales) in similar
circumstances:

> "You'd better come," Lucy had called to say. "They found him
> going the wrong way on the motorway, doing ninety, with one of
> those sleep-mask things over his eyes."[14]

The story reverses two significant aspects of the passage from the novel: here
it is the madman who makes the accusations, and they turn out to be true.
What principally interests me, though, is the act of Rushdie's rewriting itself.
His fiction often seems predicated on the need continuously to revise and to
reassemble narratives, absorbing and reworking an English and European
cultural tradition while simultaneously engaging in a process of *self*-revision.

This suggests both the multiplicity of narrative possibilities (the multiplicity of ways of understanding the world) and the fleeting transience of each. Rushdie compensates for the absence of grand narratives (the "god-shaped hole") by offering, instead, a succession of often interrelated fictions. In the remaining pages of this article, we shall be looking at how this aspect of Rushdie's writing informs his portrayal of self and, through that, the construction of social formations. Above all, we shall see how this emphasis on the contingency of each of these historical narratives is used to suggest the creative, transient historicity of the present moment, a historicity enacted in the act of reading itself.

"I have been a swallower of lives," says Saleem Sinai, "and to know me, just the one of me, you'll have to swallow the lot as well".[15] The telling of stories, the construction of a multitude of fictions, is tied inextricably in Rushdie's novels to the construction of a self: Saleem Sinai exists almost as the amalgam of the stories he tells of his family's and his country's past. *The Moor's Last Sigh* is the next of Rushdie's novels to make consistent use of a first-person narrator. Moraes Zogoiby, in a manner not dissimilar to that of Saleem, claims: "On the run, I have turned the world into my own pirate map, complete with clues, leading X-marks-the-spottily to the treasure of myself."[16] The creation of the fictions, those of Saleem and Moraes (known as "Moor"), are an act of self-assertion—or, more properly, of self-discovery. And yet at the same time these characters exist *in* and *through* the telling of their stories: so while the narrators' stories lead "X-marks-the-spottily" to the treasure of themselves, that treasure—those selves—exist only through the act of aestheticization. Here art is self-expression, but that self is "itself" shown to be yet another artistic construct.

In fact, in both *Midnight's Children* and *The Moor's Last Sigh* it is made clear that the narrators tell these stories as an attempt to keep hold of some unified self, as a method of survival. Early in *Midnight's Children* Saleem compares himself to Sheherazade of *The Thousand and One Nights*, spinning out fictions to stretch out a life expectancy. In *The Moor's Last Sigh*, too, Moor's survival in Vasco Miranda's fortress is to last the precise duration of the time he takes to write the story of his life. At the same time, that self— which survives only by the construction of successive fictions—is seen as inextricably and intimately tied to a *national* destiny: "I had been mysteriously handcuffed to history," says Saleem, "my destinies indissolubly chained to those of my country".[17] Saleem Sinai's physical fragmentation is offered as a reflection of the Indian subcontinent: the initial partition of East and West Pakistan; and the subsequent division of East and West Pakistan, after the Indo-Pakistan War of 1971, into Bangladesh and Pakistan. We find something very similar in *The Moor's Last Sigh*. Moraes Zogoiby is living his life at twice the speed he should; when he ought to be in his prime, he is already old and weakened: like post-Independence Indian democracy, he has aged far too quickly. So Rushdie constructs a triple analogy: the narrator's life reflects that of the state, but the narrator is also constructed by his form of narration. Both Saleem and Moor, in their ever more desperate attempts to make their narratives cohere, raise the question of the coherence or viability of the Indian state as a single political entity. The work of art itself, then, the very construction of these fictional narratives becomes another reflection of social construction. Self exists as an act of aestheticization, and that self is also a figure for the nation.

The series of narratives, through which the construction of both self and nation are invoked, is formed by a mish-mash of influences: some Indian, some European. While the open, free-ranging structure is intended to reflect an Indian tradition of epic storytelling (e.g. the *Ramayana* and the *Mahabharata*), and Rushdie's fiction is stylistically indebted to the writing of G.V. Desani, the novel also mimics certain European literary models: the significance of Saleem's nose and birth-date point to Laurence Sterne's *Tristram Shandy*; the name Aziz in *Midnight's Children* is borrowed from Forster's *A Passage to India*; Gunther Grass's *The Tin Drum* is another influence. And while Saleem's pickles recall Oskar Mazerath's drum playing in Grass's novel, they also point to Marcel's madeleine in *A la recherche* … It is in *The Moor's Last Sigh*, though, that the narrative's construction as a tissue of other (principally European) narratives is at its most overt:

> I have lost count of the days that have passed since I fled the horrors of Vasco Miranda's mad fortress in the Andalusian mountain-village of Benengeli; ran from death under cover of darkness and left a message nailed to the door. And since then along my hungry, heat-hazed way there have been further bunches of scribbled sheets, swings of the hammer, sharp exclamations of two-inch nails. Long ago when I was green my beloved said to me in fondness, "Oh, you Moor, you strange black man, always so full of theses, never a church door to nail them to." (She, a self-professedly godly un-Christian Indian, joked about Luther's protest at Wittenberg to tease her determinedly ungodly Indian Christian lover: how stories travel, what mouths they end up in!) Unfortunately, my mother overheard; and darted, quick as snakebite: "so full, you mean, of faeces." Yes,

mother, you had the last word on that subject, too: as about everything.

"Amrika" and "Moskva", somebody once called them, Aurora my mother and Uma my love, nicknaming them for the two great super-powers; and people said they looked alike but I never saw it, couldn't see it at all. Both of them dead, of unnatural causes, and I in a far off country with death at my heels and their story in my hand, a story I've been crucifying upon a gate, a fence, an olive-tree, spreading it across this landscape of my last journey, the story which points to me. On the run, I have turned the world into my pirate map, complete with clues, leading X-marks-the-spottily to the treasure of myself. When my pursuers have followed the trail they'll find me waiting, uncomplaining, out of breath, ready. *Here I stand. Couldn't've done it differently.*[18]

References to Vasco da Gama, *The Tempest*, Luther and *Don Quixote* litter the first few paragraphs. This is a playful celebration of cultural hybridity—which, on the one hand, stresses the textual status of the world of the novel (it is, after all, a book made from other books); and also suggests the plurality of elements in cultural construction: "was not the entire national culture based on the principle of borrowing whatever clothes seemed to fit, Aryan, Mughal, British, take-the-best-and-leave-the-rest?" asks Zeeny Vakil in *The Satanic Verses*. (Reappearing in *The Moor's Last Sigh*, Zeeny characterizes Aurora Zogoiby's painting as the expression of that very hotch-potch.)

This mish-mash of influences, the juxtaposition of the European and the Indian can be said to represent a form of multiculturalism, absorbing the historical and cultural forces of West European literary culture on colonized societies. In this sense it can be interpreted as quite a realistic portrayal of the construction of a postcolonial culture. On the other hand, it might seem remarkably akin to Jean-François Lyotard's account of the eclecticism of contemporary, consumer culture. But it seems wrong to me to insist, as Aijaz Ahmad does, that Rushdie's writing can also be identified with a commodified, postcolonial (and therefore, for Ahmad, postmodern) aesthetic through its adoption of a celebratory stance toward "inner fragmentation and social disconnection". In *The Moor's Last Sigh*, Uma Sarasvati (Moor's beloved) is the exemplar of the protean, hybridized, postmodern and postcolonial subject. Uma appears to everyone exactly as they would wish her to be—only Moor's mother, Aurora, remains unseduced. And yet it is Uma, the paragon of pluralism, who turns out to be faithless and destructive: "in the matter of Uma Sarasvati," says Moor, "it had been the pluralist Uma, with her multiple selves, her highly inventive commitment to the infinite malleability of the real, her modernistically provisional sense of truth, who had turned out to be the bad egg".[19] Likewise, for all the regenerative possibility suggested by narrative fragmentation in *Midnight's Children*, it remains difficult to witness the gradual destruction of Saleem and of Nehru's vision of a secular Indian state without detecting a deeply felt sense of loss and regret.

The fragmentary structure of Rushdie's novels is, of course, a mimetic device, reflecting (and not necessarily celebrating) other forms of fragmentation. However, Rushdie's historical narratives of the subcontinent also hint at their interconnection; (like his characters, they bleed into one another, "like flavours"). In *Midnight's Children* Saleem's son, Aadam Sinai, is depicted as a member of a new, hardier generation, perhaps better able than Midnight's Children to ensure the survival of a secular, democratic India. He reappears in *The Moor's Last Sigh*; there he is an agent of destruction. Zeeny Vakil also reappears (from *The Satanic Verses*); she, as the voice of a vigilant multiculturalism and keeper of Aurora Zogoiby's paintings, is murdered. Textual coherence is suggested. Rushdie seems to be trying to construct some kind of a continuum from *Midnight's Children*, *The Satanic Verses* and *The Moor's Last Sigh*. This alludes to, but never quite produces, that goal of *totality* which is the bedrock of Lukacsian ideas of Realism. And yet this ironic ideal of totality, of wholeness (for which both Saleem and Moor yearn), remains illusory, the construct of textual correspondences between works of imaginative literature, and the readiness of the reader to remember what has gone before. What this leads to, throughout Rushdie's writing, is a profound sense of longing, of the desire to make things anew, but the fear that such desires are hopeless. The creation of the fiction becomes then simultaneously lament and ironic wish-fulfilment, both the evocation of that Mother India which to Rushdie is now lost and the recognition that any such evocation is transient, illusory and potentially suspect (after all, the Widow in *Midnight's Children* has her own idea of a unified state). In this respect reminiscent of much modernist writing, Rushdie's work also bears a great similarity to that of the young Aurora who paints an entire room as an expression of her loss after her mother's death:

> Only God was absent, for no matter how carefully Camoens peered at the walls, and even after he climbed a step-ladder to stare at the ceiling, he was unable to find the figure of Christ, on or off the cross, or indeed any other representation of any other divinity, tree-sprite, water-sprite, angel, devil or saint.

And it was all set in a landscape that made Camoens tremble to see it, for it was Mother India herself, Mother India with her garishness and her inexhaustible motion, Mother India who loved and betrayed and ate and destroyed and again loved her children, and with whom the children's passionate conjoining and eternal quarrel stretched long beyond the grave...but above all, in the very centre of the ceiling, at the point where all the horn-of-plenty lines converged, Mother India with Belle's face. Queen Isabella was the only mother-goddess here, and she was dead; at the heart of this first immense outpouring of Aurora's art was the simple tragedy of her loss, the unassuaged pain of becoming a motherless child. The room was her act of mourning.[20]

By the end of *The Moor's Last Sigh*, Moor has lost his family and his treacherous beloved. Most of Aurora's paintings have been destroyed, and Moor himself has narrowly escaped from the murderous Vasco Miranda. He leaves Benengeli and travels to the Alhambra, monument to Boabdil, last Moorish ruler of Spain. Benengeli is the name of the fictional author of Cervantes' *Don Quixote*, whose work the novel's narrator claims merely to have translated: Cide Hamete Benengeli, a Moor. Like Don Quixote, Moor turns the land over which he travels into a fictional environment: he nails the pages of his narrative to trees, gates, to whatever he can find. The world that has colluded in his destruction is one he, like Saleem Sinai, transforms into the story of himself; but the literary allusions tell us not to take it too seriously. *The Moor's Last Sigh* dramatizes the destruction of art, but seems to show art triumphing in the end, transforming the real world around it.[21] It is also, though, reminding us of the fact that the same Christian, Spanish civilization which gave Europe the novel (in the form of Cervantes' *Don Quixote*) was also that which expelled and slaughtered the Muslims who had made their homes there. For all its textual playfulness, Rushdie's writing retains this sense of didactic purpose, constantly patching up the holes in our historical memory.

And yet there is also something else. Another of the stories in *East, West* is called "Christopher Columbus and Queen Isabella of Spain Consummate Their Relationship (*Santa Fe, AD 1492*)". This provides a further subtext to *The Moor's Last Sigh*: responsible for the Moors' expulsion from Spain, Isabella is also a key figure in Europe's discovery of the New World. The idea of a "new world"—an imaginary homeland, the Land of Oz—is a potent one in Rushdie's fiction. While also pointing allusively to Hispanic and South American literature (a source of many of Rushdie's intertexts), the conclusion of *The Moor's Last Sigh* contains an explicit allusion to the development of the American literary canon:

> *At the head of this tombstone are three eroded letters; my fingertip reads*
> *them for me. R I P. Very well: I will rest, and hope for peace. The world*
> *is full of sleepers waiting for their moment of return: Arthur sleeps in*
> *Avalon, Barbarossa in his cave. Finn MacCool lies in the Irish hillsides*
> *and the Worm Ouroboros on the bed of the Sundering Sea. Australia's*
> *ancestors, the Wandjina, take their ease underground, and somewhere,*
> *in a tangle of thorns, a beauty in a glass coffin awaits a prince's kiss. See:*
> *here is my flask. I'll drink some wine; and then, like a latter-day Van*
> *Winkle, I'll lay me down upon this graven stone, lay my head beneath*
> *these letters R I P, and close my eyes, according to our family's old*
> *practice of falling asleep in times of trouble, and hope to awaken,*
> *renewed and joyful, into a better time.*[22]

Despite this closing reference to an early text of the literature of the United States (and, importantly, a hybrid story drawing on European models), it would be naive of us to assume for even a moment that the subtext of the New World in *The Moor's Last Sigh* is unproblematically one of celebration. The history of racial exploitation in the United States is of too close a proximity to Rushdie's habitual themes for any such assumption to be credible. In fact, that history of exploitation is subtly integrated into *The Moor's Last Sigh* itself, though Rushdie is clearly interested less in the experience of slavery and subjugation than in its imaginative rendering: Rushdie's novel is a coded homage to African American literature.

"Columbus," writes Rushdie, "the invisible man who dreams of entering the invisible world."[23] *The Moor's Last Sigh* constructs a number of narrative parallels and intertextual allusions to Ralph Ellison's *Invisible Man*.[24] "I've illuminated the blackness of my invisibility," claims Ellison's narrator, "—nd vice versa."[25] "Placed beyond the Pale," suggests Moor in a near echo, "would you not seek to make light from the Dark?"[26] Ellison's nameless narrator submerges his identity in the Stalinist "Brotherhood" just as Moor is coerced into Raman Fielding's neo-Stalinist "Mumbai's Axis" (MA). The protean Uma Sarasvati echoes Ellison's indefinable Rinehart. "I yam what I am!" insists the Invisible Man,[27] "I yam what I yam an' that's what I yam," says Moor.[28] Even Aurora's paintings reinforce the association: "The Moor had entered the invisible world, the world of ghosts, of people who did not exist, and Aurora followed him into it, forcing it into visibility by the strength of her artistic will."[29]

The expression in Ellison's work of the African American experience in the United States serves as an example in *The Moor's Last Sigh* of the imagination's capacity for renewal and transformation: Isabella expels the Moors, but sponsors Columbus's discovery of the New World; the New World becomes a slave state, but the slaves' descendants produce African American literature. Neither the expulsions nor slavery are in any way redeemed, or their horror diminished, by this. But what Rushdie suggests cannot be forgotten is historical contingency and the possibility of change. The historicity of the present moment—entailing the destruction both of Aurora's art and of Moor himself—is thrust to the forefront of Rushdie's writing. The possibility that Moor might awaken, "renewed and joyful, into a better time" remains as a reminder to us too that we need not surrender the imagination to models of historical inevitability or resign ourselves to the fact that there is no alternative. There are always alternatives (next time, the pornographic fantasist may be telling the truth), and each inevitability will pass as surely as did Isabella's reign and the hide-and-seek spaceship that was due to carry us all to heaven. Grasping the present as history, *The Moor's Last Sigh* accepts the contingency of imaginative expression, while simultaneously refusing to accept that such contingency relegates art to the status of trivial textual playfulness. This is a definition of much contemporary writing that is all too common in Marxist criticism and is summarized in Fredric Jameson's comments on what he calls "the relief of the postmodern", the present impossibility and implausibility of significant aesthetic expression.[30] For Rushdie, though, that precarious status of artistic expression, those transient and fleeting moments of correspondence on which each of our readings is based, are all signs of a creative desire that is almost unbearably vulnerable and unutterably precious. "A sigh," says Moor, "isn't just a sigh. We inhale the world and breathe out meaning. While we can. While we can."[31]

NOTES

1. Aijaz Ahmad, "The Politics of Literary Postcoloniality", in *Contemporary Post-colonial Theory: A Reader*, ed. Padmini Mongia, London: Arnold, 1996, p. 276.

2. Ajaz Ahmad, *In Theory: Classes, Nations, Literatures*, London: Verso, 1992, p. 128.

3. Thomas Docherty, *Alterities: Criticism, History, Representation*, Oxford: Oxford UP, 1996, p. 57.

4. See David Harvey, *The Condition of Postmodernity: An Enquiry into the Origins of Cultural Change*, Oxford: Blackwell, 1990, pp. 301–2.

5. Docherty, *Alterities*, p. 58.

6. *ibid.*, pp. 66–7.

7. *ibid.*, p. 67.

8. Salman Rushdie, "The Harmony of the Spheres", in *East, West*, London: Cape, 1994, p. 142.

9. *ibid.*, p. 127.

10. *ibid.*, p. 144.

11. *ibid.*, p. 146.

12. Salman Rushdie, *The Satanic Verses*, London: Viking, 1988, p. 444.

13. *ibid.*, p. 432.

14. Rushdie, "The Harmony of the Spheres", p. 127.

15. Salman Rushdie, *Midnight's Children*, London: Picador, 1982, p. 9.

16. Salman Rushdie, *The Moor's Last Sigh*, London: Cape, 1995, p. 3.

17. Rushdie, *Midnight's Children*, p. 9.

18. Rushdie, *The Moor's Last Sigh*, p. 3.

19. *ibid.*, p. 272.

20. *ibid.*, pp. 60–1.

21. For Rushdie's critical comments on a less ambivalent treatment of this same theme, see Salman Rushdie, "Christoph Ransmayr", in *Imaginary Homelands: Essays and Criticism, 1981–1991*, London: Granta, 1991, pp. 291–3

22. Rushdie, *The Moor's Last Sigh*, pp. 433–4.

23. Salman Rushdie, "Christopher Columbus and Queen Isabella of Spain Consummate Their Relationship (*Santa Fe, AD 1492*)", in *East, West*, p. 116.

24. Ralph Ellison, *Invisible Man*, Harmondsworth: Penguin, 1965.

25. *ibid.*, p. 15.

26. Rushdie, *The Moor's Last Sigh*, p. 5.

27. Ellison, *Invisible Man*, p. 215.

28. Rushdie, *The Moor's Last Sigh*, p. 427.

29. *ibid.*, p. 303.

30. See Fredric Jameson, *Postmodernism, or, The Cultural Logic of Late Capitalism*, London: Verso, 1991, pp. 317–18.

31. Rushdie, *The Moor's Last Sigh*, p. 54.

AYELET BEN-YISHAI

The Dialectic of Shame: Representation
in the MetaNarrative of Salman Rushdie's Shame

> I had thought, before I began, that what I had on my hands was
> an almost excessively masculine tale, a saga of sexual rivalry,
> ambition, power, patronage, betrayal, death, revenge. But the
> women seem to have taken over; they marched in from the
> peripheries of the story to demand the inclusion of their own
> tragedies, histories and comedies, obliging me to couch my
> narrative in all manner of sinuous complexities, to see my "male"
> plot refracted, so to speak, through the prisms of its reverse and
> 'female' side.
>
> —Salman Rushdie, *Shame*

This passage from Salman Rushdie's third novel has been pivotal in most analyses of the novel, and indeed will also prove important to mine, if more peripherally. *Shame* is probably the least written-about of all of Rushdie's novels, and when they did write about it, many critics have centered their argument around his treatment of women, hence the importance of the passage quoted above. Opinions have varied, ranging from charges that his treatment is misogynist (Ahmad 144, 148; Cundy 52) to praise for his emancipatory vision (Needham). Within this range we find readings of "ambivalent" feminism (Hai 16–50) and, more complexly, "critical-

From *Modern Fiction Studies* 48, no. 1 (Spring 2002): 194–215. © 2002 for the Purdue Research
Foundation by the Johns Hopkins University Press.

therefore-emancipatory because of its ambivalence" ones (Levinson; Mufti[1]). In this paper I too take up a feminist reading, but attempt to approach it from yet another angle, one that ultimately allows for most of these interpretations but frames them according to a different question, that of representation or mediation. I wish to show that both *Shame* the novel, as well as "shame" the concept as it is articulated in the novel, are conceptualizations of a dialectic of representation, and *as such* necessarily engage a feminist dialectic. Ultimately, I argue that the novel formulates a critique of the domination of women not through the women represented, but through the representation of these women.

> The country in this story is not Pakistan, or not quite. There are two countries, real and fictional, occupying the same space, or almost the same space. My story, my fictional country exist, like myself, at a slight angle to reality. I have found this off-centering to be necessary; but its value is, of course, open to debate. My view is that I am not writing only about Pakistan.
> —Salman Rushdie, *Shame*

As exemplified in this passage, the question of representation is overtly thematized in the novel with the overarching question of Pakistan versus Peccavistan. In this and other passages, the narrator interrogates the question he posits himself, whether the novel is about the fictional "Peccavistan" named in the novel or "really" about the real Pakistan. The obvious answer is that the novel retraces the historical, real-life infamous struggle for power over Pakistan between General Zia Ul-Haq and Zulfikar Ali Bhutto, respectively portrayed in the novel as Raza "Razor Guts" Hyder and Iskandar "Isky" Harrapa. But the answer is also "not quite," for the novel—as shown in the quote above—purposefully and overtly evades an isomorphic correlation between historical "fact" and textual "fiction." Furthermore, the novel cannot be easily classified: despite its allegorical moments, the novel is not an allegory because its levels of meaning are not distinct from each other. This is not a story about an imaginary country that is meant to be understood as Pakistan but a story about Pakistan that is not quite Pakistan. Likewise, the novel cannot be classified as "historical fiction" or even the textual equivalent of a "docu-drama" because instead of striving for verisimilitude as these genres require, the narrator shies away from it. The Pakistan/Peccavistan question thus serves to foreground the centrality of the question of representation to the novel, in all its levels of form and meaning.

If this were a realistic novel about Pakistan, I would not be talking about Bilquis and the wind; I would be talking about my youngest sister. Who is twenty-two, and studying engineering in Karachi; who can't sit on her hair anymore, and who (unlike me) is a Pakistani citizen. On my good days, I think of her as Pakistan, and then I feel very fond of the place, and find it easy to forgive its (her) love of Coca-Cola and imported motor-cars.

—Salman Rushdie, *Shame*

In order to take up this question of representation, I have chosen to focus my reading on the series of narratorial/authorial "asides" that recur throughout the novel, in which the narrator, taking on the persona of the real-life Rushdie himself, addresses the reader in a metanarrative that exposes his thoughts, memories, and deliberations in the process of writing the story of *Shame*.[2] As the passages already quoted in this paper show, these asides range in character, form, and content: from postmodernist theoretical analyses of the novel; through more personal ruminations or anecdotes that appear to be true to Salman Rushdie's "real" life and his relationship with Pakistan; to the narrator's deliberations as a writer of this self-same novel. Thus, the question of representation is foregrounded in these asides by their very appearance and conceit of being somewhat more real and ontologically less fictional. However, the act of mediation between the different levels of the story is represented as transparent, and, as a result, it is elided. And indeed, some of this novel's critics have referred to these passages as conclusive in that they can provide an authoritative key to an interpretation of the novel or, alternatively, provide the (conventionally missing) link between the real-life author and his fictional text.[3]

Ascribing the metanarrative to Rushdie himself is not as unaccountable as it may seem. The form of these metanarratives works relentlessly to give the impression of "laying bare the device." Because they foreground the novel's own conceits of representation, they do seem to be ontologically absolute moments of candor, truth, and almost transparency—of very limited (if any) mediation. Aijaz Ahmad, for one, is willing to accept this conceit for his purpose of talking about Rushdie's ideology: "The narrative within the book itself is controlled *transparently* by repeated direct, personal interventions on the part of the narrator—who is for the purposes of our interpretations here, mainly Rushdie himself" (Ahmad 132; emphasis added).

However, following Althusser, I would like to read these ostensibly "transparent" moments in the text as those not least, but most, pregnant with mediation and, consequently, with ideology. How then, does the narrator mediate his representation precisely at the point of the conceit of no mediation? In other words, the "different question" I wish to pose is not whether or how this novel represents (or misrepresents) women, Pakistan, or anything else for that matter; but rather the question of what this novel says about the very possibility and meaning of the act of representation and the mediations that are elided in this very act.

I begin this inquiry by looking closely at the narrator's own definition of his mode of representation. "If this were a realistic novel about Pakistan, [...]" says the narrator over and again in one of his longer asides (65–68). He then immediately proceeds to elaborate a list of things he would have had to include had this been a realistic novel about Pakistan. This marks and creates a formal contrast between the asides and the novel proper, thus producing a correlated dichotomy between the narrative (fiction) and metanarrative (fact). The markers of the real, as pointed out by the narrator, are of two related kinds: The first is a long list of historical/cultural/political ostensibly real-life anecdotes about Pakistan, ranging from corruption—"President Ayub Khan's alleged Swiss bank account"—to "genocide in Baluchistan"; from ludicrous censorship of Western films to globally strategic anti-Semitism (67). These anecdotes mark the real by their verifiable referentiality: many of these facts are common knowledge, and the rest can be authenticated by relatively simple research. The use of such referential facts imparts a similar truth effect to the whole of the metanarrative. But the result undercuts the narrator's own stated intent: he lists the things he *would have had* to include had this been a realistic novel; this, of course, creates the opposite effect—the "realistic" is de facto included in his novel and hence not excluded. Moreover, had he restricted his novel to these verifiable facts it could not have been a novel—characterized by its fictionality—but another documentation of some sort. In other words, the "realistic novel"—as defined by the narrator—is an oxymoron and could not have, in fact, been written.

The second marker of this would-be realistic novel is the personal anecdote, in which the narrator, in his Rushdie-persona, reveals the limits of his personal perspective and shows how his story of Pakistan is specific:

> Even though I lived in Pakistan for a long time, I have never lived there for longer than six months at a stretch. [...] I have learned Pakistan in slices, the same way as I have learned my growing sister. [...] I have felt closer to each successive incarnation [of my sister] than to the one before. (This goes for the country, too.)

> I think that what I am confessing is that, however I choose to write about over-there, I am forced to reflect that world in fragments of broken mirrors, [...]. I must reconcile myself to the broken bits. (66)

A number of things combine here to create a realistic effect. First is the confessional, autobiographical mode—we always tend to sound more "truthful" when we confess our limitations. The narrator seems to create a sense of candor and honesty by professing an inability to produce a complete narrative about Pakistan, due to his inconsistent residence in the country. But this candor is also ironic, for *Shame* is heavily invested, both thematically and formally, in fragmented, radically subjective narrative technique, as is much of Rushdie's fiction. The text itself implies that the narrator's inadequacy is shared by all human perspectives and narrators. In other words, neither he nor a full-fledged Pakistani resident could have created a comprehensive narrative. This is especially true in light of the repeated allusions to Pakistani censorship, rendering the "outsider" more, not less, capable of telling the "truth" about Pakistan. Thus, while the narrator is ostensibly confessing his limitations, he is at the same time showing that he is just as reliable a narrator as any other—his fragments are as good as the next; the "reconciliation" is a celebration. The same is true for the academic tone the narrator takes here and elsewhere in his asides, analyzing the narrative by means of the metanarrative. This seems to lay bare the device of the narrative, deconstructing the text, but yet again, the deconstructive moment turns on itself, exposing its very textuality as opposed to its referentiality. The result is that textuality, rather than referentiality, has become the marker of the reality-effect.

The second reality-effect component of the "personal" marker of the realistic novel is specificity. The narrator writes about his sister, "[w]ho is twenty-two, and studying engineering in Karachi; who can't sit on her hair anymore, and who (unlike me) is a Pakistani citizen" (65–66). This specificity and personal tone (as well as the production of the Rushdie persona) lends an autobiographical—hence non-fictional——tone to the text. But this marker is also short lived: the sister is almost immediately allegorized (in one of the most banal of allegorizations—woman-as-nation) as Pakistan. Nevertheless, this equation of specificity with the realistic is further supported by the text when the narrator states, two pages later, that

> By now, if I had been writing a book of this nature, it would have done me no good to protest that I was writing universally,

not only about Pakistan. The book would have been banned, dumped in the rubbish bin, burned. All that effort for nothing! Realism can break a writer's heart.

Fortunately, however, I am only telling a sort of modern fairy-tale, so that's all right; nobody need get upset, or take anything I say too seriously. No drastic action need be taken, either. (67–68)

This passage affords us a closer look at the reason given in the text for the separation of fictional narrative from its factual "realistic" metanarrative asides. Once more, the dichotomy of representation is thematized: a text can only be fictional or factual—either obscure to reality or transparent to it, realistic or "fairy-tale." It is in this vein that the reader is instructed to approach this text. Or maybe not? For in its sarcastic tone, the text subverts this fact/fiction dichotomy, alluding to its very impossibility. Moreover, in implicitly assigning this notion to the much-derided Pakistani censors, he emphasizes the over-simplification and ludicrousness of the very idea of such a dichotomy. Yet again, the text subverts the premises it establishes; turning a mirror onto both the transparency of the "realistic" metanarrative as well as the fictional "fairy-tale" narrative—and more importantly, to representation itself.

Representation is thus established as a troubled concept, central to the novel as a whole and specifically to the metanarrative within it. It constantly subverts the seemingly natural categories that it sets up; calling the concept of representation itself into question. Therefore, the "different question" that I have posited above regarding the very possibility and meaning of the act of representation and its mediation is pointed out by the text itself. What then, is represented by the novel's concern with representation? What might the meaning of this concern ultimately be? I approach these questions of representation through various theoretical and critical texts that inform my understanding of the intertwining dialectics of representation and feminism in *Shame*. In doing so, I will articulate my argument by differentiating it from these other texts, tracing, in a negative way, its own contours.

The first type of reading I would like to distance myself from in this context is the postcolonial deconstructionist reading espoused by Homi Bhabha in *The Location of Culture*.[5] Granted, the reading by which representation always already subverts and refracts its own ability to represent is one to which the text lends itself with great ease. The narrator's arguments for fragmented representation are convincing, for as I have shown they appear to be more truthful and "real." As a result, it becomes commonsensical, indeed almost natural to end by saying that we, like the narrator, must "reconcile" ourselves to the broken bits and fragmented mirrors through which we represent the world. For Bhabha, this would seem (as I have hinted it might seem for the narrator as well) a moment of celebration, "an empowering condition of hybridity; an emergence that turns 'return' into reinscription or redescription; an iteration that is not belated, but ironic and insurgent" (227). Thus the impasse of representation becomes an empowering moment, produced and reproduced through its rearticulation. The metanarrator (the Rushdie-persona) certainly seems to read his work that way. However, this paper follows the methodology of questioning that which seems natural. So, while Rushdie's prose does seem to go hand-in-hand with Bhabha's theory, I would like to attempt to release that clasp and read Rushdie's representation as a negative dialectic of shame constituting a dialectic of mediation because of its stakes for feminist reading.

Enter shame. It is the metanarrator who establishes the notion of shame as a dialectic, though he does not use the specific term: "What's the opposite of shame? What's left when *sharam* is subtracted? That's obvious:shamelessness" (33). First, we must note that the positioning of shamelessness opposite shame is not an obvious one. The lexical and semantic opposite of shame is not shamelessness but rather honor;[6] while the "opposite" of shamelessness would be shamefulness. Opposing shame and shamelessness in this text is, of course, hardly a mistake or misunderstanding, but rather an indication that the relationship between the two concepts is not one of opposites, but one of negation (subtraction) and hence a dialectic. The dialectic of shame in this novel is not with its opposite—honor, but with its lack—shamelessness. The antithesis is not distinct from the thesis, but rather inscribed within its production: shameless behavior produces shame.

Having (tentatively) identified shame as the thesis and shamelessness as its antithesis, the narrator continues, "Between shame and shamelessness lies the axis upon which we turn [...]. Shamelessness, shame: the roots of violence" (118). What then is the nature of this dialectic, which, fierce and destructive, can only generate violence? I would like to show that it can be read in three ways, all of which are supported by the novel itself. The first is a dialectic that consists of a juxtaposition of two opposites and an ability to contain them both at the same time; the second is one that establishes a self/other dependency between its two components and then internalizes that relationship in order to overcome it; the third form is related to Horkheimer and Adorno's negative dialectic, wherein the dialectical relationship necessarily produces excess or residue, thus providing its own undoing and/or critique.

The key to the first reading can be found in the last metanarrational aside of the novel, opening a chapter entitled "Stability": the narrator recounts discussing a play, Büchner's *Danton's Death*, which he has seen with "visitors from Pakistan": "'The point is,' one of my friends argued, 'that this opposition exists all right; but it is an internal dialectic.' That made sense. The people are not only like Robspierre. They, we, are Danton too. We are Robeston and Danpierre. The inconsistency doesn't matter; I myself manage to hold large numbers of wholly irreconcilable views simultaneously, without the least difficulty. I do not think others are less versatile" (256). The narrator understands the dialectic to be the subject's ability to hold or embody two or more inconsistent and even irreconcilable views at the same time. It is, in his mind, a matter of versatility, reminiscent once again of Bhabha's empowering notion of the hybridity of the migrant whose ability to be many things at once is his advantage over others.[7]

Against this understanding of dialectic-as-hybridity the metanarrator shows a different understanding, again gleaned from the opposition between Danton and Robespierre in that same play, of the nature of the dialectic. He comments: "This opposition—the epicure against the puritan—is [...] the true dialectic of history. [...] Virtue versus vice, ascetic versus bawd, God against the Devil: that's the game" (254). What is forcefully implied is that the last, unnamed, item in this list of oppositions is that between shame and shamelessness. This relationship between the puritan and the epicure, and hence between shame and shamelessness, is more complex than the mere juxtaposition of the irreconcilable. For the two entities in this reading of a dialectic are dependent upon each other for their very existence—the epicure can only be defined as such or become one against an existing notion of puritanity that he or she can then transgress. Hence the dialectic between shame and shamelessness—the latter is and can only be defined against the former, which is in turn constituted by the latter. There is no unmarked term upon which the relationship hinges. In other words, shamelessness can only be defined against shame, whereas it is through shameless behavior that shame is created. I will continue elaborating on this point, but not before the (belated) introduction of Sufiya Zinobia Hyder, shame incarnate; and her husband Omar Khayyam Shakil, the embodiment of shamelessness.[8]

Sufiya Zinobia is born into shame for being a girl instead of a boy. At the age of almost two, she contracts brain fever; the cure leaves her mentally retarded. As Ahmad correctly observes, in the course of the novel, her shame "comes to refer less and less to herself (her femaleness, her mental retardation) or to her family and becomes increasingly focused on the world as Sufiya finds it; she becomes, almost literally, the conscience of the shameless world" (146). Her allegorical marriage to Omar Khayyam, forbidden by his three shameful mothers to feel shame, reinforces the interdependence of the two concepts they embody.

The above second reading is, indeed, dialectical in portraying the dependency of the two opposites on each other, the metanarrator now adopting a more Hegelian view of the dialectic—"the true dialectic of history" (254). The result of this dialectic is overcoming its opposition by progressing to a third term that preserves that which it overcomes. Thus the dialectical opposites are contained within a trajectory of progression. In this case, the metanarrator takes "shame" and "shamelessness" and pits them against each other, creating the narrative that preserves them both, but contained, now understood as "the game." Shame and shamelessness are no longer as threatening since they are contained by their very dependency on each other; they can be transcended, grasped from without.

But this view from without carries its own dangers. First and foremost, the position of exteriority gives the observer the privilege of not being implicated in or by the dialectical terms. The metanarrator assumes he recognizes the dialectic for what it is and that "it" is extrinsic to himself. Having the power of comprehension, he is able to transcend the dialectic; he is on the outside looking in. He is not part of shame or shamelessness because he is able to explain them. This can lead (and, I argue, does lead) to a reification of the concepts of shame and shamelessness. And indeed, shame is represented as an object whose meaning is sealed, independent and exterior to its user; hence it is reified and, ultimately, fetishized as "Eastern": "This word: shame. No, I must write it in its original form, not in this peculiar language tained by wrong concepts [...] *Sharam*, that's the word. For which this paltry 'shame' is a wholly inadequate translation. Three letters, *shin rè mìm* (written naturally, from right to left)" (33). Shame is (or was) a pure "natural" Eastern (Oriental?) concept, before it was "tainted" by the English language. This quote assumes, of course, that concepts exist originally in pure form, untainted by a subject position from which they are uttered.[9]

All things considered, this version of the dialectic does not, in my mind, account for the mediation at work within it. The ideas of shame and shamelessness are not unmediated concepts or received notions simply reflecting an external, pre-existing concept. Rather, it is only in their articulation from concrete subject positions that they become meaningful. In the above, second, reading of the dialectic, shame and shamelessness are perceived as hermetic unequivocal concepts; this reading thus lacks an awareness of the subject position that creates their meaning.

If we want to go beyond a description of the personification of shame towards an explanation of it—to distinguish between what shame is and the way it manifests itself—we must first acknowledge that a double set of mediations is at work in the conceptualization of shame in the novel. One is the representation of shame as a reified object; the second, of course, the personification of this construct in Sufiya Zinobia. Following the methodological steps of Moishe Postone in his essay "Anti-Semitism and National Socialism," we can recognize that the two mediations present themselves antinomically, as the opposition of the abstract (concept/word) and the concrete (the character).[10] Postone argues that "[b]ecause, additionally, both sides of the antinomy are objectified, each appears to be quasi-natural" (308). As I have shown, both the mediations in the novel— shame as a reified object as well as Sufiya as shame personified—have indeed been objectified and naturalized. It is exactly a wariness of the naturalness of these two representations that leads me to the third, most productive way to read the dialectic in this novel: looking at these mediations *through each other*, in a negative dialectic.

This methodology can be traced to Horkheimer and Adorno's *Dialectic of the Enlightenment*. Their dialectical approach is characterized by the use of the self same concept as both object and subject position. In fact, according to Martin Jay, it is the ability to include both these moments, negative as well as positive, which is presented as the very strength of the concept (*Begriffe*) by Horkheimer and Adorno (261). In their critique, the Enlightenment is both the object and the subject position for their project. This is not to say that the two—enlightenment as historical object and enlightenment as theory—are identical. In fact it is the way they both "escape" this identity that creates their dialectic in the form of reflective opposition. A similar move can be located in their reading of Homer's *Odyssey*; the text serves both as an object of their reading and at the same time as the source of theory for that very reading. Finally, the notion of sacrifice within the *Odyssey* is elaborated as an ultimate dialectical moment; Odysseus is both sacrifice and priest (Horkheimer and Adorno 50), a nexus for their reading of the *Odyssey* as the "inherent relationship between self-renunciation and self preservation" (Jay 264). Thus, the same dialectical move is traced in three different levels of *Dialectic of the Enlightenment*: in its overarching project (the dialectic of enlightenment); in its approach to the literary (the reading of the *Odyssey*); and in its analysis of trope within the literary text (the analysis of sacrifice). This provides a methodological understanding of the negative (cultural) dialectic as the use of subject matter (object) as theorizing its own conceptuality. In other words, closer to those of Horkheimer and Adorno, this method negates the object with its own perception, while maintaining their "reflective opposition" (Jay 267).

An invitation to take this third approach can also be located in the novel. Since *Shame* is not a purely allegorical novel, both Sufiya and Omar Khayyam are but *representations* of shame and shamelessness; the characters do not embody that which they represent, because they cannot do so. Due to this very act of mediation, they are in excess of their corresponding concepts as well as of each other. Ahmad makes this precise observation, but fails to follow through on its meaning: "[T]he very dialectic—of shamelessness and shame, and their condensation in eruptions of violence—which governs the conceptual framework of the novel is fundamentally flawed; symbolic values that Rushdie assigns to Sufiya Zinobia simply exceed the terms within which he has fashioned her whole existence" (146). Moreover, and at the same time, her existence exceeds the symbolic value she embodies. It is this excess that is the marker of mediation—of the impossibility of a complete allegorical identification between the character and what she purportedly represents. Thus, this excess is not a "flaw" in the conceptual framework of the novel, but is the inevitable residue, intrinsic to the negative dialectic, according to Horkheimer and Adorno.

This approach accords with that of Marjorie Levinson, who takes Ahmad to task for a Marxist reading of *Shame* that "reproduces the false antithesis identified by Lukàcs as the foundation of capitalist science: namely, immediacy and abstraction" (103). Levinson argues that Ahmad's reading is not dialectical, thus espousing a "binary, moralistic, transcendental critique" (107). Reading Sufiya Zinobia and Omar Khayyam as transparencies through which one can see shame and shamelessness and their dialectic, ultimately results in a reification, wherein the abstraction of shame is naturally perceived to *be personified* or actualized in Sufiya Zinobia, shamelessness in Omar Khayyam, and the dialectic at work in their relationship.

We return to shame, now approached as a negative dialectic. We no longer need shamelessness to create this dialectic, because the negation of shame is already contained in its conceptualization. In other words, the dialectical relationship is no longer that of shame and shamelessness but rather of shame as object and its perception as such. Since neither of these representations is transparent, they must be "detoured through another transparency"—observed through each other—for "unless they are so produced, they remain abstractions masquerading as particulars" (Levinson 115). Only when we look at shame as a nontransparency, as a reified construct, through another nontransparency, the mediated characters, can we examine its naturalization by asking *why* and *how* Sufiya Zinobia is incarnated as shame.

The best place to do so is the aside in which the metanarrator describes his real-life and imaginary sources—his how and why—for his "heroine." Sufiya Zinobia was initially created "out of the corpse" (118) of a Pakistani girl in London who was stabbed to death by her father for making love to a white boy and bringing "such dishonour upon her family that only her blood could wash away the stain" (117). Two more "phantoms" join the first girl in the making of Sufiya Zinobia, both from London, another girl and a boy. The girl, "'Asian' again," is beaten up by a group of white teenage boys, and "afterwards, remembering her beating, she feels not angry but ashamed." In the narrator-as-writer's imagination the violence that is the result of shame unleashes in the second girl great fury and strength far beyond her physical ability, as she "thrashed the white kids within an inch of their lives" (119). The boy, "from a news clipping" had been found "blazing in a parking lot" (120). Apparently (and unaccountably) he had ignited of his own accord.

How do these three sources work against or with each other in the implied writer's mind? How are they perceived and objectified? Let us begin with the first girl. The narrator recounts how the story of her murder "appalled" him not only because of the infanticide itself, but because of the family's friends and relatives who refused to condemn the father's actions and understood the man's point of view, and went on supporting him even when it turned out that the girl had never actually "gone all the way" with her boyfriend (117).

The narrator's horror is increased when he realizes that the girl did not really "go all the way," which implies that had she done so, her death would still have been unjustifiable, but a little less so, perhaps because in his eyes the shame is real, even if the means of its eradication are wrong. Further explanation is given when the narrator candidly admits: "But even more appalling was my realization that like the interviewed friends etc., I, too, found myself understanding the killer" (117).

This moment of great honesty and self-reflection speaks for an understanding of the subjective nature of shame, for its location in the mind of the beholder. But the narrator is quick to externalize this understanding: "The news did not seem alien to me. We who have grown up on a diet of honour and shame can still grasp what must seem unthinkable to peoples living in the aftermath of the death of God and of tragedy: that men will sacrifice their dearest love on the implacable altars of their pride" (117–18).

The narrator resists personal agency and responsibility and ascribes it to his own socialization, thus separating this cultural conditioning from his "real" self. But at the same time he does something more subtle but still of crucial importance—he shifts his focus of inquiry from the concept of shame to its consequences. It is the murder that obsesses the narrator, and not shame, which is left as an unanalyzed given; a commodity to be consumed: "a diet of honour and shame." This is supported by the conclusion of this paragraph, which I have already quoted: "Shamelessness, shame: the roots of violence" (118). The narrator's thesis, and, to some extent, the novel's, is about the connection between shame and violence and not, despite the text's repeated claims, about the origin of shame itself. The latter is perceived and presented as an immediate fact, not a social construct.

Even more tellingly, the narrator describes his obsession with shame as manifested in the girl's dead body: "Wanting to write about shame, I was at first haunted by the imagined spectre of that dead body." The description of the (imagined) body that follows reads like a clichéd buildup to a detective novel,[11] once again reifying the specific in the generic. The description continues in biblical form, using "And" for narrative progression, culminating in "And the father left with blood-cleansed name and grief" (118). This too serves to reify the murder, placing it within a mythological order, before the death of God, evoking the story of Ibrahim/Abraham's sacrifice of Ishmael (in the Islamic tradition) or Isaac (in the Judeo-Christian tradition).[12] The tone of this passage is severely censorious; there seems to be no possible reading that would sanction this murder in any way. In fact, the inclusion of these two disparate genres—crime fiction and biblical register—serves to critique and implicate them in the death of the young girl. However, in the process of doing so, the girl is distanced, effaced, and the text refocuses—uncritically—on the idea; on shame as a reified construct.

It seems that the narrator feels that he has "lost" the girl and attempts to return to her in the next passage:

> I even went so far as to give the dead girl a name: Anahita Muhammad, known as Anna. In my imagination she spoke with an East London accent but wore jeans, blue brown pink, out of some atavistic reluctance to show her legs. She would certainly have understood the language her parents spoke at home but would obstinately have refused to utter a word of it herself. Anna Muhammad: lively, no doubt attractive, a little too dangerously so at sixteen. Mecca meant ballrooms to her, rotating silver balls, strobe lighting, youth. She danced behind my eyes, her nature changing each time I glimpsed her: now innocent, now whore, then a third or fourth thing. But finally she eluded me, she

became a ghost, and I realized that to write about her, about shame, I would have to go back East, to let the idea breathe its favourite air. Anna, deported, repatriated to a country she had never seen, caught brain-fever and turned into a sort of idiot.

He names her. The real-life girl about whom he had read in the papers, must have had a name and, since the story was so publicized, one that should have been relatively easy to find out. But the narrator is no longer interested in the girl herself but in the concept of shame she has come to embody for him. His final move of abstraction from the specific woman is done, paradoxically, by personifying her as concept; appropriating her to himself. She now exists only in his imagination as his "private dancer." This is the dialectical moment where the concept—shame—reveals both its abstraction from its underlying misogyny (its "labor process") and its objectification in the reified personification of the girl.[13]

What can we then discover about shame through this moment when the two mediations are superimposed on each other? We find that in order to conceptualize shame the narrator had to rid the girl of her specificity and to internalize and appropriate her. The girl, object of shame, does not have a subject position within the dialectic, for it is contained within the male gaze. She is trapped between the (male) imperative for her to be attractive and the "danger" (also from men) of being so. Her status as object is further illustrated when the narrator describes her changing nature as a succession of "things" that are already inscribed by the very idea he is analyzing: "innocent" or "whore" assumes shame. The changing nature of the girl moves from one category of shame to another but does not question the categories themselves. We seem to have a variant of the Hegelian master-slave dialectic. The narrator has internalized the girl; in looking at her he finds himself, manifested in his (socialized) perceptions of received categories.

However, the passage is more complex. Even trapped inside his imagination, a figure seemingly identifiable with his conception of shame, the girl manages to elude the narrator: she dances *behind* his eyes and then becomes a ghost—a magic that, according to Horkheimer and Adorno, is the residue and excess of the dialectic. She thus escapes identification as shame. In order to recapture her the narrator/writer takes her "*back* East" and she turns into "a sort of idiot." The narrator never answers the question he asks of himself: "Why did I do that to her?" (119) We can only conjecture that this too was an attempt to empty her of a subject position, make her conform to the idea she is supposed to embody, by turning her into a sheer victim. But

Sufiya Zinobia refuses to comply. In her furious (though unconscious) outbursts she kills and mutilates, avenging shame—both hers and others'.

This second quality of shame, that which avenges its own shamefulness, is not left abstract by the metatext either, but is personified by the second girl. However, she who is given agency, is not named. This vengeful quality of shame is described by Rushdie—both in the narrative and in the metanarrative—as the regenerative possibility for women, and, as others have noted, a very bleak option at that. In any case, the important thing to note at this point is the necessity of splitting the two qualities of shame, personifying them in two girls. The incommensurability of either girl with shame, their relegation into the supernatural, to magic, is the marker of negative dialectic—that which negates the object through its own perception.

We find ourselves at an impasse: despite the narrator's honest attempts to give a voice and a central place to women and the shame that oppresses them, his narrative ultimately circles back on itself, generalizing the singular, turning oppression into abstraction. Is this, then, simply an "honorable failure" as Gayatri Spivak would have it? ("Reading" 223). I have suggested that this need not necessarily be the case. Our way out of this impasse is indicated by Marjorie Levinson: "the appropriate Marxist move is to search out the historical conditions of that representation of *arrested dialectic*. [...T]he contradictions and arrests that deform Rushdie's novel, keeping it from assuming some received utopian shape, also give it the power to shadow forth its culture's immanent and founding negation" (124–25, emphasis added).

In order to perform this search, we must return to the idea of sacrifice, constitutive both of Rushdie's *Shame* and of Horkheimer and Adorno's *Dialectic of Enlightenment*. In the former, shame is repeatedly referred to as a form of sacrifice.[14] Of the father who murdered his daughter the narrator says: "men will sacrifice their dearest love on the implacable altars of their pride" (118). In this description, men are subjects while their "love" (again an abstraction of the woman/daughter as defined by men's regard) functions as the object (15). This is the difference between Rushdie's sacrifice and Horkheimer and Adorno's, where it is Odysseus who embodies both sacrifice and priest, thus obliterating the subject/object split.

In order to do the same, Rushdie's father must kill the girl. In his perception he is sacrificing part of himself—"his dearest love"—he too is both sacrifice and priest. The subject (man)/object (woman) split is ultimately internalized in the father as a dialectic. Once again, Rushdie shifts the focus from the woman, whose plight he is trying to underscore, to the struggles of the man. Andrew Hewitt finds that Horkheimer and Adorno do the same: "That male domination involves a certain *self-immolation* on the part of the male may well be true—very probably it is—but the thrust of the argument here is to bypass man's domination of woman in the rush to get at the crux of the issue, the "real" heart of the matter: man's alienated domination of himself" (154–55, emphasis added).

So we arrive at the third source of Sufiya Zinobia, as elaborated in the metanarrative, the boy who burns to death, apparently from self-combustion. Anna is the victim, or object, of shame; the second, nameless, girl turns shame into agency, a subject position; but it takes a boy to put the two together.

In her seminal essay "Can the Subaltern Speak?" Gayatri Spivak has shown that a woman cannot be represented as both priest and sacrifice of her own sati. The practice of sati, argues Spivak, has been represented, time and again, by various dominant discourses (whether "brown" or "white," feminist or not) but in all those discourses the sexed subaltern is always the *object*, never the *subject* of her self-immolation, not to mention both at once. Her argument is corroborated by this novel. Rushdie needs the boy to incorporate both subject and object positions. The boy is both subject and object of his pyre; both priest and sacrifice of his self-immolation. He is the one who discovers "the truth" (120).[15]

Linked thematically as well as theoretically through the motif of self-immolation, this argument—of the gendered subject/object split internalized within man—resonates with Andrew Hewitt's feminist reading of the *Dialectic of Enlightenment* where he traces the exclusion of women in the internalization of the dialectic by man: "in focusing upon the category of (masculine) self-domination. Horkheimer and Adorno ignore the persistence of outer-directed domination—man's domination of woman, for example. The central role played by the category of alienation [...] allows them to focus, among other things, upon: 'male domination, which—as a permanent deprivation of instinct—is nevertheless a symbolic self-mutilation on the part of the man [Adorno and Horkheimer 72]'" (Hewitt 154–55).

According to Hewitt, man interpolates himself, through sacrifice, from the realm of domination to that of power, which is domination by representation. "[Man] trades off his subordination to a network of power in order to maintain his own direct privilege" (144). As we have seen in *Shame*, man indeed sacrifices one part of himself—"his dearest love"—in order to gain power (represented as pride) over the woman. However, by so doing, argues Hewitt, he loses the *experience* of domination, which is relegated to women, instrumentalized as the representation of exclusion. (The woman, by the way, loses her life.) He points out that Horkheimer and Adorno, although cognizant of the exclusion of women as a category, "are obliged to repeat the generalizing gesture they condemn. How can it be asserted that 'woman' is denied the honor of individualization without once again denying her the honor of individualization, by forcing her into the singular yet generic category of 'woman'?" (148)

If we agree that power is domination as representation then we have to conclude that Rushdie's women characters—represented as they are in both in narrative and metanarrative—are certainly unemancipated. But, as Hewitt shows, there is no way for them to be represented as emancipated for it is the very representation that dominates them. Moreover, even if this were possible it would result in a liberation from domination into a more complex system of power (157).

However, the solution to yet another variant of the impasse described above is the foregrounding of representation itself. This, argues Hewitt, is suggested by the *Dialectic of Enlightenment*: "The 'way out,' which is really a 'way in,' a way into the very heart of representation—that Horkheimer and Adorno offer consists in articulating in and through the figure of woman a critique not only of social relations made possible within a certain system of representation but a critique of the representational system itself" (157). Thus, the novel formulates a critique of the domination of women not through the women represented, but through the representation of these women.

Rephrasing this argument in the terms set by Spivak, I can say that the sexed subaltern subject still does not speak. The novel does not give a voice to Anahita/Anna, or to the unnamed "Asian girl" or even to its fictional characters, foremost Sufiya Zinobia. However, its representation of these women can be read as exposing the violence and the silencing imposed on their voices by the selfsame representation—ultimately echoing Spivak's own argument.

What I have tried to represent in this paper is the double mediation at work in Rushdie's representation of shame. I have shown that this concept is both a reified abstraction of the social forces dominating women *as well* as a cause for this domination of women. The metanarrator does not seem to be cognizant of this distinction. Thus, while declaring his interrogation of the concept he is, in fact, questioning the causal connection between shame and the violence (domination) it generates. In this he is unsuccessful: the connection cannot be severed because the domination is inherent in the concept itself. On the other hand, the concept cannot be interrogated because it is a naturalized abstraction of the social forces at work.

However, through the excess accrued in the process of this naturalization in the text, Rushdie marks its non-immanent, representational quality, or, if you will, its negative component. Focusing on these moments of this text, we can defamiliarize them, gaining access to their "mode of production." By superimposing these two mediations upon each other we find an entering point into what initially had seemed like a vicious circle. Thus, the novel's radical critique is located in the narrative's *inability* to embody shame in one character, in Anna's evasion and disappearance, in the residue and excess accompanying each and every attempt at representation—and especially that of women—in the novel. Shame, in this case, is a reified abstraction of men's domination of women; its failure to be represented reveals its abstraction and thus harbors its own critique.

NOTES

I would like to thank Colleen Lye, Shai Ginsburg, Amy Huber, Irene Perciali and Jenny L. White for their rigorous and encouraging comments on earlier versions of this paper.

1. Mufti makes this claim in his discussion of Rushdie's fourth novel, *The Satanic Verses*, but I think that it can be easily applied here with the same degree of success. (My critique of Mufti's argument will be implied in a later stage of this paper.)

2. While the narrative implies that this metanarrator is indeed the real-life Salman Rushdie, he is not the implied author of this narrative, hence my decision not to refer to him as such. The implied author is commonly understood as a construct of the text "inferred and assembled by the reader from all the components of the text" (Rimmon-Kenan 87). The narrative voice I quote throughout this essay is not implied by the text or inferred from it. Rather it has a distinct narrative *presence* in the novel. I have called it the metanarrator to distinguish this voice from that of the narrator of the diegesis itself. The metanarrator narrates the process of narration of the diegesis.

3. See for instance Ahmad, who writes in reference to the meta-narrative passages, "we should recall what Rushdie himself tells us [...]" (133).

4. A good case in point is the genre of the *realist* novel in the tradition of Eliot, Balzac, and Dickens, which, paradoxically, achieves its reality effect in its fictionality (which enables its narrative omniscience and detailed specificity) and not in its fidelity to reference. See Gallagher.

5. Especially 223–29, where he discusses Rushdie's *The Satanic Verses*.

6. As attested by Rushdie himself: "Because shame and its opposite, which is honour, seem to me kind of central to the society I was describing, to such an extent that it was impossible to explain the society except by looking at it through those concepts" ("*Midnight's Children*" 54).

7. Most would argue, and I would agree, that this is not a *dialectic* relationship. But since it is explicitly named so in the novel, I have decided to leave it, possibly in the interest of a future observation of the post-structural, deconstructive adoption and (mis)use of the dialectic concept.

8. Since my paper focuses specifically on the metanarrative asides in this novel, I will in no way be giving a comprehensive reading of these characters, who are at the center of the narrative itself. They are presented here briefly, in order to introduce the discussion of how these characters are represented and talked about in the metanarrative.

9. Or may be untainted as long as they are uttered by those who were "naturally" meant to use the concept in its "pure" form.

10. My indebtedness to Postone's essay goes much farther and wider than its specific contribution here; it has influenced and indeed shaped my argument throughout this paper.

11. À la Raymond Chandler, or a scene in the film noir genre of cinema.

12. The girl's throat is described as "slit like a halal chicken" implying the God-instructed purifying process this murder brings about.

13. And note the narrator's shame at his own "understanding" of the murder.

14. Elsewhere, the narrator says of Sufiya Zinobia, "What is a saint? A saint is a person who suffers in our stead" (146).

15. However, though the boy can embody both the subject and object of his sacrifice—internalizing the dialectic—he is not directly linked to shame. This, I would argue, is due to his maleness—since shame is a category used (as I have shown) for the domination of women.

WORKS CITED

Ahmad, Aijaz. *In Theory: Classes, Nations, Literatures*. London: Verso, 1992.

Althusser, Louis. *Reading Capital*. Trans. Ben Brewster. London: Verso, 1997.

Bhabha, Homi K. *The Location of Culture*. New York: Routledge, 1994.

Booker, M. Keith, ed. *Critical Essays on Salman Rushdie*. New York: Hall, 1999.

Cundy, Catherine. *Salman Rushdie*. Manchester: Manchester UP, 1996.

Gallagher, Catherine. *Nobody's Story: The Vanishing Acts of Women Writers in the Marketplace 1670–1820*. Berkeley: U of California P, 1994.

Hai, Ambreen. "'Marching In from the Peripheries': Rushdie's Feminized Artistry and Ambivalent Feminism." Booker 16–50.

Hewitt, Andrew. "A Feminine Dialectic of Enlightenment? Horkheimer and Adorno Revisited." *New German Critique* 56 (1992): 143–170.

Horkheimer, Max, and Theodor W. Adorno. *Dialectic of Enlightenment*. 1947. Trans. John Cumming. New York: Continuum, 1998.

Jay, Martin. *The Dialectic Imagination: A History of the Frankfurt School and the Institute of Social Research 1923–1950*. Berkeley: UC Press, 1973.

Levinson, Marjorie. "News from Nowhere: The Discontents of Ahmad Aijaz." *Debating in Theory. Spec.* issue of *Public Culture: Society for Transnational Cultural Studies* 6 (1993): 97–131.

Mufti, Aamir. "Reading the Rushdie Affair: 'Islam,' Cultural Politics, Form. "Booker 51–77.

Needham, Anuradha Dingwaney. "The Politics of Post-Colonial Identity in Salman Rushdie." *Massachusetts Review* 26:4 (1988–89): 609–24.

Postone, Moishe. "Anti-Semitism and National Socialism." *Germans and Jews since the Holocaust: The Changing Situation in West Germany*, Ed. Anson Rabinbach and Jack Zipes. New York: Holmes, 1986. 302–14.

Rimmon-Kenan, Shlomith. *Narrative Fiction: Contemporary Poetics*. New York: Routledge, 1983.

Rushdie, Salman. *"Midnight's Children and Shame." Kunapipi 7.1* (1985): 1–19.

———. *Shame*. New York: Knopf, 1983.

Spivak, Gayatri Chakravorty. "Reading The Satanic Verses." *Outside the Teaching Machine*. New York: Routledge, 1993. 223.

———. "Can the Subaltern Speak?" *Marxism and the Interpretation of Culture*. Ed. Cary Nelson and Lawrence Grosberg. Urbana: U. of Illinois P, 1988. 271–316.

Chronology

1947	Ahmed Salman Rushdie is born in Bombay, India to Anis Ahmed Rushdie and Negin Rushdie. Pakistan divides from India at the end of British colonialism in South Asia.
1961	Moves to England to attend Rugby (school).
1962–64	Lives with his family in Kensington, England.
1965–68	Attends King's College in Cambridge, England.
1968	Receives an M.A. in History with Honors from King's College. Works in both Pakistan and London in television production, publishing, and advertising.
1968–69	Works as an actor in the Fringe Theater, London.
1970-73	Works as a freelance advertising copywriter.
1975	Publishes *Grimus*.
1976	Marries Clarissa Luard.
1976–1980	Again works as a freelance advertising copywriter.
1976-1983	Serves as executive member of the Camden Committee for Community Relations, assisting emigrants from Bangladesh. Begins to develop sensitivity for the plight of the South Asian emigrant.
1981	Publishes *Midnight's Children*, which gains him fame in both Britain and South Asia. The novel wins the Booker McConnell Prize for fiction, the English-Speaking Union

Literary Award, and the "Booker of Bookers" prize for the best novel to win the Booker prize in its first twenty five years.

1982   *Midnight's Children* wins the James Tait Black Memorial Prize.

1983   Publishes *Shame*.

1984   *Shame* wins the French Prix du Meilleur Livre Etranger in postmodernist fiction.

1985   Produces the documentary film *The Painter and the Pest*.

1986   Travels to Sandinista Nicaragua.

1987   Publishes *The Jaguar Smile: A Nicaraguan Journey*, a diary of his travels. Divorces estranged wife Clarissa Luard.

1988   Produces the documentary film *The Riddle of Midnight*. Marries American writer Marianne Wiggins. Publishes *The Satanic Verses*, which wins the Whitbread Prize in Great Britain and Germany's Author of the Year Award. The novel is banned in a dozen countries and causes protests and riots in India, Pakistan, and South Africa, leading to eleven deaths and sixty injuries.

1989   The Ayatollah Khomeini accuses Rushdie of blasphemy and denounces him in a *fatwah* (death sentence). Rushdie divorces Marianne Wiggins.

1990   Publishes *Haroun and the Sea of Stories*. Publishes *Imaginary Homeland: Essays and Criticism, 1981-1991*. Japanese translator of *The Satanic Verses* is stabbed to death.

1993   Is honorary Visiting Professor of Humanities at Massachusetts Institute of Technology. Appears with other writers in a BBC documentary *In Search of Oz*.

1994   Publishes *East, West*.

1995   Publishes *The Moor's Last Sigh*, which wins the Whitbread Novel of the Year Award and is shortlisted for the Booker Prize.

1996   Marries Elizabeth West.

1997   Publishes the anthology *The Vintage Book of Indian Writing, 1947-1977* with Elizabeth West to coincide with the fiftieth anniversary of the founding of India.

1999   Publishes *The Ground Beneath Her Feet: A Novel.*

2001   Publishes *Fury: A Novel.* Publishes essay entitled "Fighting
            the Forces of Invisibility" in Giorgio Baravalle's anthology
            *NEW YORK SEPTEMBER ELEVEN TWO THOUSAND
            ONE.*

Contributors

HAROLD BLOOM is Sterling Professor of the Humanities at Yale University and Henry W. and Albert A. Berg Professor of English at the New York University Graduate School. He is the author of over 20 books, including *Shelley's Mythmaking* (1959), *The Visionary Company* (1961), *Blake's Apocalypse* (1963), *Yeats* (1970), *A Map of Misreading* (1975), *Kabbalah and Criticism* (1975), *Agon: Toward a Theory of Revisionism* (1982), *The American Religion* (1992), *The Western Canon* (1994), and *Omens of Millennium: The Gnosis of Angels, Dreams, and Resurrection* (1996). *The Anxiety of Influence* (1973) sets forth Professor Bloom's provocative theory of the literary relationships between the great writers and their predecessors. His most recent books include *Shakespeare: The Invention of the Human* (1998), a 1998 National Book Award finalist, *How to Read and Why* (2000), and *Genius: A Mosaic of One Hundred Exemplary Creative Minds* (2002). In 1999, Professor Bloom received the prestigious American Academy of Arts and Letters Gold Medal for Criticism, and in 2002 he received the Catalonia International Prize.

M. D. FLETCHER has taught at the University of Queensland, Australia, and is the editor of *Reading Rushdie: Perspectives on the Fiction of Salman Rushdie*.

HENRY LOUIS GATES, JR. is W.E.B. Du Bois Professor of the Humanities, Chair of Afro-American Studies, and Director of the W.E.B. Du Bois Institute for Afro-American Research at Harvard University. His many works include *Figures in Black: Words, Signs, and the Racial Self* (1987) and *The Signifying Monkey: Towards a Theory of Afro-American Literary Criticism* (1988).

CATHERINE CUNDY has taught at the University of Kent, England and is the author of *Salman Rushdie*.

K.M. NEWTON has published several books on George Eliot and on literary theory. Most recently, Newton is the co-author of *George Eliot, Judaism and the Novels: Jewish Myth and Mysticism* (with Saleel Nurbhai).

NICHOLAS D. ROMBES, JR. is Associate Professor of English at the University of Detroit Mercy, where he co-founded the journal *Post-Identity*. He has published several essays on American literature in the Federalist period.

VIJAY MISHRA is Professor of English and Comparative Literature and Head of the School of Arts at Murdoch University, Perth, Western Australia. He is the author of many books and articles on literature, aesthetics, cultural studies and film theory, including *Dark Side of the Dream: Australian Literature and the Postcolonial Mind* (with Bob Hodge) and *The Gothic Sublime*.

ELENI COUNDOURIOTIS is Assistant Professor of English at the University of Connecticut and the author of *Claiming History: Colonialism, Ethnography, and the Novel*.

PAUL A. CANTOR is Professor of English at the University of Virginia and a member of the National Council on the Humanities. He is the author of *Shakespeare's Rome* and *Hamlet*, as well as *Creature and Creator: Myth-Making and English Romanticism*.

JOSNA E. REGE is Assistant Professor of English at Dartmouth College, where she teaches postcolonial literature and theory and twentieth-century British fiction. In addition to her work on Salman Rushdie, she has published articles on Anita Desai and Doris Lessing.

BRIAN FINNEY is Lecturer at California State University, Long Beach, and has taught literature at the University of London, University of California, Los Angeles, and University of Southern California. He has published books on Samuel Beckett, Christopher Isherwood, D. H. Lawrence, and modern autobiography.

JOHN CLEMENT BALL is the Editor of *Studies in Canadian Literature /
Etudes en litterature canadienne*. He has published articles on Hanif Kureishi,
Derek Walcott, Janet Frame, Robert Kroetsch, and others.

STEPHEN BAKER is Lecturer in English at South Bank University in
London, England. He specializes postmodern fiction and theory, and has
published essays on Alasdair Grey and Martin Amis.

AYELET BEN-YISHAI is a Ph.D. candidate in the Department of
Comparative Literature at the University of California, Berkeley. She is
currently working on her dissertation, "Establishing Narrative Authority:
Representation of Reality in Legal Narratives and the Realist Novel in
Nineteenth Century France and England."

Bibliography

Akhtar, Shabbir. *Be Careful with Muhammad!: The Salman Rushdie Affair*. London : Bellew, 1989.

Al-Raheb, Hani. "Religious Satire in Rushdie's *Satanic Verses*." *Journal of the Fantastic in the Arts* 6, no. 4 (1995): 330-339.

Appignanesi, Lisa, and Sara Maitland, eds. *The Rushdie File*. Syracuse, NY: Syracuse University Press, 1990.

Baker, Stephen. "'You Must Remember This': Salman Rushdie's *The Moor's Last Sigh*." *The Journal of Commonwealth Literature* 35, no. 1 (2000): 43-54.

Ball, John Clement. "Pessoptimism: Satire and the Menippean Grotesque in Rushdie's *Midnight's Children*." *English Studies in Canada* 24, no. 1 (March 1998): 61-81.

Ben-Yishai, Ayelet. "The Dialectic of Shame: Representation in the MetaNarrative of Salman Rushdie's *Shame*." *Modern Fiction Studies* 48, no. 1 (Spring 2002): 194-215.

Bhabha, Homi. *The Location of Culture*. London and New York: Routledge, 1994.

Booker, M. Keith, ed. *Critical Essays on Salman Rushdie*. New York: G.K. Hall, 1999.

Brennan, Timothy. *Salman Rushdie and the Third World: Myths of the Nation*. New York: St. Martin's Press, 1989.

Cantor, Paul A. "Tales of the Alhambra: Rushdie's Use of Spanish History in *The Moor's Last Sigh*." *Studies in the Novel* 29, no. 3 (Fall 1997): 323-341.

Challakere, Padmaja. "Migrancy as Paranoid Schizophrenia in Salman Rushdie's *East, West*." *South Asian Review* 20, no. 17 (December 1996): 66-74.

Coundouriotis, Eleni. "Materialism, the Uncanny, and History in Toni Morrison and Salman Rushdie." *LIT: Literary Interpretation Theory* 8, no. 2 (October 1997): 207-225.

Cundy, Catherine. "'Rehearsing Voices': Salman Rushdie's *Grimus*." *The Journal of Commonwealth Literature* 27, no. 1 (1992): 128-137.

———. "Rushdie's Women." *Wasafiri: Journal of Caribbean, African, Asian and Associated Literatures and Film* 18 (Autumn 1993): 13-17.

———. *Salman Rushdie*. Manchester, UK: Manchester University Press, 1996.

Durix, Jean-Pierre. "The Artistic Journey in Salman Rushdie's *Shame*." *World Literature Written in English* 23, no. 1 (Winter 1984): 196-207.

Ellerby, Janet Mason. "Fiction Under Siege: Rushdie's Quest for Narrative Emancipation in *Haroun and the Sea of Stories*." *Lion and the Unicorn: A Critical Journal of Children's Literature* 22, no. 2 (April 1998): 211-220.

Finney, Brian. "Demonizing Discourse in Salman Rushdie's 'The Satanic Verses.'" *ARIEL: A Review of International English Literature* 29, no. 3 (July 1998): 67-93.

Fletcher, M. D. "Rushdie's *Shame* as Apologue." *The Journal of Commonwealth Literature* 21, no. 1 (1986): 120-132.

Fowler, Bridget. "A Sociological Analysis of the Satanic Verses Affair." *Theory, Culture & Society* 17, no. 1 (February 2000): 39-61.

Gates, Henry Louis, Jr. "Censorship and Justice: On Rushdie and Soyinka." *Research in African Literatures* 21, no. 1 (Spring 1990): 137-139.

Goonetilleke, D. C. R. A. "*Haroun and the Sea of Stories* and Rushdie's Partial/Plural Identity." *World Literature Written in English* 35, no. 2 (1996): 27-37.

Grant, Damian. "*East, West*: Home's Best? Salman Rushdie's Cultural Questioning." *Ateliers* 2 (1995): 33-39.

Hamilton, Ian. "The First Life of Salman Rushdie." *New Yorker* 25 December 1995: 90-119.

Harrison, James. *Salman Rushdie*. New York: Twayne Publishers, 1992.

Heffernan, Teresa. "Apocalyptic Narratives: The Nation in Salman Rushdie's *Midnight's Children*." *Twentieth Century Literature* 46, no. 4 (Winter 2000): 470-491.

Israel, Nico. *Outlandish: Writing between Exile and Diaspora*. Stanford, CA: Stanford University Press, 2000.

Kalliney, Peter. "Globalization, Postcoloniality, and the Problem of Literary Studies in *The Satanic Verses*." *Modern Fiction Studies* 48, no. 1 (Spring 2002): 50-82.

Khan, Fawzia Afzal. *Cultural Imperialism and the Indo-English Novel: Genre and Ideology in R. K. Narayan, Anita Desai, Kamala Markandaya and Salman Rushdie*. University Park, PA: Pennsylvania State University Press, 1993.

Kuortti, Joel. *The Salman Rushdie Bibliography: A Bibliography of Salman Rushdie's Work and Rushdie Criticism*. Frankfurt am Main and New York: Peter Lang, 1997.

Leonard, Philip. "Degenerescent Lections: Legal Fictions in Rushdie, Derrida, and Bhabha." *New Formations: A Journal of Culture/Theory/Politics* 32 (Autumn-Winter 1997): 109-119.

Levy, Leonard William. *Blasphemy: Verbal Offense against the Sacred, from Moses to Salman Rushdie*. New York: Knopf, 1993.

Mishra, Vijay. "Postcolonial Differend: Diasporic Narratives of Salman Rushdie." *ARIEL: A Review of International English Literature* 26, no. 3 (July 1995): 7-45.

Moss, Laura. "'Forget those damnfool realists!': Salman Rushdie's Self-Parody as the Magic Realist's 'Last Sigh.'" *ARIEL: A Review of International English Literature* 29, no. 4 (October July 1998): 121-139.

Netton, Ian Richard. *Text and Trauma: An East-West Primer*. Richmond, U.K.: Curzon Press, 1996.

Newton, K. M. "Literary Theory and the Rushdie Affair." *English: The Journal of the English Association* 41, no. 171 (Autumn 1992): 235-247.

Parameswaran, Uma. *The Perforated Sheet: Essays on Salman Rushdie's Art*. New Delhi: Affiliated East-West Press, 1988.

Pipes, Daniel. *The Rushdie Affair: The Novel, the Ayatollah, and the West*. New York: Carol, 1990.

Rege, Josna E. "Victim into Protagonist? *Midnight's Children* and the Post-Rushdie National Narratives of the Eighties." *Studies in the Novel* 29, no. 3 (Fall 1997): 342-375.

Rombes, Nicholas D., Jr. "*The Satanic Verses* as a Cinematic Narrative." *Literature/Film Quarterly* 21, no. 1 (1993): 47-53.

Semminck, Hans. *A Novel Visible but Unseen: A Thematic Analysis of Salman Rushdie's The Satanic Verses*. Ghent, Belgium: Studia Germanica Gandensia, 1993.

Singh, Sujala. "Secularist Faith in Salman Rushdie's *Midnight's Children*." *New Formations: A Journal of Culture/Theory/Politics* 41 (Autumn 2000): 158-172.

Taheri, Amir. "Pandora's Box Forced Open." *Index on Censorship* 18, no. 5 (May-June 1989): 7-9.

Taneja, G. R., and R.K. Dhawan, eds. *The Novels of Salman Rushdie*. New Delhi: Indian Society for Commonwealth Studies, 1992.

Acknowledgments

"Rushdie's *Shame* as Apologue," by M. D. Fletcher. From *The Journal of Commonwealth Literature* 21, no. 1 (1986): 120-132. © 1986 by *The Journal of Commonwealth Literature*. Reproduced with the kind permission of Cambridge Scientific Abstracts, part of Cambridge Information Group.

"Censorship and Justice: On Rushdie and Soyinka," by Henry Louis Gates, Jr. From *Research in African Literatures* 21, no. 1 (Spring 1990): 137-139. © 1989 by the Indiana University Press. Reprinted by permission.

"'Rehearsing Voices': Salman Rushdie's *Grimus*," by Catherine Cundy. From *The Journal of Commonwealth Literature* 27, no. 1 (1992): 128-137. © 1992 by *The Journal of Commonwealth Literature*. Reproduced with the kind permission of Cambridge Scientific Abstracts, part of Cambridge Information Group.

"Literary Theory and the Rushdie Affair," by K. M. Newton. From *English: The Journal of the English Association* 41, no. 171 (Autumn 1992): 235-247. © 1992 by The English Association. Reprinted by permission.

"*The Satanic Verses* as a Cinematic Narrative," by Nicholas D. Rombes, Jr. From *Literature/Film Quarterly* 21, no. 1 (1993): 47-53. © 1993 by Salisbury State University. Reprinted with permission of Literature/Film Quarterly © Salisbury University, Salisbury, MD 21801.

"Postcolonial Differend: Diasporic Narratives of Salman Rushdie," by Vijay Mishra. From *ARIEL: A Review of International English Literature* 26, no. 3 (July 1995): 7-45. © 1995 by The Board of Governors, The University of Calgary. Reprinted by permission.

"Materialism, the Uncanny, and History in Toni Morrison and Salman Rushdie," by Eleni Coundouriotis. © 1997 from *Literature Interpretation Theory* 8, no. 2 (1997): 207-225. Reproduced by permission of Taylor and Francis, Inc., http://www.routledge.ny.com.

"Tales of the Alhambra: Rushdie's Use of Spanish History in *The Moor's Last Sigh*," by Paul A. Cantor. From *Studies in the Novel* 30 (Summer, 1998). © 1998 by the University of North Texas. Reprinted by permission of the publisher.

"Victim into Protagonist? *Midnight's Children* and the Post-Rushdie National Narratives of the Eighties," by Josna E. Rege. From *Studies in the Novel* 29, no. 3 (Fall 1997): 342-375. © 1997 by the University of North Texas. Reprinted by permission of the publisher.

"Demonizing Discourse in Salman Rushdie's 'The Satanic Verses,'" by Brian Finney. From *ARIEL: A Review of International English Literature* 29, no. 3 (July 1998): 67-93. © 1998 by The Board of Governors, The University of Calgary. Reprinted by permission.

"Pessoptimism: Satire and the Menippean Grotesque in Rushdie's *Midnight's Children*," by John Clement Ball. From *English Studies in Canada* 24, no. 1 (March 1998): 61-81. © 1998 by John Clement Ball. Reprinted by permission.

"'You Must Remember This': Salman Rushdie's *The Moor's Last Sigh*," by Stephen Baker. From *The Journal of Commonwealth Literature* 35, no. 1 (2000): 43-54. © 2000 by *The Journal of Commonwealth Literature*. Reproduced with the kind permission of Cambridge Scientific Abstracts, part of Cambridge Information Group.

Ben-Yishai, Ayelet. "The Dialecti of Shame: Representation in the MetaNarrative of Salman Rushdie's *Shame*. *Modern Fiction Studies* 48, no. 1 (Spring 2002): 194-215. © 2002 Purdue Research Foundation. Reprinted by permission of the the Johns Hopkins University Press.

Index